JOHN MOE: DOUBLE AGENT

JOHN MOE: DOUBLE AGENT tells for the first
time the story behind one of the Second World
War's most important and effective double
agents — the man who operated under the
codename "Mutt" and whose successes
included the diverting of the German High
Command's attention away from the planned
Allied Forces' landing in North Africa.

In 1978 when journalist and historian Nigel West
was commissioned to write a history of MI5 he
began an attempt to trace some of the
organisation's double agents. In October 1979
he eventually received information regarding
the enigmatic "Mutt" and was astonished to
find him living quietly in Sweden. At first Moe
refused to break the pledge of lifelong silence
imposed by MI5. Only after a great deal of
persuasion and receiving official permission did
John Moe agree to publicise his amazing
experiences. JOHN MOE: DOUBLE AGENT is
the result.

John Moe was a young man living in Manchester when World War II broke out. Although his mother was English, he was Norwegian and regarded Oslo as his home, so it was natural for John to make his way there. He had not been in Oslo long, though, before Norway was occupied by the Germans. John grew restless. He had to do something — anything — to strike back at the enemy.

So John Moe and his friend Tor Glad began to play a deadly dangerous game with the Germans. By a combination of nerve and guile they eventually managed to get themselves sent to Britain as Nazi spies and saboteurs. After a dramatic landing in Scotland, they were arrested, interrogated and almost shot as spies before the British finally accepted them as agents — the double agent team of "Mutt" and "Jeff".

John Moe's true role in the war has never been revealed until publication of this book. In fact, rather than break MI5's secrets he even let himself be accused of being a Nazi sympathiser.

He now lives in Norway.

John Moe
Double Agent

Jan Moen

NEW ENGLISH LIBRARY
Hodder and Stoughton

Copyright © John Moe and Jan Moen 1986

First published in Great Britain in 1986 by Mainstream Publishing Company (Edinburgh) Ltd.

New English Library Paperback edition 1987

This translated edition of the Swedish original title *Jon Moe, Dubbelagent* is published by arrangement with Wiken Publishing House, Höganäs, Sweden.

Translated into English by Helen Jackson

British Library C.I.P.

Moen, Jan
  John, Moe, double agent.
  1. World War, 1939 — Secret service
  I. Title II. John Moe, dubbleagent. *English*
  940.54'85   d810.S7

  ISBN 0-450-41909-6

Printed and bound in Great Britain for Hodder and Stoughton Paperbacks, a division of Hodder and Stoughton Ltd., Mill Road, Dunton Green, Sevenoaks, Kent TN13 2YA. (Editorial Office: 47 Bedford Square, London WC1B 3DP) by Richard Clay Ltd., Bungay, Suffolk.

ACKNOWLEDGEMENTS

Acknowledgements are due to members of the Imperial Security Service (MI5); officers of the Special Branch who aided me in my 'sabotage' operations; the many members of the Intelligence Corps and the British police force who did everything they could to make my task successful; to the late Ted Ingram, my dear friend, who was in charge of the radio room at Aberdeen City Police Headquarters; and last but not least, sincere thanks are due to my friend Rupert Allason (Nigel West) whose diligent research enabled me to give a true account of my wartime experiences to my co-author, Jan Moen, in Sweden.

John Moe, July 1986.

In memory of eleven-year-old Laurence McKay Kerr of Fraserburgh, who was killed on 20 February 1943 when a German aeroplane dropped supplies for me near Loch Strathbeg.

Introduction

by Nigel West

The first official mention of the two Norwegian double agents whose codenames were Mutt and Jeff appeared in 1972, when Sir John Masterman published *The Double Cross System of the War of 1939-45*. We now know that their real names were John Moe and Tor Glad. Contrary to most Nazi spies caught by the Allied Forces, these two young Norwegians had decided from the very start to use spying as a means of escaping the brutal occupation forces in their native country. When they discovered that their mission to England was to comprise both spying and sabotage, they saw a unique opportunity to double-cross the enemy. That is why they were fully prepared to co-operate. The risks that both these young men faced when they undertook this dangerous task should not be under-estimated and the families which they left behind them remained potential targets. Despite the obvious hazards, they established contact with the British Secret Service as soon as they arrived and offered their services as double agents.

Christopher Harmer of MI5 helped Mutt and Jeff to make radio contact with the Germans in April 1941 and this contact was maintained without interruption until February 1944 when Mutt joined the regular army. Sir John Masterman writes that 'Mutt and Jeff appeared to us and to their case officer to be sometimes on the crest of a wave, and considered as valuable sources of information as well as lucky though not skilled saboteurs'.

Despite the fact that the Germans occasionally seemed doubtful as to Mutt and Jeff (Ja and Tege, as they were referred to by the Germans), their dual roles continued for thirty-three months. During this period, Mutt took part in a series of skilful strategies intended to mislead the Germans. One of the most difficult and important was Solo 1, a carefully planned cover operation for Operation Torch, the Allied Forces' landing in North Africa. It was executed so well that the North African campaign went ahead with little loss of life. The German High Command was totally convinced that the military concentration at the English ports was part of a planned manoeuvre against the Germans' northern flank in Scandinavia. As a consequence, the Germans maintained a large section of their forces in Norway, and could therefore not use them to defend against the North African campaign. The same ploy was repeated in 1944 to help cover the D-Day landings in Normandy.

In 1978, I was commissioned to write the history of the British Civil Service (MI5), and so it was that I began an attempt to trace some of the organisation's double agents. Clues that could lead to their true identities were deliberately difficult to find, since MI5 was always very thorough in providing protection for those who had helped in their work. However, I had previously read of Mutt and Jeff's achievements in some earlier publications, without learning of their true identities.

It was not until October 1979 that I eventually received information regarding the enigmatic Mutt, and I managed to trace him to his home in Sweden, where I had the opportunity of speaking to him for the first time. After such a long silence, Mutt was unwilling to talk about his role during the war, except in general terms. Mutt is an unassuming man, and he was determined not to say anything that might compromise an old colleague, or pass on any information that had remained secret since the war. It was only after he had spoken to his former English contact from MI5 that he became more frank and began to write his own account of his important role in wartime espionage.

John Moe and Tor Glad were eventually given the opportunity to fly to England in October 1981 for a reunion with their old friends from MI5. It was held in the Hyde Park Hotel, London, the Secret Service's favourite meeting place during the war years. The reunion between Mutt, Jeff and their old colleagues was an emotional one. They exchanged stories and relived the extraordinary adventures which they had all shared.

After a good deal of persuasion, Mutt has agreed to publicise his amazing experiences of the war in this book. In my opinion, it ought to have been done years ago; there are so many of the Allied troops scattered around the world who have him to thank for their lives. It was his brave decision to fight the Nazis, in his own extremely dangerous way, that helped ensure their survival. Some have perhaps wondered at the comparative ease with which some of the operations, such as Torch, were executed. They will now be given an explanation. In his own writings about World War II, Mutt has finally revealed his contribution to history, and he can now be given the credit he so richly deserves, and the recognition which was previously impossible owing to the strict security surrounding his real identity.

Nigel West

1

The Manchester to Newcastle train was absolutely packed. All of the seats were taken and the corridors were filled with rows of people swaying in time to the rhythmic movement of the coaches.

I had arrived at the station in good time and managed to find a seat with a few spare inches in the corner. I tried to curl myself up as small as possible on the dusty seat, but I was still firmly wedged between the compartment wall and a stoutish woman with two young children on her knee. Upon my trying to strike up a conversation with her, she replied in a language I could not understand — perhaps Finnish or Estonian. I just shrugged my shoulders and started to leaf through an old *Daily Mirror* that I had found on the luggage rack.

The articles were all old-hat. Nothing is as old as yesterday's news, but I re-read the familiar items just to pass the time. Chamberlain's radio speech to the British nation: 'This country is at war with Germany. We have a clear conscience that we have done all that a country could do to establish peace. . . . You can imagine what a bitter blow it is to me that all my long struggle to win peace has failed.'

I had listened to the speech in grandfather's billiard room when I had gone to spend the weekend with him away from my temporary job just outside London. Although it was only late morning the house was full of people. Grandfather's old friends from the Officers Corps had come to take part in their weekend billiard match, but at 11.15 the Prime Minister was to address the British public.

They finished their game in good time and put away their cues. There we all stood, waiting — my grandfather, the colonel, the other greying veterans of the First World War and myself, the young lad who dabbled in something as dubious as the film industry. The announcer made his introduction and Chamberlain began, assiduous and deeply shaken: 'I am speaking to you from the Cabinet Room at 10 Downing Street. . . .' The elderly officers stood to attention, remaining silent and serious, while the Prime Minister's speech issued from the loudspeaker, broken at times by a series of clicks, scratches and interference.

That particular scene remained engraved in my memory — those quiet solemn men. They had experienced this once before and they understood the implications. When the speech was over and grandfather had switched off the radio, the room remained completely still. The old soldiers just looked at each other. After a long pause, grandfather spoke: 'We'll just have to make sure you get home as soon as possible, John. Norway is a neutral country, you'll be safe there.'

War had been expected really. Ever since the end of August, when the tension had risen along the German-Polish border, people had started talking of war, a war that certainly would follow Chamberlain's failure to ease the situation. It still came as a shock. After all, earlier conflicts had been resolved by concessions and promises. Why shouldn't Chamberlain succeed again? But this time Hitler had gone too far. There was no turning back now.

For me, the outbreak of war meant returning home, and I wasn't the only one. Thousands of foreigners were trying to catch the first available boat. They gathered at the docks and mobbed the travel agencies and shipping offices. They had to get home. They had to find a boat going back to their own particular country. The hotels in Hull and Newcastle were overbooked with long waiting lists. I was lucky. Grandfather had arranged my passage on the Bergen ship *Leda*, which was to depart from Newcastle, and I was now on the train together with several hundred other people, all with the same objective of reaching the Tyneside docks where the ship lay which would take us home.

The compartment door opened and a troubled-looking face peered in. 'Excuse me, are all the seats taken?'

It was a girl, about twenty years old. She was struggling with two weighty suitcases and was breathing heavily. Her face was flushed bright red with exertion. She quickly glanced around the compartment and saw that all the seats were already occupied. 'I apologise for bursting in like this,' she said, 'but I haven't been able to find a single seat in any of the other compartments.'

I could tell she wasn't English by her intonation. I suddenly remembered the slogan on the trams in Oslo which said that if you're young and fit, you should give up your seat for someone who needs it. 'Sit down and take a rest,' I said.

She stared at me, then smiled. She put down one of her suitcases and held out her hand. 'I'm Rachel,' she said. 'Thank you, I'm so exhausted.'

I introduced myself, placed her suitcases under the seat and stood aside to let her sit down.

Opening her handbag, she took out a handkerchief, wiped the perspiration from her brow and cleaned her face and neck. When she had finished she looked at her handkerchief which was completely black. 'So this is the England Hitler wants — covered in soot.'

'It's the coal,' I explained. 'There's a cloud of soot over every city. But there's a more pleasant England too.' I was thinking of grandfather's England, with its green meadows, stone-walled farmyards, and small villages with their country pubs. That was the England where I had spent the summers of my childhood as a well-loved addition to grandfather's house outside Manchester.

'I've only seen London, and then this dreadful train with its thick soot, smoke and dirt.'

'In England, you have to wear detachable collars and cuffs,' I said.

'I thought that had gone out of fashion.'

'You should see the poor men who have to go to work wearing white shirts. A lot of them have to change at lunchtime if they have not taken an extra collar and a pair of cuffs. Celluloid ones are really popular. They are easy to just wipe clean or wash in the sink.'

Suddenly I realised that mine was the only voice to be heard. There were twelve people crammed into the compartment, including two restless children, but they were all perfectly silent, deep in thought, deep in themselves. A harshly made up middle-aged woman sat dozing opposite me. Beside her was a man with a small face and pointed beard. He held her hand and stared at the floor, stiff and taut, as if ready to jump up and find a place to take cover.

Take cover from what? Who was he? Where was he going? He wasn't English — his clothes gave that away. Perhaps he was Greek or Turkish, Yugoslavian or even Hungarian? He was also going back home. He too was seeking protection, both for himself and for the woman to whom he gave a sense of security with his tiny hand.

Another man sat by the window. He must have been there in very good time since he had the best seat. He chainsmoked and continuously ran his hand over his bald head. Every few minutes he would pull out a silver watch from his waistcoat pocket, look at it, tap it, as if wanting it to go faster and then put it away with a sigh.

I became aware of an atmosphere of discomfort. My fellow passengers were scared and on the run, their sights set on a ship headed for a neutral country. Perhaps they felt uncertain as to whether or not they would ever get home.

On the very first day of real war, Monday, 4 September 1939, the British liner *Athenia* was sunk by a German U-boat. On the same day there were reports of a British air-raid on the German port of Wilhelmshaven. Would the Germans bomb Newcastle?

'It's a strange country,' said Rachel. 'I don't think I would be happy here. I'm glad I'm only passing through. I've just come over from Paris and this seemed the best way

way back home. I couldn't travel through Germany.'

'Do you have a reservation?' I asked.

'The *Leda*. Bergen.'

'Me too. We can keep each other company.'

We both nodded. Maybe she felt as relieved as I did at finding someone to share the rigours of the journey with.

'Are you from Norway?' she asked.

'Oslo,' I replied.

'How long have you been in England?'

'A few months. I was working on a film.'

'That sounds interesting. What did you do?'

'I'm a make-up artist. I was in charge of the harem.'

She laughed. The bald-headed man turned round and looked at us, took several drags of his cigarette, shrugged his shoulders and then continued to look out through the dirty window of the compartment. It was obviously unfitting to laugh out loud at the very moment of the London evacuation, and when German troops were at Wisla and drawing ever closer to Warsaw.

'I found a job in a studio just outside London. They are doing a film called *The Thief of Baghdad*. It's directed by Alexander Korda. Have you heard of him? Conrad Veidt, John Justin, Sabu, Rex Ingram and June Duprez are starring in the major roles. And then there are a host of exquisitely beautiful and flimsily clothed ladies.'

'That you take care of?'

'That was part of my job,' I said.

Less than a week had passed since I had left the set for what I thought would be a short weekend visit to my grandfather's house. I should have gone back really, for I had a contract for the entire film. My services were free as the job was all part of my training. But I never returned to Joan, Mildred, Jeanette and the other London girls — those Eastern beauties of sinful Baghdad. Instead I was sitting in a train, on the first stage of my journey back to Norway.

'And you're now on your way home?' asked Rachel.

'I'm afraid so. I was happy here.'

'I can understand that,' she said, and looked as if she meant it.

'It will become difficult for foreigners here,' I said. 'Apparently you have to report to the local police station. The Germans and Austrians have already been accounted for, and placed in detention camps.'

In fact that was one of the reasons I agreed to my grandfather's wish that I leave England. I had no desire to be looked upon as a *persona non grata* in the country I regarded as my second home. I had grown up in Oslo, of course, and my father was Norwegian, but every year for as long as I could remember, I had travelled across to England, alone or with my mother, to visit her parents.

Mother hadn't been an only child. She had a brother called Jack who was to follow in his father's footsteps. He became a lieutenant in grandfather's regiment and they both received orders to go to Gallipoli during the First World War. Grandfather survived the ordeal but his son never returned. He had been shot by a Turkish sniper.

Perhaps this was partly why grandfather was so determined that I should return home. He didn't want me to enlist in the British Army, as I could have done. I was the right age, having just turned twenty-one, and I also had the right connections: a colonel and regimental commander's word carried considerable weight. Although I was a Norwegian citizen, I was born in London and could therefore gain British citizenship. Besides, English was my second language.

The train chugged through a tunnel. The smoke from the coal-fired engine was forced downwards, swirled around the carriages and seeped in through the chinks of the doors and the half-opened windows. A girl sitting opposite the bald-headed man leaned to look out of the window. All she could see was her own reflection and the lines of soot being driven past the window. Then the train rattled out into the open again. There was little improvement in the view but it became a bit lighter in the compartment.

It was drizzling outside. The soot from the coal-black

smoke that billowed across the compartment window mingled with the raindrops beating against the window-pane, forming rivulets and creating a fresh pattern.

'Does it always rain in England?' asked Rachel.

'Almost every day,' I replied.

I looked at my watch. It was lunchtime. When I had boarded the train in Manchester I had noticed that there was a restaurant car a few carriages along.

I asked Rachel if she would join me. She agreed and so we forced our way through the jam-packed carriages. The corridors were lined with suitcases, many of them with labels marked 'Bergenske' and *SS Leda*. There were clearly a lot of us going to Bergen.

We eventually found the restaurant car. Despite the fact that it was full of people, the head waiter managed to find us a couple of places at a table where three others were already seated: a young couple and a dark-haired man. We squeezed ourselves in. There was only roast beef and leg of lamb left on the menu and the head waiter felt obliged to apologise for the service not being up to standard. Apparently several of the waiters had been called up.

I still hadn't seen much of the war, except for grandfather's serious war friends and the crowded train. Of course, the newspapers were full of good advice on such things as how to use sandbags as a protection against bomb blast. I had seen a couple of cinemas and theatres close down for a few days because of the danger of air-raids, and the Home Guard had received their helmets and had begun to organize groups of rescue parties should their services be required.

But none of these things really affected me. Neither did the reorganisation of the government have anything to do with me. It didn't affect me that on the first day of fighting Churchill was appointed Minister of War. Nor the release of a thousand prisoners from the three London prisons after only a short gaol sentence. To me it was just another newspaper item.

The one stark reminder that I had of the war was the gas-mask that grandfather had given me, and which I had packed in one of my suitcases.

And then there were the restaurant car waiters who were now dressed in an all too different uniform. We managed all right, even if we did have to set the table and serve ourselves. It was of little importance but, to me, it was very symbolic. The war wasn't just something that happened in faraway places. It affected the whole community and changed the everyday routine of life.

The roast beef was excellent. The cook obviously hadn't been called up as yet. We even had a good quality beer to drink; but the stocks wouldn't last very long.

I chatted with Rachel. I gathered that she was Jewish and born in Austria. She had gone to Paris and then spent a few days in London. Now she wanted to leave this Nazi-threatened country. *Anschluss* and the German invasion of Austria were still fresh in her mind. She was eighteen, small and slender, and very frightened — that much I understood. It took some time before she was able to tell me anything about herself.

The train suddenly jolted to a halt, steam hissed from the engine and iron clashed with iron, like hammer against anvil, when the carriages thundered against one another.

At the sudden crash of a plate that fell to the floor, Rachel threw up her hands as if to protect herself from shrapnel. It was neither a bomb nor a machine-gun attack. She had been frightened by the noise and for a few seconds I had seen the look of terror in her eyes. After a short while the engine started to billow forth smoke in short sharp puffs, and the train soon built up to its normal speed.

'It is OK now,' I said.

She nodded and tried to smile.

We were two different people, two different nationalities, with our sights set on the same goal — except that our reasons for making the journey were very different. Rachel was on the run. For her it was a question of life or death: the concentration camps and labour camps intended for those not born of the superior race. And me? I had reluctantly agreed to grandfather's wish that I leave my harem ladies in the hands of another make-up artist.

We decided to stay together during the journey, and I became a sort of guide. After all, I had more experience of British bureaucracy, which although it hadn't wormed its way into every nook and cranny of social life, could still be very trying. We had to change trains at Newcastle and settled ourselves in a carriage that would take us to Tyneside where the *Leda* was moored. A shipping officer checked our tickets and within the hour we were at the docks.

The quayside was crawling with people. We realised how fortunate we were in having reservations to board. Hundreds of people were queuing in the hope of getting a place, and the air was thick with foreign tongues, whose swearing echoed across the water. This was war all right. Everyone wanted to get home. They had placed all their hopes on the Bergen ship, on a faint promise that maybe there was room. We elbowed our way through the crowd towards the gangway, pushing aside the masses of people with our suitcases and shoulders. People were waving their tickets and passports in the air, stumbling towards the edge of the quay where a couple of policemen tried to control the heaving mob.

Suddenly a voice on board sounded through a loud hailer. 'This is the captain speaking. I'm sorry, but we can only take those passengers who already have tickets. There aren't enough lifejackets and lifeboats for everyone. We have received reports that German U-boats have been sighted in the North Sea. Even though we have Norway emblazoned along our hull, and we shall be travelling with our lights and lanterns fully lit, we cannot run the risk of allowing more passengers on board when we cannot provide for their safety. We have to be prepared for every eventuality.'

The loud hailer crackled and fell silent. The captain knew there was a danger of being torpedoed. Even if the *Leda* was from a neutral country, he couldn't be totally certain of its safety. Mistakes can be made, and a German U-boat commander could easily assume the *Leda* to be a British ship and therefore a viable target. The Norwegian flag was made up of the same colours as the British: red, white and blue. It would be all too easy to make a mistake.

Rachel stood beside me, listening to the booming voice. She was shaking as she huddled closer to me. I put down one of the suitcases and placed my arm around her shoulder. She looked at me and tried to smile. The queue slowly shuffled forward. We were carried along every foot of the way until we finally reached passport and ticket control.

'Do you have a gas mask, sir?' asked the passport controller.

The question surprised me, but I told him that I had one in my suitcase. He asked to see it. 'My grandfather gave it to me,' I explained. 'I had thought of taking it home as a souvenir.' Norway wasn't at war, so I'd certainly have no use for it there.

"I'm sorry, sir,' said the controller, 'but you will get it back upon your return, I cannot allow you to keep it.'

'In that case I shall never see it again,' I said. In fact I never did, even though I was to return to Britain.

2

We were jostled up the gangplank by the pressure of the crowd, myself with two heavy suitcases to carry and Rachel half a step in front of me. Noises from the quay echoed against the hull of the ship. A shrill, taut cry broke through the din of the crowd. The voice belonged to a Norwegian woman.

I looked up towards the bridge where one of the crew members of the *Leda* was standing, watching over the evacuation. He surveyed the unruly scene below. I could see that he was trying to find the screaming woman in the crowd. He couldn't pick her out, so he shrugged and glanced away.

Rachel stopped suddenly, causing me to bump into her with my case. She turned her head and looked at me. 'What did that poor woman want?' she asked.

'She wanted to go to Bergen, like everybody else,' I replied, 'to be with her children.'

'The captain ought to make an exception for her.'

'There is nothing we can do,' I replied.

The queue behind us lurched forward and I bumped into Rachel again. She struggled on, taking a few quick steps up the swaying gangplank and filling the gap that had been made when she stopped.

At last we were on board. I put down my suitcases and searched for my ticket to show the steward who was allocating cabins. In my pocket I found a couple of letters which I'd written whilst waiting for the train to leave Manchester and which I'd forgotten to post. I left my luggage and began to squeeze my way towards the stream of people on the gangplank.

'Where are you going?' Rachel shouted after me, her voice laden with anxiety.

'I'll be back soon,' I yelled.

'Please come back.'

'I'm just going to post these letters.' I turned round for a second and saw her give a smile of relief. That was the first time I saw her smile.

I wasn't allowed on shore. I was stopped by a guard at the end of the gangplank. Customs and passport formalities had already been finalised and according to regulations I had already left English soil. In order to get to a postbox I would have to have my passport stamped for entry into the country and then stamped again for the outward journey. The guard was adamant.

'I just want to post a few letters,' I said. 'It'll only take a few seconds.' I showed him the envelopes and pointed to a letterbox that I had noticed beside an office building, not more than a hundred yards away. The guard shook his head.

'It's important,' I said. 'Can't I at least find someone to do it for me?'

'You will have to wait until you get to Bergen,' he answered. Then he leaned forward and looked at the letters. When he saw that one of them was addressed to a colonel he straightened up. 'Your father, sir?' he asked.

'My grandfather,' I replied.

'Well, I'll gladly take care of these,' he said, reaching for them.

I left them in his care and offered him a shilling for his kindness. He refused the money. I laughed awkwardly, put the money back and thanked him for his help.

Rachel had disappeared when I came back on board. I went up to the steward and asked about my cabin number. He pointed me in the right direction and I set off, squeezing past a bewildered group of fellow passengers who had got lost along the stairs and corridors. Needless to say, I ended up in the wrong place and had to heave my luggage back half the length of the ship before I eventually found my cabin and started to put away my suitcases.

I opened one of my bags, intending to unpack and hang up my clothes in the old wardrobe. But then I stopped, shut the case and put it on the floor. What if the German U-boats really did have hostile intentions? What if in the dead of night a commander mistook the *Leda* for an enemy ship? A couple of ready-packed suitcases would make things quicker in the event of the alarm sounding.

For a moment I felt slightly uncomfortable. I wondered if I should go on shore again, say that I had changed my mind and give my ticket to that woman who wanted to go home to her children. It was safer in England than on board the *Leda*. But at the same time I realised that this could be the last available boat back to neutral Norway. I wanted to get home. I decided to stay on board.

I washed the grime from my face and hands, changed my shirt and put on a suitable tie. Then I went up on the deck to look down at the quay. Everyone who had a ticket was obviously aboard, for the gangplank had been drawn up. A rumbling noise came from the engine room, the dockers loosened the moorings and the *Leda* was ready.

While the passengers who had gathered by the railings were waving goodbye, a member of the crew appeared and requested that we all make our way to the lounge immediately. No one was to remain on deck. The lifeboats were to be lowered over the side of the ship in readiness for the journey.

The lounge was packed with people. Some were seated in the broad armchairs, but most of them stood in silent groups and listened to the captain. He remained serious. We were urged to study the instructions in our cabins as soon as possible. We also had to find out where our lifejackets were situated and to which lifeboat we had been assigned.

All in the interests of safety. In theory, the risk of a neutral ship being attacked was minimal, but it was better to be well prepared; just in case. We were not to panic even if the worst were to happen. It wasn't that dangerous, he smiled. The water was still warm and there were no sharks in the North Sea.

Someone began to applaud, but it was a half-hearted attempt. Although the captain had tried to make light of the danger, it couldn't stop one's imagination working overtime; a sudden explosion, the sound of a wailing siren, a lifeboat swinging down towards the dark waters alongside a burning ship, the black waves beating against the frail hull, the night, the cold, the driving rain, and the unnoticed distress flares.

The captain left the lounge. There was a long, unbroken silence. All that could be heard was the hum from the engine room, and the swing doors which flicked to and fro. One hundred and twenty-five people were frozen in complete stillness; whatever our individual reasons for leaving England, we were bound together by the thought of escape.

Somebody lit a cigarette; another coughed; there were faint whisperings to neighbours. Slowly the tension eased, and some passengers left the lounge to map out their escape route to the lifeboats.

I caught sight of Rachel. She was standing pale and alone in a corner. I pushed my way through to her and took her hand. She squeezed it hard.

'Let's find the bar,' I suggested. It was late afternoon and the *Leda* was just leaving port, but she hadn't got up speed as yet. We could feel her swaying very softly, but she would certainly start rolling once we reached the open sea.

It was time for afternoon tea, as a matter of fact — a typically English habit that not even an old military man like my grandfather could live without. I needed something stronger, however, and when we found the bar I ordered a whisky. Rachel had a Martini, and we managed to find a nice comfortable sofa. When I opened my wallet to pay, a small picture fell out on to the table; it was part of a 1920s cigarette collection.

Rachel picked it up. 'Do you collect pictures of film stars?'

'As a child I did,' I replied. 'I had several shoe boxes full of them.'

'Do you still have them?'

'I think they're in the attic at home in Oslo.'

'But you keep this picture close to your heart?' She read the name under the picture. 'Ida Mae. Who is she?'

'That's my mother,' I said. 'She's an actress.'

'She's very beautiful,' Rachel said handing me the picture. 'Tell me about her.'

I put my mother's picture back in my wallet, reached for my glass and took a drink.

'She's English,' I said. 'She met my father in London, where he was working as a hairdresser. They got married, moved to Oslo and she began working in the theatre. Revues and musical comedies mostly. It wasn't thought very highly of by her rather conservative family. Her mother showed some understanding, but appearing on the stage wasn't considered suitable in their circles. Neither was her marriage to a hairdresser — a foreigner too — not exactly what had been expected of their only daughter. But, she was strong-willed.' After all these years grandfather had either forgotten or accepted it.

I fell silent and looked at Rachel. Some colour had returned to her cheeks. She tucked away a strand of black hair and laid her head to one side. I looked into her dark-brown eyes.

'Go on,' she said.

'I don't know what you want me to tell you,' I said.

'About yourself. Everything. About your mother.'

I thought there was probably more to say about my mother. In her day she was a celebrated actress. After every performance there were flowers from admirers in her dressing-room. Perhaps that was one of the reasons why my parents got divorced after only a few years of marriage. 'She lives alone in Oslo now. Sometimes I stay with her, sometimes with my father.'

'Is she still just as beautiful?'

I thought about Trygve Lie who always used to visit my

mother on her birthday, and always with a huge bouquet of carnations. 'Yes,' I said. 'I know at least one man who still thinks she's the most beautiful woman ever. He's the Norwegian Home Secretary. Well, I've talked more than enough about my family. Now it's your turn, Rachel.'

Her face clouded; she turned and stared through the salt-crusted window. The light was fading, dark clouds drifted by. A pair of seagulls were gliding on the wind.

'I'm someone,' she whispered, 'someone searching desperately for a little peace.' She tried to smile. I stroked her cheek. 'It's almost time for dinner,' she said. 'Did you want to change?'

I had a dinner suit packed away in one of my suitcases; grandfather was strict about dinner dress. 'I always like to dress for dinner,' I said.

We got up and went back to our cabins. My dinner jacket was neatly creased, but had been slightly crumpled in packing; what did it matter — we were in the middle of the North Sea.

Just as I found the dining-room, someone called out my name. I stopped and turned to see the first mate waving at me. We had met a couple of times in Oslo, and he was serving on board when I had travelled to England in the early summer.

'So you've joined us for the last journey then?' he said, shaking my hand. I stared at him. Did he believe that the Germans would engage in an all-out U-boat strategy? Or did he already know something? He noticed my astonishment. 'Don't misunderstand me,' he said. 'I just meant that there won't be many more tourist trips. Who's going to have the time for holidays, and who would be crazy enough to make the crossing?'

'You had me worried,' I said. 'How dangerous is it in the North Sea?'

'The winds are moderate from the south and there's a possibility of light rain. It might blow up later in the night. The temperature is barely ten degrees.'

'You know very well what sort of danger I mean,' I answered.

'I don't know, John. Nobody knows. All we hear are rumours. Our orders were to sail. Why would they want to attack an unarmed passenger ship from a neutral country?'

'What about the *Lusitania*?' I said.

'That was a one-off.'

'I hope you're right.'

We went out on deck. The last of the evening light was fading. Dark clouds loomed ahead of us, and the air was heavy with moisture even though it wasn't raining. The *Leda* was rolling a bit more now in a kind of pendulous motion. The wind was warm and not particularly strong and the swell rose all but a metre high; but it wasn't the weather that troubled us.

'If you hear anything, let me know,' I said.

'About what?'

'About what's happening in the world.'

He understood what I meant. 'All right, I will. I promise,' he said and rushed away.

Rachel was already seated when I arrived. A bottle of Løitens was opened on the table. I filled our glasses and we drank a toast, although Rachel clearly didn't want to.

I felt myself relax as the meal went on. After all, I was dining in the company of a beautiful brunette; we enjoyed each other's company. It was a good meal: turtle soup and Tournedos Rossini accompanied by a ruby red Burgundy. There had obviously been plenty to drink at the other tables too, for the dining-room was soon filled with noise and laughter. Only at the captain's table did the meal proceed in an orderly and calm fashion.

After dessert had been served, the third mate entered the room. He approached the captain's table, gave him a piece of paper and stood quietly to the side as the ship's commander read the message.

I looked over at the captain and tried to read his face: what was so important as to warrant him being disturbed during dinner? It occurred to me that everyone had fixed their attention on him; the laughter and chatter faded away. We all stared at the captain's table. He read the message twice, then reached for a pen from his inside pocket and wrote something. He returned the slip of paper to the third mate, who straightened up, turned and disappeared.

Suddenly aware of the silence, the captain looked up to meet everyone's attention. 'Just the weather report,' he explained. 'The wind will blow up a bit towards morning.' I could tell he was lying. The message had read something else. 'To make the journey a bit more comfortable, I will see that the bar stays open all night, or until you've all had enough,' he added.

After a significant pause, people began to relax once again. A little while later we felt the ship change course as the *Leda* turned sharply to starboard. The gentle and familiar rocking stopped, and glasses began to slide, prevented from falling only by the table-rim. The ship then adjusted herself, regained her balance, and began to rock once more, but this time in a different rhythm.

Why had we changed course?

I excused myself and went to find the first mate. He was with the radio officer, and waved to me to be quiet while the Morse equipment tapped out its staccato message. Then he took me into the corridor.

'What's going on?' I asked.

'Nothing,' came the reply.

'Why have we changed course?'

'The weather,' he tried feebly, but he saw me shake my head and he smiled. 'OK, we just heard that two freighters have been sunk in the waters just off Bergen. We're sailing towards Stavanger instead, and then we'll follow the coast northwards. Unfortunately we'll be a few hours late.'

'How does it look?'

'I know as much as you do. Remember this is just between the two of us. We don't want a panic on board.'

'I promise.'

Rachel had moved to the bar by the time I returned. She was curious to know what had happened, but I told her they wanted to avoid a storm, and that we would be arriving in

Bergen a little later than expected.

I don't know if she believed me.

The atmosphere remained a happy one as the evening grew late. By midnight it seemed as if everyone in the bar had forgotten just where we were. None of us were concerned about the prospect of U-boats or ghost-like torpedoes stalking us through the murky waters; we were all too wrapped up in the noise of the tuneless singing and chatter that filled the bar. I had learned to play the piano as a child, so I promptly sat myself down at the keyboard. I was always more inclined towards classical music, but I still knew a good collection of contemporary numbers.

By the early hours of the morning I felt unable to keep awake any longer. I returned to my cabin, lay down on top of my bunk and, still fully dressed, tried to sleep. Eventually I succeeded, to the accompaniment of the droning throb of the engine, the ship's gentle rocking and the rise and fall of the prow.

When the engine pitch rose, I woke up. There was a loud rattle and we slowed down. I got up and tried to peer out of the small round porthole. The glass was thick, but you could still manage to see out of it. I noticed a ray of sunlight flicker on the water through a break in the scurrying grey clouds.

There was another faint sound; an engine whirred angrily. I looked out onto the water; there couldn't possibly be a motorboat in the middle of the North Sea?

It took some time before I realised that it wasn't a boat, but an aeroplane. I jumped up from my bunk, found the shoes that I'd kicked off, buttoned up my dinner jacket and rushed up onto the deck. There was a plane circling the *Leda* —a British bi-plane. When it flew over the ship I saw the circle of blue, red and white on the underside of her wings. Only then did I begin to relax. I yawned, and realised that I was freezing cold and very tired.

I met Rachel in the corridor. She ran to me and I opened my arms out to her and pulled her close. I felt her shaking.

'What's wrong, Rachel?' I asked.

'Nothing,' she whispered.

'Don't worry, it was an English plane. What it was doing, I don't know, but it was English.'

I took her to my cabin and we lay down on my bunk fully clothed. She drew herself up across my arm and after a long while I felt her breathing soften. Soon we were both asleep. We didn't wake until late in the afternoon.

By that time we were very close to the Norwegian coast. We could just make out the dusky coastline for a while before night fell. Late in the evening we reached the port of Bergen.

3

We managed to find an empty compartment on the morning train from Bergen to Oslo, which stopped for half an hour in Finse, up in the Hardanger region. I took the opportunity of phoning home to let them know I was all right. I could tell by mother's voice that she was happy and relieved.

Both my mother and father met me at the station. Their welcome was more emotional than it ever used to be after my trips to England, but I knew they had been anxious.

'Did you spot any U-boats?' father asked. I shook my head. 'The Germans have sunk another British ship,' he continued. 'I heard it on the radio. The crew were shot in their lifeboats.' He was clearly upset, and shook a clenched fist in the direction of Hitler's Germany.

We booked Rachel into a hotel and when we'd seen to her luggage we found a taxi.

'Who am I going to stay with?' I asked.

'With us,' said mother, laughing.

'Both of you?'

'We're back together again.'

I couldn't believe it, but father nodded and gave the driver an address that I didn't recognise.

So, they had moved house for the umpteenth time. They were now living in Observatorie Terrase next to the university library. They'd found a large flat in a well-to-do area with a well-tended lawn at the back and a decorative fountain in the middle of the garden. They hadn't mentioned this new arrangement in any of their letters.

I wasn't completely happy about their reconciliation,

probably because I knew it wouldn't last very long. After their divorce they had remarried, but even that didn't last. Over the years I had come to realise that they were too different to be able to live together for any great length of time. To be honest, I preferred it when they lived apart; it suited me a lot better. As a child I could get pocket-money from both of them. As a teenager I had valued the freedom that their arrangement gave me. When I was out enjoying myself, father thought I was at my mother's, and she likewise thought that father was keeping an eye on me.

When my father had returned home from England with his young bride, he set up a hairdressing business. He was highly skilled, due to the experience he had gained in London, and he was soon running one of the leading salons in Oslo. He now had two of them; a large salon in Tivoli-hallen and a smaller one in Majorstuehuset. There was a total of eighteen employees, among them Antonio, a German who had been there for several years now, and an Austrian, Josef Dellmondo, who hadn't joined them until some time later. Antonio, Josef and I had spent a great deal of time together, and it was thanks to them that I learned to speak German.

Before I left for England I had become my father's right-hand man. I had to help out setting and adding the final touches to a hairstyle when the salons got too busy. I even took care of the bookkeeping, and was responsible for the takings: on one occasion I had to run the whole show.

During the early period of my involvement, I noticed that in spite of my youth the others treated me with a certain respect. I was Junior, the only son. The idea was that I would eventually take over the business, and when Dellmondo left to run another salon, father renamed the business Helge K. Moe & Son.

Mother had left the theatre some years earlier and established her own salon. She had had absolutely no experience and so she had employed a top-class hairdresser to ensure the best treatment for her customers at Hövik.

But Antonio and Dellmondo were something special.

They were artists. The fashionable styles were created by clipping the hair up, followed by perming. Antonio and Dellmondo created their own fashions using more natural methods. Somehow they had managed to cut their own style which was very different. They became well known and attracted the wealthier women who could afford to keep up with fashion trends. Their creations did not last as long as the permed styles, but the customers returned more regularly, and that couldn't ever be bad for business.

In the 1930s Oslo was still a city divided by class, a call back to the early 1900s. The working-class quarter lay to the east of the Akerselva river, the middle class to the west. Karl Johan, the main street of Oslo, acted as a type of frontier between the two areas, and during the May festival it became the site for great celebrations.

But with the outbreak of war, class differences seemed no longer to be of any great importance. The Akerselva developed into a type of dialectic barrier, and the contrast between east and west owed more to history than to present realities.

I myself grew up on the west side. My parents were fairly well-off and I was probably rather spoiled. I never really paid much attention to the class differences that existed between the two areas. They were there to be seen, but I was barely aware of them. I seemed to keep to my side of the fence and was consequently exposed to the artistic circles round my mother — actors, musicians, writers and even politicians. My friends from the salon introduced me to the *demi monde* of the restaurants and cafés around the Karl Johan, which meant that I knew a good cross-section of people and managed to avoid becoming prejudiced.

Towards the end of the 1930s, Norway had established its own film industry and father decided that we should try our hand at it. No one in Oslo was experienced enough in the make-up business, so Ingrid Jensen, one of our stylists, was sent to Stockholm to learn the basics from a man named C. M. Lundh and, not long after, I found myself in London for six months on a similar course. I received tuition from Max

Factor who, at the time, were the market leaders in that particular field. And so I learnt the art of make-up for the film industry; I picked up the little tricks of the trade: how to create a deep gash on the cheek, how to mix up a browny-red liquid to look like genuine blood.

Father had also started producing shampoo and beauty products under his own name, and this eventually became my responsibility. Myself and Gunnar Boedtker-Naess, a chemical engineer, worked in a cellar blending salves and creams. We created perming lotions and even a synthetic shampoo to compete with the German-made Schwarzkopf which was extremely popular. It was a non-alkaline product, which meant weeks of frustrating hard work before Gunnar hit on the right formula for production. Face creams, day creams and night creams were also blended, and even though the day cream tended to degenerate after a very short while, we still maintained healthy sales figures.

·I moved into my parents' new flat and invited Rachel home on the first evening. She had decided to stay in Norway, at least for the time being. Father helped her to find lodgings in a boarding house and also to get a job as a waitress. She and I kept in regular contact, but she rarely talked about herself. All I knew was that her family had been in a prison camp since the Nazis invaded Austria, that she had left home and was now trying to start a new life for herself.

The day after my arrival back home I started back at work, and relieved my father of the accounting which he had taken care of during my absence. I also paid a visit to the film company to offer our services.

During the winter I helped organise a fashion show at the Regnbuen, a nightclub opposite the National Theatre. A large fashion house was showing its latest collection and we were responsible for the hair and make-up. My particular job was to ensure that everything ran smoothly. Dressed in a morning coat, I introduced the various selections and entertained the audience with small chat during the intervals.

A lot of my evenings were spent in restaurants in the company of friends. We would go to the Ritz, the Regnbuen or the Bristol, and sometimes Gunnar and I would disappear off to a restaurant on Drammensveien. At lunchtime father and I usually ate together at the Theatercaféen restaurant.

Nothing much happened during the autumn. I just worked and enjoyed myself. Thanks to the fashion show, I had gained a certain amount of notoriety. I suppose I appeared quite cocky at times. I certainly liked the attention, but I suppose that's youth for you.

Rachel and I saw less and less of each other. Perhaps she was put off by my behaviour, or maybe she just found the company of my friends and I less than appealing. She appeared to be coping, however. She had learnt some Norwegian, even if she spoke with a strong accent, and after a few months she could make herself easily understood.

During these months I lived a hectic, carefree life. It was probably a natural reaction to the fact that I had been close to the war even if I had not witnessed it at first hand and that I had felt the atmosphere of fear and uncertainty. Perhaps that was exactly what I was trying to forget by throwing myself into my work and leading a hectic social life that occasionally led to sharing a girl's inviting bed. Sometimes it would be a new acquaintance, but more often a girl from the salon whose nickname was Pus and who was regarded by all as my fiancée.

I kept abreast of the world news. Every evening my father would turn on the radio to listen to the BBC broadcast; we heard of the Germans' swift triumph over Poland, the entry of the Soviet troops into the war, the bombings in Warsaw, battles fought in the North Sea, the disappointment when Hitler survived the attempt on his life in a Munich beer-hall.

Our sympathies clearly lay with the Allies. Father was openly pro-English and never missed an opportunity to express his hatred for the Germans — and there were plenty of opportunities. There is always plenty of time for a chat when cutting hair, and before the customers were handed to the assistants for perming and setting the war always featured as a topic.

Christmas was drawing near. In fact it had already begun at the end of November when mother bought her presents and started wrapping them. Christmas was a big occasion. It never changed. Friends and relatives could not be forgotten, so parcels were sent over to England, and to the north of Norway where most of father's family lived.

Father had been born in Bodö and grandfather owned a bakery and liked to be known as "Scandinavia's biggest baker". Maybe it was true that he provided half of the fishermen in the north with their daily bread. Batches of parcels were sent to Bodö, Namsos, Steinkjaer and Mo i Rana. As Christmas Eve approached, the postman would put notifications of the arrival of parcels in our letterbox and I would be sent to the local post office to fetch them. I always remember that every year we received two kilos of goat's cheese in good time for Christmas dinner.

This Christmas wasn't that different from those before the war. There was a chill in the air, snow on the ground which crunched underfoot as you walked along the ill-kept pavements. We hadn't really been affected by the war. Our petrol was rationed of course, but that only affected our yacht, which had been brought up on to dry land. The shops were still well stocked, and Christmas dinner was spent with my parents, our good friends Arnesen and Silvander, their English-born wives and the girls, Eva and Eleanor, playmates from my younger days. It was just as much fun as it always was.

After Christmas the domestic bliss ended. My parents decided to separate once again. Mother found a hotel apartment on Wergelandsveien, where she knew the architect, and moved into the eighth floor of the newly built block. Father found a flat in Therese's Gate not far from Bislet. There was room for me there, and for father's sister, Ragna Måkestad, who was a widow of a parliamentary stenographer. I continued with the bookkeeping and the production of shampoo and creams. I needed a qualification before I could run a professional business so I enrolled for a course at the College of Commerce.

At the end of the day I sometimes paid a visit to Möllhausen's café on Bogstadveien and soon became one of the regulars. People working in the neighbourhood would sneak in for a cup of coffee and a piece of cake while having a chat for a couple of hours before it was time to go home.

Yngvar Fyhn was another of the regular customers. We got on well together, discussing literature and music, often late into the night. Fyhn was one of the leaders of a small political group known as the NNSAP (Norwegian National Socialist Labour Party). They were right-wing though not too extreme; the party symbol was the swastika, but they were nothing to do with Quisling's National Assembly.

Fyhn lived in Bislet and we would occasionally accompany each other home from the café. One evening he asked if I would like to join his party. I told him that my sympathies lay in the other direction. After all I was half-English and it was impossible for me to become a member of a group that used a swastika as its emblem. Besides, father had warned me against holding any political allegiance. Not that he had anything against the Left or the Right, it was simply that he felt it might adversely affect business. It was best to be neutral. Given that we ran one of Oslo's leading beauty salons, it might just have put off some of the customers. Fyhn seemed to appreciate my point of view and we never touched on the subject again.

One evening in February I succeeded in getting Rachel to go out with me. A great deal of persuasion was required. I felt it was as if she didn't want to be seen out. I thought she was avoiding me, but I later discovered the real reason. We ended up at the Regnbuen and had a good meal. She didn't say much, but did reveal some details about herself that I hadn't known before.

She'd been on her way to Poland when the war broke

out. Her relatives in Krakow had promised to look after her when her father and mother had been taken by the Germans. She had intended to get to Poland from Paris, but never made it.

'I'm Jewish,' she said. 'And I have a French passport. What do you think will happen to me when the Germans arrive?'

'The Germans won't come here,' I said both honestly and with conviction. It was totally unthinkable to me that the Germans would dare to attack Norway. What possible interest could Hitler have in us? It was England and France he was at war with. A huge show of strength was expected in the West, so the Germans couldn't afford to waste soldiers, planes and ships on an operation in the North. Norway was a neutral country and Rachel could feel safe here.

On our way out I met a friend in the cloakroom, so Rachel went on ahead of me. When I came out into the clear, cold winter air, I noticed that she was surrounded by some youngsters who were obviously a bit drunk. I shoved them aside and took her by the arm. As we hurriedly walked away, one of them swore after us.

'What did they want?' I asked.

'Nothing,' she replied, 'but I couldn't help thinking what things would be like if I was still in Austria.' We walked into Karl Johan street, crossed the small park that was now covered in snow, turned off the path and trudged through deeper snow there. She stopped unexpectedly, took a deep breath, drew herself closer to me and buried her face into my shoulder. I could feel her sobbing quietly. Eventually, when she had calmed down, I took her home. I only ever saw her once again after that.

The weather became milder and the midday thaw made the streets and pavements slippery and slushy. Spring was slowly coming. We were currently involved in filming at a studio in Jar, just outside Oslo. The film was entitled *Tante Pose*, and once again we had taken charge of the make-up. Ingrid Jensen and I had been contracted by the film company. Every morning they would arrive to collect us in a large limousine, a huge eight-seater Buick.

During the evening before filming, we packed everything we would need for the day. We had gone over the specifications for each actor and knew what make-up to use, the different shades for lips and eyebrows, and all the other facial disguises that were needed.

The car arrived at six in the morning. We climbed in, huddled together with the lighting crew and the sound technician, still yawning and half asleep. We lurched from side to side as the car drifted over the tracks and furrows of melted snow cleared from the roadway. On arrival several hours of hard work lay ahead. Everyone had to be ready for filming at nine; Hans Bille, Ellen Isefjaer, Eva Lunde and the others had to have their hair set and their make-up looking fresh. It took over an hour to create a beard and I was far from being a total professional, but the actors helped me out. They had been involved in the profession for a long time, and many of them, over the years, had had to do their own make-up whilst touring with theatre companies. Hans Bille, one of my mother's old friends, often put me right and if he saw me hesitating he did it himself.

Father regarded the film work as a complement to the other activities of the company. We now had both gentlemen's and ladies' salons, a beauty expert, a masseuse, and people trained as manicurists and pedicurists. The laboratory was in full swing, and we could now add film work to the list.

March passed by with the daily routine work at the film studio. Father and I listened to the BBC broadcasts during the evening when the reception was far better than in daytime. The war continued in its quiet way. The news flashes were rarely major, but the tension was mounting. I spent Sundays working on our yacht, christened *Ada* after my grandmother. Soon it would be time to return her to the water, and like every other year she had to be sanded down and repainted, which was my job.

On the afternoon of 8 April there was an atmosphere of unease in the film studio. Someone had heard that the English had laid mines off the west coast, that there were minefields in three different spots inside territorial waters. I refused to believe it. However, when we returned home after the day's filming, we discovered that the rumours were true. Small groups of people stood huddled together in the streets; the Foreign Secretary had apparently spoken in Parliament, saying that the Western powers had now taken the war into Norwegian territory. Others had heard that the British Navy was on its way to Bergen, Trondheim and Narvik, but nobody could say for definite.

I went to find my father. He had also heard the rumours — a hairdresser is always well informed. He didn't say very much, but I could see that he was shaken. He tried to defend their actions: it was just a precaution; the mines were meant for the Germans, not us; the Allies had to prevent offensive action rather than defend against it.

He didn't carry it off. He was disappointed. His people, the English, had broken Norway's neutrality.

That evening we sat, as always, listening to the radio. The BBC confirmed that the mines had been floated, but this, we were assured, in no way indicated an offensive against Norway.

Father turned off the radio, slamming his fist down on the square box. Without a word he walked quietly into his room.

4

Just after midnight, we were woken up by a deafening noise. The air-raid sirens were wailing outside, a hoarse, piercing sound.

I got out of bed, went over to the window, and pulled up the blind. Down on the street I saw some late-night walkers standing, looking up at the sky. When I opened the window, the noise from the sirens filled the room. Father padded through in his slippers and we stood listening for a while, staring down on the illuminated street, and searching the black skies. The siren stopped as abruptly as it had begun. The people below scurried away, and soon the street was empty and quiet.

'I don't understand why they have to test the sirens in the middle of the night,' father said. 'The whole of Oslo has just been woken up.' He drew his dressing-gown round himself and shuffled back to his bedroom.

I closed the window again to shut out the cold night air. It had made me feel wide awake and irritated. In a couple of hours' time I would need to feel alert and full of energy. I sat down in an armchair and tried to relax. The sirens had frightened me. Just like father I didn't understand why they had to test the defence system in the middle of the night.

Then the light went out, so I got up and groped my way into the hall to the fuse box. It didn't take long to realise that it wasn't the fuses which had blown. The whole street lay in darkness, without even the light from the street lamps. It was pitch black outside. I felt my way back to my room, lay down and tried to sleep, tossing and turning for what seemed like ages. Eventually I fell asleep, but it only seemed as if a few minutes had passed when my alarm clock went off.

So it was back to work. I set the table for breakfast and got ready to leave. By six o'clock I was down at the corner of Bislet waiting for the car to pick me up. I walked over to a policeman who was standing talking at an emergency telephone fixed to the wall of a house.

'That was some din last night,' I said. He nodded, closed the box and turned towards me. He smiled and replied, 'The word is that the Germans are on their way up the Oslo fjord.'

'The Germans?' I stared at him. It couldn't possibly be true, I could tell by his smile that it couldn't possibly be true.

'I heard it at the station. The Germans are on their way to Oslo. Bergen and Trondheim have already fallen. It's almost certainly a hoax.'

'Thank God for that,' I replied.

'Probably just another rumour,' said the policeman. 'You shouldn't believe everything that you hear. Besides, what would the Germans want with us?'

He strolled off just as the car arrived, and I climbed in. One of the lighting technicians and two of the actors sat half asleep in the cushioned seats. I repeated what the policeman had told me and we all agreed that it was impossible; one of the many rumours that had been circulating over the last few days. A German invasion of Norway was unthinkable. None of the others had heard anything about the Germans advancing, and no declaration of war had been issued either.

The car made a couple more stops to pick up Ingrid Jensen and Ellen Isefjaer at Frogner Plass. Nobody had heard the latest reports, but we were still worried about the English mines. Someone suggested that a minesweeper had already been sent out, the danger would soon pass, and the episode be forgotten. The Norwegian defence was on its guard.

When we arrived at the film studio we began the usual

routine. Conversation was never very bright in the morning as most of the actors were sleepy and took the opportunity to relax during make-up. Eventually we were ready for the first take of the day. The camera was in place, the actors prepared themselves, rehearsing their lines. I checked their make-up one last time, and the spotlights were switched on, lighting up the studio. Director Sinding gave the go-ahead. The camera started rolling, the sound technician signalled from his glass box and put on his bulky headphones, then at last he gave the thumbs up. The man with the clapper-board placed himself in front of the camera. Action.

Before the actors could begin, the sound technician pulled off his head-set and shouted: 'Hold it, I'm getting some sort of engine noise. It must be a car.'

We listened, but we couldn't hear anything. The microphones on the booms were obviously more sensitive than our hearing.

'I can't hear a thing,' said Sinding. 'Let's get on with it.'

But the noise could still be heard by the technician. 'It's a motor,' he said. 'It's as clear as a bell. There must be an engine still running outside.'

Sinding ordered an assistant to run out and check. We waited. He soon returned to report that there was no sign of any car. 'Let's go,' said Sinding.

The procedure was repeated. The actors stood in place, Ingrid went round with the make-up sponge and brush to freshen up cheeks and hair. The camera started, the man with the clapper-board did his job and the action began. They managed a couple of lines before the sound technician gave up.

'It won't work,' he said. 'The noise is still there.'

Sinding rose from his director's chair, waving his arms about angrily, then he rushed into the sound box, grabbed the earphones away from the technician and listened intently. We watched him, saw him concentrate hard, after which he slung the earphones away, took a couple of quick steps, raised his arms and pointed to the door. 'There must be a car out there,' he shouted. 'Tell that bloody idiot to turn off his motor!'

The assistant crept out again and I followed him. The courtyard outside the studio was empty except for the company limousine, but the motor wasn't running. There were no vehicles to be seen on the road and not a sound came from the forest. We listened attentively and searched around us. Everything was quiet and calm, so we went back inside. 'We can't see a thing,' I said. 'There are no cars running.'

'I can still hear that engine,' the sound technician retorted.

'There must be something wrong with your equipment,' said Sinding.

'So far it has worked without a hitch,' said the sound technician.

'There must be something,' shouted Sinding. 'Are the cables attached in the right sequence?'

'Exactly as they should be,' replied the sound technician.

Sinding was furious, but he'd run out of arguments. He remained quiet as we all stood still and waited. Then we heard it. A faint whining noise; the regular turn of a running engine. Sinding turned round slowly, listening anxiously. It was definitely an engine. The noise grew louder and we knew it was coming closer.

'You can hear it for yourself,' said the sound technician.

Sinding strode over to the door, opened it and yelled, 'For God's sake turn off that motor!'

Nothing happened. The noise just got louder and louder. It echoed through the studio and the air vibrated with its drone. Then all at once we realised what it was. We ran out into the gravel yard, stopped and looked up at the sky. An aeroplane thundered low over the treetops. It was grey and bore the Germans' familiar emblem on its underwing. It was followed by another plane, then another two — swastikas at the end of the tailfins.

The rumour was true: the Germans were in Norway. The four planes thundered past and we even caught a glimpse of the pilot in the last plane. Then the sound of the motors died out. We didn't know where they were headed; they would land at Gardermoen, or so we supposed, since they were flying in that direction.

We didn't say much to each other, but stood there for a long time, staring up at the sky, watching the wispy clouds drift by.

'They were Germans,' one of the actors affirmed.

We nodded. We had all seen that. We'd all realised that they were armed war machines, and we were scared and worried. What would happen now? Had the Germans really launched an offensive?

Sinding went back into the studio. Slowly we followed him inside, listening all the time for more engine sounds, explosions, the rattle of gunfire and anti-aircraft flak. But there was nothing. Why didn't our troops open fire on the German planes?

There was a radio in the kitchen where we used to gather during our coffee breaks. Someone turned it on and it crackled into action. But no voice could be heard.

'Does anyone have a newspaper?' asked the clapper-board man. None of us had read the morning paper. They hadn't been delivered by the time we'd been collected.

'Well, we can't film any more today,' I said to the director. I had to get home as quickly as possible. I wanted to know what had happened and what was to be done. Would those of us who hadn't yet joined military service be drafted? Where could we turn to?

'We'll suspend filming for the time being,' said Sinding, 'but we'll be in touch.'

We cleared up as quickly as we could. Everyone wanted to get back to Oslo to find out what was happening. I gathered up my jars and flasks, put them into their cases, and then our party clambered into the Buick.

Oslo didn't look quite the same. People stood together at street corners, involved in animated discussion. The driver stopped outside a newsagent and one of the team jumped out and bought the *Tidens Tegn*. He held up the front page so that we could read the headlines: FOREIGN WARSHIPS FORCE THEIR WAY INTO THE OSLO FJORD DURING THE NIGHT. We read in silence. Someone swore. The story expanded on the headline's impact. Norway was at war.

I was dropped off downtown and decided to visit my mother. I half ran past the university and continued up the hill towards Wergelandsveien. Oslo was definitely transformed. The atmosphere was strange. Planes could be heard in the distance, and I thought I could distinguish the sound of an anti-aircraft gun. People were rushing about in a panic; dashing about in random directions. An old man hurried aimlessly around, trying to find someone who knew more about it, someone who could tell him what to do.

Exhausted, I reached Wergelandsveien where mother lived. The lift wasn't working, so I had to walk up the eight flights of stairs. I rang her doorbell, my heart pounding. She opened the door and gave me a hug. I could feel her shaking. 'Did you know the Germans are in Norway?' she whispered.

'I know,' I said. 'We just stopped filming. What are we going to do?'

She could just as easily have asked me that. None of us knew the best thing to do. Should we stay in Oslo? Should we try and get to the countryside? Would it be safer there anyway? Nothing had been planned since we hadn't thought that we would suddenly be drawn into the war.

'I wonder what grandfather will think when he finds out,' mother said.

I leafed through a bundle of morning papers she had bought. Some were full of information, others hadn't had the time to print much of the night's happenings. Some of the reports were conflicting, but one thing was clear: the Germans had attacked Norway.

Shooting had been reported in Bergen and there were German warships in the Oslo fjord. Just how far had they managed to get during the morning? Mother's voice came from the kitchen. 'Help will come soon,' she said. 'They

say that the British Navy is already on its way. Our troops
will be able to hold out until they arrive.'

I don't know if she believed that, or if she was just trying
to convince herself that what had happened was simply a
temporary threat, a mere diversion that would soon be
swept aside when the British arrived to restore peace.

An aeroplane flew overhead and I went out on to the
terrace. I looked over the Palace Park to the cranes in the
harbour and then further out to sea. Maybe that was a
warship I could see on the horizon; but whatever it was,
cruiser or destroyer, it was almost totally obscured by an
islet. The planes flew low in formation, their motors
growing louder and louder as they swooped over the city
centre.

Mother came out and stood beside me. The aeroplanes
flew closer, almost passing right over the house, and then
we heard something hit the tin roof. It took some time to
realise that it was shrapnel clattering over our heads. Pieces
of metal rained down on the block, splinters bouncing off
the roofs. The Norwegian anti-aircraft defence was in
action. I quickly grabbed mother by the arm and dragged
her inside. Bombers thundered past and then disappeared.

I think that was the first time that I fully understood our
predicament. The war was not simply a cursory newspaper
article about something intangible that took place far away.
It was no longer a radio broadcast along the lines of a mere
sports commentary, ourselves the interested spectators.
The war had also reached Oslo. We'd been dragged into
the fight, and now it was a question of holding out.

'We'd better stay inside,' I said. 'The planes might come
back this way.'

She nodded and went to the kitchen. I could hear the
clinking of coffee cups and the biscuit tin. Before long, she
came back into the lounge with a well-laden tea-tray.

'I'll have to find father,' I said. 'He might be wondering
where I am.' Besides, he would certainly know a lot more
about what was going on.

'I'll come with you,' my mother replied.

Since their last divorce they had met only very rarely. They could still talk to each other, as good friends, and when they were together on my birthday and other such special occasions the atmosphere was always a happy one. This was one of those special occasions.

When we came down into Wergelandsveien we decided to cut through the Slottsparken towards the Tivolihallen. The lawns were becoming more lush and the trees in the park would soon have their new foliage. It was cool, but spring was in the air. A flock of finches hopped across the gravel path in search of food.

Once again there was the distant drone of planes; more of them on their way to the heart of the city. They thundered over the park, followed by the splinters of flak raining to the ground. We took shelter under a tree and watched the downpour of metal as it covered the lawns and paths. We just stood and waited. I realised that we had little protection but I couldn't see anywhere safer, and anyway it was impossible to guess on which side of the tree the shrapnel would fall. The aircraft shortly disappeared. We had escaped unhurt, and hurried along to Tivolihallen.

The salon was closed; the staff had gone home, but we found father sitting in the office. He was at his desk, his head buried in his hands. He looked up and pulled over a chair for mother. 'The Germans will be here soon,' he said. 'Oslo has surrendered — I just heard. We hoisted the white flag when they threatened to bomb the city.'

'What about the rest of the country?' I asked.

'Still fighting. The King has gone, along with the Government and the Storting. They're supposed to have set up a base in Hamar.'

'What's going to happen?' asked mother.

'The Germans will lose the war,' said father. 'Oslo will soon be free again.'

'Are you sure?'

He straightened up and went out into the hall. We followed him to the pavement and looked towards the National Theatre. A truck drove past, then an elderly couple walked by, an old man leaning on a stick, whilst his wife held his arm. They were pulling a small cart after them, loaded with knotted and badly wrapped bundles. They hurried along, downcast.

'The Germans haven't marched into the city yet,' said father. 'That's something to be happy about. I'll buy you lunch, or have you eaten?'

I hadn't thought about food all day but I felt hungry now. We crossed the road to the Theatercaféen and as usual were served by Hernaes, the head waiter. Father ordered a meat dish; we drank a bottle of wine and chatted about our plans for when the Germans would enter the city.

'Life must go on,' said father. 'We'll continue as if nothing had happened. Tomorrow we'll open the salon at the usual time. After that we'll have to grit our teeth and wait.'

Hernaes came to our table. 'They're here,' he said.

We knew who 'they' were. The Germans were on their way into Oslo. We settled the bill and walked out into Stortingsgaten and through 'Studenterlunden'. We heard the steady beat of marching as a unit of Germans came tramping into Karl Johan street, all in complete uniform.

We stopped and watched them. We weren't alone. Rows of silent people lined the pavements watching the entrance of our new occupiers.

I felt unsure of myself. How were you supposed to react when enemy soldiers suddenly appear, marching through the streets of Oslo? I clearly wasn't the only confused spectator. Some cried, some turned away, some swore under their breath, others shook their fists at the soldiers. But that was the sum total of our protest: no one rushed forward to fight off their advance. It was as if we all understood our helplessness. The sight of marching troops instilled in us a feeling of total resignation. We were paralysed.

I thought of 17 May, when schoolchildren paraded through the very same streets waving their miniature flags. I'd been there several times, singing together with the other spectators. We had cheered for the fatherland then. This parade was met with silence. No one cheered — or could I hear the clapping of hands? I turned. A bit further along some people stood beaming at the scene. They were quietened, but I understood that there were those who didn't feel the same as us.

'I can't stand this any longer,' father whispered. I looked at him. His face was ashen, his eyes blank; he was having trouble holding himself back.

Slowly we made our way up towards the Palace. The King was no longer in residence. Perhaps he was organising the counter-defence. Tomorrow, or perhaps in a few days' time, Oslo would be liberated.

We took mother to Wergelandsveien. Then we walked home. There were German soldiers everywhere, small platoons marching along the middle of the road. Here and there a group stood outside a shop to look at the displays in the window. On Pilestredet a couple of soldiers stepped out of a sweet shop with handfuls of chocolate. One of them had a packet of butter under his arm. They looked happy. We watched them as they moved into a street doorway and started eating. One of them even spread butter on a bar of chocolate and ate it like a sandwich.

'They obviously don't have chocolate or butter in Germany,' said father.

When we got home we turned on the radio. It was silent, but we left it on, hoping we might just catch a message later in the evening. We prepared dinner together. During the meal we exchanged few words, but our minds were active.

Suddenly the radio crackled into life. We listened, and father turned the sound up: 'Major Vidkun Quisling will now address the Norwegian people,' came the announcement.

'Quisling?' shrieked father. 'What's he got to do with it?'

A piece of background music struck up. We waited impatiently, then finally we heard Quisling's voice: 'Fellow Norwegians, since England broke Norway's neutrality by planting mines in Norwegian territorial waters, an act met only by tame protests from the Nygaardsvold Government, the German Government has offered . . .' The doorbell rang. I got up and crept into the hall whilst trying to listen to the monstrous, strained voice.

I opened the door and found Rachel standing outside. She was dressed in a casual jacket, a long skirt and heavy shoes. She wore a woollen hat and carried a rucksack on her back. 'I have to get away,' she whispered. 'I need a bicycle. Can you help me?'

In the drawing-room Quisling droned on: '. . . under these circumstances it is the National Assembly's duty and right to replace the government . . .'

'I've only got a man's bike,' I said, 'but I'll try and get hold of a lady's bike for you. Where are you going to go?'

'Sweden. The Nazis haven't reached there yet.'

'Surely the trains must still be running?'

'It's safer to cycle. Trains can be inspected. There are several of us together.'

One of our staff lived close by so I asked Rachel to come inside and wait. Then I put on my coat and ran off. A quarter of an hour later I returned with a bicycle. It wasn't new, but it was in good working order. Father was looking after Rachel, giving her some dinner.

'The day the Germans lose the war is not far off,' he said. Rachel tried to smile.

I followed her out into the street, where it had begun to grow dark. She tried the bike out and I adjusted the saddle for her. Then I held her close. 'Good luck,' I said.

She pushed off with her foot, climbed up and started pedalling. I stood there and watched her disappear into a side street.

I don't know what happened to her. Perhaps she found peace somewhere. I hope so.

5

Oslo was an occupied city, but life went on. The German occupation didn't give rise to any immediate, earth-shattering changes. Everything was pretty much the same as usual: people set off for work as normal. Father reopened the salons, the staff returned to work, serving the customers just as before. During those first few days there were understandably fewer appointments, but after just a week it was all back to normal.

Filming also restarted after a short break. Sinding received permission to continue from the newly formed leadership, and even managed to obtain some extra petrol rations. The Buick arrived to pick us up just as before.

The only noticeably new aspect of city life was the presence of the German soldiers who marched through the streets in their blue uniforms. We didn't much care for the Germans. After all, they had conquered us and captured Oslo. But there was no directly expressed hatred of them for a considerable time. They now had military superiority; we had yielded to their arms and as occupiers of the city they behaved very correctly. They were even polite in the shops.

On the other hand, we detested Quisling and his fellow compatriots more than ever. They were traitors and belonged with the Fifth Column who had paved the way for the Nazi invasion.

Every evening was spent listening to the BBC. We learnt of the fighting which was still carrying on to the north of Norway, of the landing of British troops in Narvik, and that the King and his government were still in hiding.

The present atmosphere was established by these snippets of news. It all seemed to be going in the Germans' favour. UFA at the cinemas depicted recent victories. We wanted to believe that it was all propaganda, but the BBC confirmed the worst; the Allied Forces really were retreating.

There was soon a shortage of provisions in the shops. Our captors bought up everything they laid their eyes on, in what were comparatively well-stocked stores, so we began hoarding food and in just a few weeks the shelves were empty. At the same time we tried to adapt to the new order of things. We reluctantly came to realise that Oslo would not be liberated next week, or next month, and the Germans were here to stay for a lot longer than we'd anticipated. Our yearned-for victory would have to bide its time.

I had plenty to keep me busy. Every morning I prepared for my journey to the film studio, and if I had time in the afternoon I made myself useful at the salon. Once *Tante Pose* had been completed, our presence was no longer necessary and I could now spend all my time at the salon. The conversation there always seemed to come back to the same question: what should we do? We certainly had a lot to do, but salon work seemed somehow unfulfilling. I wondered if something could be done to help the Resistance movement.

Father made his opinions quite clear. As far as he was concerned the German success would be short-lived. It was just a matter of putting a brave face on it and waiting until the nightmare was over. In the meantime, he would take care of the business as best he could; ensure that the staff had work, and that they received a wage. At the same time he offered hope and consolation to those who felt there was no way out.

Our regular customers knew which side of the fence father stood on. His optimism was openly expressed for all to hear, together with his conviction that the Germans would eventually be defeated. However, our circle of

customers slowly began to change, for Oslo had given birth
to a new social strata, a new upper class. The wives of
Quisling's ministers tried to live up to their position as the
first ladies of the new government. They made their
appointments in the salon at Tivoli. They were never
turned away. Father maintained that you should never mix
business and politics, but when they arrived our staff just
happened to be busy with other clients and they were
politely asked to wait. Father generally took care of these
new ladies himself. He treated them no differently from
any of his other customers; he was polite and courteous,
but should the conversation turn to the war, he always
spoke his mind.

I tried to warn him. I told him to be a bit more careful.
His opinions could be seen in a bad light and get him into
serious trouble. He couldn't understand because his belief
in a British victory was more like a religious conviction and
he saw it as his duty to preach this simple but irrevocable
truth.

I should really have been quite content. The salons were
doing well, our products were proving immensely
successful. We were making money, we lived well, our
lifestyle had barely changed at all. But I felt I had to do
something. What though? Spit in a German's face? Drag
some officer into a dark alley and beat him half to death?
Such protests were meaningless. Why did no one from the
Resistance approach me? I waited, continued with my
work, but grew ever more determined to find something
different.

One particular summer evening I had gone to the Ritz, to
a dance. I had asked a girl I had met for a date. She was
there with a girlfriend and asked if I would join them. A
tall, thin man sat with them. He was a few years older than
I and introduced himself as Tor Glad. We exchanged a few
words, everyday chit-chat about the weather and the
orchestra. I had learnt to be cautious with strangers.

We all danced and once the musicians took a break I
continued talking to Tor. He seemed a sympathetic chap

with a pleasant sense of humour, and I found myself liking him.

He told me of the officers' training course for engineers in which he had taken part on 9 April. His detail had been kitted out and sent off to fight, but he had been captured by the Germans. 'We were released after a couple of days,' he said. 'I can't complain of ill-treatment, but it was an awful experience. We surrendered almost immediately, just when we should have been strengthening our defence, not weakening it.'

'If you had done, you wouldn't be sitting here tonight,' I said.

'You've no idea what it's like being a prisoner-of-war.'

'You should be grateful that you survived. Now at least you can live to fight another day.'

'I know,' came the reply.

The conductor called up the orchestra. The girls had been listening and grown bored with our talk. They wanted to dance, so we shuffled, turned and waltzed for a while. The dance-floor was crowded and we kept bumping into people, but I held my date close and tried to keep in step.

When I returned to the table I asked Tor what he did for a living. 'I was Sam Eyde's personal secretary for six months before I was called up.'

I had heard of Sam Eyde. He was a well-known scientist, one of the founders of the Norwegian Hydro.

'It must have been quite interesting,' I said.

'Well, I was happy.'

'Are you still with him?'

'No.' Tor turned to the girl beside him, got up and led her on to the dance-floor.

'We really should be doing something,' I said.

'Well, you can start by dancing with me.'

'I meant about the Germans. I don't know what exactly, but there must be something.'

'I know what you meant, but what?'

'Dance,' I replied. I took her hand as we walked on to the floor for the last dance.

Soon the orchestra were packing away their instruments, so we made our way to the foyer. Before we parted company Tor asked if we could meet the following day. I was a little taken aback — we weren't exactly close friends, but I quite liked him, so we arranged a rendezvous.

The following evening I stood outside the National Theatre waiting for him. As it was quite a warm night I sat on a bench. A German soldier strolled past with a young girl on his arm — I turned away. Tor then appeared; serious, frightened almost. Quietly he sat down beside me and tried to smile.

'I enjoyed last night,' he eventually said.

'Me too,' I replied.

'It went on a bit late though, I've been tired all day.'

'Same here.'

There were plenty of people out for a stroll. Groups of Germans in uniform, families out for an evening walk, youngsters.

'Shall we walk a bit?' Tor asked, getting on his feet. 'We'll look for somewhere quieter,' he added. 'There's something I want to talk to you about.'

I knew there was something on his mind from the moment he arrived. He hadn't wanted to see me just to talk about the previous evening's little romance.

We made our way to the Slottsparken. Tor made sure that there was nobody within earshot and began. 'I've heard a lot about your father, and how he feels about the Germans.'

It was clearly common knowledge.

'What about you? What do you think?' he continued.

'I thought you knew. My grandfather is English, so is my mother. I spent half my life over in England.'

'Well, you never know who you could be talking to,' said Tor. 'But I think I can trust you. I felt I could rely on you after last night.'

'You've nothing to worry about as far as that's concerned. But what's this all about? What do you want?'

He stopped and looked around again. I thought I could

detect a trace of fear in his eyes.

There was nobody about. Slottsparken lay enshrouded by the summer evening dusk. The noise of traffic could be heard in the distance but there were only a few cars on Karl Johan. He stuck his hand into his pocket and pulled out a scrap of paper. It was folded up small, but he opened it out and handed it to me. There was some writing scrawled on it, but I couldn't read it.

'What is it?' I asked.

'Names,' Tor replied. 'Norwegian companies that the Germans are checking out. They have to be warned.'

'You mean, you want me to warn them?'

'You could pass the list on to someone with the right contacts.'

'I don't know anybody.'

'What about your father? I don't have contacts either. I can't even write to someone — the letter is bound to end up at the censor's.'

I had heard about the post censor. Under the circumstances the Germans would certainly be checking the post. The letters we received from relatives and friends had been read and resealed, and stamped to say that they had been opened by the German authorities.

We strolled towards a street lamp, the gravel crunching beneath our feet. I held the paper in my hand, not knowing what to say. For a moment I thought it might have been a trap. Tor could have been sent by the German authorities to see if there were any underground organisations who could handle this type of thing, and trying to make contact with me would be an obvious move. My father was a well-known opponent of the occupiers and the Quisling Government. But Tor didn't look like an *agent provocateur*. He had been altogether too honest and frank, and what's more he was scared. He was also a true Norwegian. He had been a sergeant and had even spent time as a prisoner-of-war.

'How did you get hold of the names?' I asked.

'I wrote them down,' he whispered. 'I work at the

censor's office.'

'You work there? For the Germans?' I stopped and stared at him. He was slightly taller than myself. His face was gaunt, his body thin and gangly.

'Yes. I work for the Germans as a censor. I read people's letters, and . . . well . . . I make a note of those who are treading on dangerous ground, to warn them. But I don't know how to and I thought your father might be able to help.'

I could quite easily have handed him back the list of names. I could have said that I wouldn't know how to go about it either and I wouldn't have been lying. Despite the fact that only a few months had passed under German occupation, suspicion and mistrust were widespread. Who could you trust? Who could make sure that the list ended up in the right hands? I had no idea what to do, but I folded up the paper and put it in my pocket. 'I'll try,' I said.

Tor looked relieved. It was only then that I decided I could trust him. He must have felt the same way, because if he was speaking the truth he could be putting himself in grave danger too. I could easily take the note to the authorities.

'Thanks, John,' he said. 'I expect you're wondering why I ended up at the censor's?'

'Why did you take the job?'

'I wanted to help in some way.'

We carried on walking, turning off down one of the many badly kept side streets that led to the harbour. Tor continued with his story.

Before the war he had been employed by Sam Eyde. He lived in Wiesbaden for six months while Eyde was very ill. Eyde died during the first year of occupation. Tor was unemployed and at a loose end. By pure chance, during a trip to Holmenkollen, he met a German with exceptionally high connections. They got talking and when the diplomat heard how good Tor's German was, he asked if he would like to work for the German authorities. Tor replied that he had a low opinion of the Nazis. In Wiesbaden he had witnessed a mob of Hitler's *Jugen* destroy a shop owned by a Jew. Something he would never forget. The diplomat told him that people were needed to censor the post, people with a sound knowledge of languages. The authorities had nothing to do with the Nazis anyway; it was just a necessary function at a time of war.

'So you joined them?'

'I thought about it for a few days and then decided to accept. It was at least a chance to do some good.'

'By collecting names?'

'At the time I didn't really have much of an idea. I thought I might be able to allow dangerous letters to pass through. Only it wasn't that easy. If only we could get in touch with these people.'

He said 'we'. 'We' were going to work together. He would collect the information and I would pass it on. The two of us would contribute to the war effort as a team. We could build up our own resistance unit. I felt that this could lead to something. It was what I had been waiting for. Perhaps the start of something big.

I searched for reasons not to help: Tor worked for the authorities, and he was paid with their money. But he wasn't a Nazi sympathiser. He had taken the job to help reduce the impact of censorship. The end justifies the means. I felt that he had been particularly courageous, putting his head in the lion's mouth, so to speak.

'I'll see what I can do,' I said. 'I won't give up until I find a way.'

Tor stopped, held out his hand and shook mine hard, holding it fast. It was almost as if we had sworn an allegiance although we didn't mix blood. We would do whatever we could to undermine the Germans' hold on Oslo, and in our own way, albeit somewhat amateurish.

I was well aware that our efforts would be extremely limited. We wouldn't drive the Germans from Norway. In fact we could do little to disrupt their impressive efficiency. But we might help spare some Norwegian patriots from the Gestapo and that was reason enough.

It was late evening by the time we parted company. Father was asleep when I arrived home, so I had to wait till morning to tell him about the list of names I had been given. He asked if it could possibly be a frame-up. I replied that I could vouch for Tor's trustworthiness. Although I hadn't known him long, I trusted him implicitly.

Father was hesitant. I realised this was something he himself would love to do but, at the same time, he was keen that I should do something by myself. I had always been allowed to make my own decisions, to go my own way. Perhaps that was why I had so much respect for him. I knew I could always go to him for advice. He would give me his own opinion, but it was up to me to make the final decision.

'Perhaps you could try at the Travellers' Club,' he said, 'along Trampelaget? There are people there with contacts. Ask for Erling Jörgensen, he might know someone.' Father had been a member of the club for some years. He had taken me there on several occasions and I had got to know a couple of the other members. They knew me well enough — every 17 May we all got together after the festival procession.

I set off at lunchtime. Erling Jörgensen wasn't there, but I bumped into Åge Berg, a dentist from Nordland, a large red-haired gentleman whom I had met previously. I asked to talk with him in private, as I thought him the sort of man I could trust. I explained why I had come, but avoided mentioning Tor, and showed him the slip of paper—'from a reliable source'.

Åge Berg read the names, scratching his head, and read the list again. Then he put it away in his breast pocket. 'I think I can arrange it,' he said.

'What if there's more?' I asked.

'Come to my house, but make it evening time once I've shut up the practice.'

I left him and went back to the salon. I nodded to father but said nothing. From his expression I could tell that he thought I had made the right contact.

Tor and I met every night. We made plans, most of them

totally impractical. We were extremely enthusiastic. At last
we had found our niche, Tor collecting the lists and myself
passing them on. We would spend the evenings dancing
with girlfriends, taking long evening walks, and planning
ahead. Every now and then we would collect some more
information and I would go to see Åge Berg at his house in
Camilla Collets Vei. They were brief visits; I would be
shown into the hall, hand over the list and be on my way.

As time wore on I decided to try and get work at the
censor's office. Two of us could do twice as much good.

'It's impossible,' Tor told me.

'Why?'

'With your background? With a colonel grandfather in
the British army?'

'An ex-colonel.'

'Forget it. We'll carry on as we have done. It's worked
well so far.'

'But I'm good at languages. I can speak English and
German. It's got to count for something.'

'The Germans will look into your background. And
don't think they won't be thorough. As soon as they find
out that your mother's English, they won't want to know.
They may even hand you over to the Gestapo for
questioning.'

Tor was right, of course. Anyone in my position trying
for a post with the German administration was doomed to
failure. 'You just don't have the right background,' Tor
continued.

But I wasn't going to give up the idea. 'Then I'll get the
right background.'

'Oh, come on. How?'

'I'll join the party.'

6

I was not referring to Quisling and his National Assembly when I mentioned becoming a party member. I had been thinking of Yngvar Fyhn and the time he had asked me to join the NNSAP. If I could show proof of membership, a swastika and a party card, the Germans might think better of me, and it could allay any suspicions they might have. So he's half-English they might say, but he's one of us. He is wearing our emblem on his lapel, a member of a party which is on a par with Hitler's own.

It was hopelessly naïve, of course. I could not pretend I did not have a background, but by openly displaying Nazi sympathies I might just get away with it.

I phoned Fyhn. He remembered me and was sorry that we had not seen each other for such a long time. I mentioned our previous conversations and that I desired to meet him, in private, as there was something I would like to discuss with him. He invited me over to his house. We arranged a time, and I set off immediately up the steep slope to Rosenborgsgatan and rang at his door on the second floor.

Yngvar Fyhn was a large, blond man. He looked Aryan, whatever they look like, but perhaps a bit too well built to pass as a model for the Nazi ideal, even if those deep blue eyes and broad shoulders did make up for the beginnings of a paunch.

He greeted me warmly, smiling broadly, and helped me off with my coat. He had a two-room flat with a small kitchenette. The furniture was plain; you could tell that Fyhn was a bachelor as the place lacked that woman's touch. 'Good to see you, John,' he said. 'Come in.' He offered me some sherry and went to fetch the bottle and two glasses as I sat myself down on a well-worn sofa. 'How are things?' he asked.

'I can't complain.'

'Times are hard.'

'We've got problems. Business is slow; every day brings fewer customers because people can't afford the luxury of getting their hair done as often as they used to.'

He nodded understandingly. He didn't visit any of our salons, so he could hardly know that things had never been better. 'I'm sorry to hear that,' he said. 'No doubt business will improve once things have settled down. It just takes a bit of time.'

'There's hardly anything for me to do anymore,' I moaned. 'I can't just sit around doing nothing and get paid for it. It's an uncomfortable feeling just living off my parents. I don't enjoy it.'

He raised his glass and we drank a toast. The sherry was awful. 'You should try to get another job,' he suggested. 'With your qualifications it shouldn't be too difficult, although I have to admit it's not all easy these days.'

'I heard of a job that's going; but there are a few complications.'

'What's the problem?'

'I want to try for a job with the military post censor,' I replied.

He looked at me inquisitively, put down his glass and sat back in his armchair.

'I heard that they're on the look-out for people with language skills,' I continued. 'I can speak both German and English but, as you know, there are a couple of snags. Grandfather, for example, and mother. The Germans won't take me on just like that.'

'It depends on the way you handle it.'

The conversation was beginning to take shape.

'A while back you asked me to join your party, but I said no.'

'Yes, I remember.'

'It was stupid of me and I regret it now, but at the time I felt obliged to follow my father's principles. Running a hair salon, you can't afford to be too involved in politics. Eilif Hammerö asked me to join the FNF, but I turned him down flat too, and for the same reasons.' It was true — I had been asked to join the voluntary association of Norway's defence.

'I understand your position,' said Fyhn. 'I understood it then and respected your decision. You can accept an honest motive. Better that than take on people who feign their beliefs.'

He got up and walked behind his chair. He wore a pair of grey baggy trousers held up by wide braces. He shuffled over the cheap dining-room carpet in his brown slippers.

'I need the job,' I said. 'I need work desperately. I don't want to be a burden any longer.'

He turned and looked at me. 'I'm afraid I don't really understand why you have come to me. I like you, but I can't really help. I have no contacts at the censor.'

'I want to join the party.'

He sat down in his armchair and put his hands behind his head. 'It no longer exists,' he said.

'What do you mean?'

'It sounds odd, I know, but we've disbanded. When the Germans arrived we put an end to our activities.'

'Why?'

'Because we're Norwegian. We're no traitors. We have our political views, and stand for National Socialism — but first and foremost we're patriots, and there's no way we'd allow ourselves to be run by the Nazis.'

'So the party is defunct?'

'Yes.' He leaned across the table, took the sherry bottle and filled our glasses.

I was astonished; my visit had been all for nothing. The conversation had lost its purpose; I might as well leave. I wasn't going to get anywhere. Or maybe I might. 'Just my luck,' I said. 'It might have done some good, being in the party for a couple of years.'

'Yes, I know, but that's just the way it goes. The party has been disbanded for good.'

'I don't suppose you've got any membership badges left, have you?' I asked. 'You did ask me, and I could always pretend to have joined the first time.'

'There's bound to be some in the drawer, but we burned all the records and other papers.'

'What about membership cards?'

He got up again and walked over to the chest of drawers which stood against one of the longer walls; he opened a drawer and began rummaging through the old papers. Then he lifted out a sizeable box, shut the drawer and placed the box on the table. I just looked at it, trying to calm my enthusiasm and not show too much curiosity.

'This isn't strictly right,' he said. 'However, I understand your problem and, since we're old friends, I'll help you out. I hope it'll prove some good.' He sat down, opened the box and revealed its treasures: papers, glittering swastika badges and membership cards. 'I saved these,' he said. 'Everything else was destroyed. I kept these as a sort of souvenir.'

He took one of the membership cards and carefully printed my name on it. 'You joined us when . . . what date shall I put down?' he asked.

I gave it some thought. I could ask him to write 1938, or the spring of 1939. That would probably be the safest bet. It would show that I had joined up long before the outbreak of war. Perhaps it was tempting fate. It might look better if we made it just after the outbreak. Well, it would be in line with the argument I would put forward for wanting to work for the Germans. 'Put down October 1939,' I said. 'Just after I returned from England. That was when you asked me to join up.'

Yngvar nodded and noted that I had paid my first subscription in October 1939. Following that, I had kept up the payments until the party disbanded. He allowed the ink to dry, then handed me the card which I put in my wallet.

'Take a badge too,' he said.

From the box I removed a large swastika. The black cross was surrounded by a bright red background. Leaning forward, he pinned the badge to my lapel. For a moment I thought of standing to attention. It would have been more ceremonious but Fyhn might not have appreciated it. I was the last to join the party and it didn't exactly have much of a future.

'You'll have to pay for the badge, I'm afraid.'

'Of course,' I said. 'And the membership fee?'

'No, there's no need for that, we don't have a petty cash box any more. It's just the badges; I paid for them myself.'

The enamel swastika cost twenty kroner, which I duly paid. It was a worthwhile investment.

Yngvar Fyhn collected together what was left of Norway's National Socialist Labour Party, put the pieces in a box, and laid it at the bottom of the drawer. A solitary swastika had been left on the table. He picked it up, tossed it in the air and caught it. 'This is worth a few coffees at Mollhausen's,' he said. 'Twenty-five badges lying there, worthless. All cash on the table.'

It was the second time he had mentioned the expense. Was he short of money? An extra badge might come in handy. 'I wouldn't mind another one. If you don't mind.'

Before I had a chance to fetch my wallet he had thrown the badge across to me. I caught it and put it in my trouser pocket. Two more ten kroner notes changed hands. I got up and walked over to him. He was almost a head taller than myself. I looked into his blue eyes. 'Thanks, Yngvar.'

'If it works,' he said fumbling for words, 'I mean, should there be any questions, you'll have to stick to your story. I recruited you last October. If I'm asked, I promise to back you up.'

I nodded and put out my hand. He took it and held it firmly in his large fist.

I felt sorry for him. He had held on to his convictions amongst all the confused ideas about a pure race and a superior being. He had genuinely hoped for a better future.

When the Germans came on the scene, prepared for battle, he realised that he had been a mere puppet. He was suffering the consequences. What could he do now? He would most probably join the National Assembly; it seemed the only possibility left open to him. He had compromised himself, and once Norway was liberated he would have to bear the consequent retribution.

I fetched my coat and left. He watched me as I went down the stairs. When I reached the ground floor, I heard the door close behind me. I stopped, removed the badge and slipped it into my pocket. Only when it was absolutely necessary would I wear the swastika, but right now I had to try and infiltrate the German Military Intelligence.

I showed Tor the membership card and badge. He studied the card carefully, shaking his head. 'It looks genuine enough,' he said.

'It is. I bought you one as well.' I handed the badge over to him. He paused, thoughtful, and then put it away. 'So, what's our next move?'

'It won't work,' replied Tor. 'No one will believe you. You are what you are, no matter how many badges you wear. What are you going to say at the interview?'

'That I detest England and that I'm ashamed of my background,' I said.

Tor laughed. 'That doesn't sound too convincing. Why don't you just tell them that the English sent you over here to get information about the German occupation? That's what they'll think anyway.'

'I'll tell them about Mitchell,' I replied.

'Who's he?'

'Grandfather's chauffeur.'

'What's he got to do with it?'

I told Tor the story I had remembered since my childhood. I was convinced that the Germans would believe it.

Grandfather owned a Daimler which Mitchell had been employed to drive. It was a large car with a spacious rear seat. Mitchell sat in front of a glass partition which separated him from the rear. I was often allowed to sit beside him. One summer's day we went to visit Eliza, who had been nanny to both myself and mother. Almost all her life had been spent living with some poor relatives who took care of her. Grandmother sent her a couple of pounds every month. It was common practice when faithful servants had been forced to retire because of old age.

Mitchell made his way to the house in a rundown, working-class district on the outskirts of Manchester. I remember looking around, wide-eyed: I had never seen a slum at close hand before. Dirty, neglected children in tattered sweaters ran barefoot after the car. I asked Mitchell why they were so dirty.

'They have nothing to wash with, and nowhere to do it anyway.'

'I bet they're pretty hungry too,' I replied.

Grandfather's servants called me Master Jack, as I was the privileged grandson, both protected and cherished. Mitchell treated me with the utmost respect, but on this occasion he gave me a lecture. 'There are two Englands,' he said. 'You, Master Jack, are one of the lucky few. These children belong to the other England. Their parents are either unemployed or their fathers slave away in a mine for a mere few shillings a day. They live in draughty, shabby houses, about four or five to a room. It's seldom they have enough food to last a day, there's no running water and they can barely afford to buy coal to keep them warm during the winter.'

Mitchell was a committed socialist. He made his beliefs quite clear during the car journey. I was shocked. This was a totally new world he was showing me, and from my seat at the front of the Daimler I could see he wasn't lying.

We arrived to find Eliza lying in bed in a cold, dark room. The whole house reeked of cabbage soup. I gave her a hug, and she cried upon seeing me. She was overjoyed and at the same time embarrassed that we had taken so much trouble for her sake. I handed her the pound grandmother had given me for her. Then we drove back and Mitchell continued his lecture.

'What's this got to do with your job application?' asked Tor.

'I'll tell the story to the Germans,' I said.

'I don't see how it'll make things easier.'

'Don't worry. Let me deal with it, just make sure that I get to meet your boss.'

'How am I supposed to do that?'

'Ask if he needs more staff. Then say that you've got a good friend who's gifted at languages and trustworthy, who would like to try for the job.'

Tor hesitated. If I failed to convince the Germans of my honest intentions, then he would get into deep trouble, get the sack or, even worse, be taken to the Gestapo for questioning. It was risky. Together, Tor and I could do so much more than he could by himself. As things stood, we had to take the chance. 'I'll try,' he said finally. 'I'll go to Major Schacke and tell him you're interested.'

'Thanks,' I said. 'See him as soon as you can.'

He kept his promise. The next day he informed me that the head of the German military censor's office wanted to meet me. The time was already arranged. I was to take my identity papers and school certificates with me.

The days of waiting made me nervous. I was working at the salon, but I couldn't concentrate on the job. I prepared myself over and over again. I went over what I would say and do, what details to highlight, how I could phrase my answers to make them sound plausible. Then the big day arrived. I put on my best suit, a white shirt and a new tie.

'Where are you going? father asked.

'To look for a job.'

'Job? You've got enough to do here.'

'I'm going to try and get a position with the post censor,' I said.

'With the Germans?'

'Yes.'

He looked at me, clearly irritated, but then his expression softened. 'You know what you're doing?'

'Yes,' I said. 'It could work. I think it's worth a try.'

'I don't like it,' he said. 'There'll be talk, and you could get into trouble. But it's up to you.'

'I know I am doing the right thing,' I said.

He put his hand on my shoulder. Someone called him. He stood a while, looking at me, then he left without another word. I went over to a mirror, combed my hair and pinned the swastika badge on to my lapel. Then I put on my raincoat, making sure it covered the badge.

The censor was situated in the main post office on Dronningens Gate. It was a magnificent brick building, built in the 1920s. Tor had given me instructions. I was to enter by a side entrance and go up the stairs to the floor which Major Schacke and his censors had taken over.

When I entered the post office I undid my raincoat, making sure that the badge could be seen. Then I went up the stairs and looked for the board to see on which floor the censor authorities had their offices. There was a guard in German uniform sitting at the door. I saw from his stripes that he hadn't managed to advance too high up the military hierarchy. I gave him my name and said that I had an appointment with his superior. He asked me to wait, went over to a door and knocked, then waited until he heard a shout from inside to open it. He came out again, and Major Schacke invited me into his office.

The head of security was sitting behind a large desk. He had grey hair and was wearing a pair of round spectacles. He also had a little moustache. I could tell straight away whom he was attempting to emulate, and it wasn't successful. His uniform bulged over his large stomach. He was fat and although he made no move to stand, I could tell that he was short. He sat low in the leatherbound chair. 'Sit down,' he said, pointing to an uncomfortable wooden chair. 'So, you're Mr Moe?'

'John Moe,' I said, handing over my documents. He looked at them, reached for a pen and began filling out a form. I sat quietly, listening to the pen scrape across the paper. I turned slightly so that the swastika could be seen more easily.

When he'd noted down my name and date of birth he stopped and looked at me. 'I see you were born in London,' he said.

'My mother's English,' I said. 'My grandfather is a retired colonel. He was a regimental commander during World War I and took part in the fighting at Gallipoli.'

Major Schacke looked out of the window. The sky was a dull grey; some seagulls flew by. I realised that even he had taken part in that war. Perhaps he also was haunted by memories. Perhaps he cursed the day when he was forced once again to put on his uniform and had received orders to leave for Oslo? He returned to the present. 'Why do you want to work for us, Mr Moe?' he asked.

'I need the job,' I said. 'I'm good at languages.'

'Your German is quite acceptable.'

'Of course, I speak English fluently,' I added.

'Languages aren't enough,' said Major Schacke.

'I want to make my own contribution,' I said. 'I want a position where I can be of use — for Norway, for the New Society and the New Age. I believe in your philosophy, Major.'

I thought he seemed slightly interested, but he maintained his air of formality. 'You're half-English, Mr Moe,' he said.

'Not by choice,' I replied. 'You cannot choose your background, sir.'

He had to agree with that.

'I'm not happy about my past,' I continued. 'I've seen too much of the injustice in England. The society is rotten, but it will soon crumble, and then you will be hailed as the saviours of the repressed millions. I want to be there on that day, and I want to be on the right side.'

Major Schacke leant back in his chair, toying with his pen, but writing nothing. Maybe he was thinking forward to the day when German troops would march into London just as they had in Oslo and Paris.

He stared at me. I felt he was beginning to trust me. I

told him the story about Mitchell, albeit a shorter version to
the tale I had related to Tor. He nodded in agreement. He
could see that I had been incensed by the decadence and
the inherited class differences.

'I left England when war broke out. I asked myself whose
side I should take. There was no question. The Germans
represented Europe's future justice.' I had learnt many of
the propaganda slogans by heart; the newspapers were full
of them. UFA newsreels laid it on thick when victories
were gained.

The major nodded. This was no propaganda to him, it
was the truth. I was a Norwegian who had perceived his
truths and held to them. I decided to play my next trump
card. 'The first thing I did on my return was to get in touch
with the Norwegian National Socialist Labour Party,' I
said. 'After a few weeks I became a member.'

I stuck my thumb under my lapel to reveal the swastika.
Then I took out my membership card and laid it in front of
him. He briefly examined the document and gave it back.
He got up, came round to my side of the table and offered
his hand. It was a symbolic gesture. I took it.

'Thank you for your visit, Mr Moe,' he said. 'I'll give it
some thought; if you could come back in a week's time?
Let's say the same time next week.'

'Thank you, Major,' I said, standing to attention.

I felt that I had won him over, even though I hadn't had
the opportunity to proclaim my indignation and disappointment over the British mine affair. It would have
been another good card to play.

I realised that he would not make the decision alone. His
report would be sent for further examination, perhaps even
to Berlin. I tried to think of anything I might have
forgotten. I had mentioned grandfather and not hidden the
fact that I had spent a large part of my childhood in
England. It seemed to be enough.

'I'm pleased to have met you, Mr Moe,' said Major
Schacke.

'Until next week, sir,' I bowed.

7

The days passed slowly. Tor and I made plans, but we were both very frightened. Would I get the job? Would the Germans guess our real motives? Would Tor get into trouble for having recommended me?

The day finally came when I was to meet Major Schacke for the second time. I left early, dressed as last time, but I was more nervous. I removed my coat on the stairs, making sure that the swastika could be seen, and then carried on my way.

When I entered Major Schacke's office he stood up to meet me. He hadn't done that the last time. It was a good sign. 'Welcome back, Mr Moe,' he said.

'Thank you.'

'I'd like to welcome you to your new job,' he continued. 'As from this moment you're working for the Military Intelligence.'

I could have hugged him. He had helped me get a foot inside the enemy's door. But I simply bowed and clicked my heels in as German a fashion as I could muster.

He gave me my instructions. Work was to be both long and demanding; breaks would be short. Food was served in the canteen or, if I preferred, I could bring a packed lunch. Total secrecy was demanded. I wasn't to speak to any outsiders about my work, and I was encouraged to keep discussion to a minimum during working hours. I was to be efficient, thorough and honest. He repeated that I was never to forget professional secrecy. I was told how much I would earn and I said I was quite happy. It was not much, but money was not my prime objective.

He then called for my immediate superior. A short man with mousy grey hair appeared. He stood to attention and was informed as to who I was, and that I would be working under his guidance. His name was Horn, and I took an immediate dislike to him. He was unsympathetic in every way, a typical prototype of the Germany we detested — arrogant, superior, vulgar, loud and openly ambitious. It did not take too long to discover his bad points.

Horn represented the classic underling who used his position to persecute those beneath him. He was un-intelligent to the point of stupidity, and I wondered how he had landed a job at the censor's office of all places.

'Do you know who I am?' he asked.

'No, Mr Horn, I don't.'

'I am one of the Führer's oldest friends,' he explained, and pointed to the brooch-like medal pinned to his coat. 'I wear the golden party emblem.' He looked self-important and proud. He was clearly expecting me to show my admiration.

Horn had been there since the very beginning. He had been a part of the Old Guard from Munich and when the party was being built around its leader, he had been there. Now, he was stuck in Oslo doing a subordinate's job. He must have been a totally impossible man; otherwise he wouldn't have been sent to Oslo and placed beneath an army major who probably wasn't even a party member.

'Congratulations, you are honoured, Mr Horn. It must feel very good to experience all the success that the Führer and his old friends have found.'

He stared at me as if he was unsure whether I had been sarcastic or serious. Deciding to take it as a compliment, he snorted and straightened up. 'Follow me, Moe,' he ordered. 'I'll show you what you're to do.'

The room was small, the window looked out onto the yard. The walls were bare, and a square table stood at the centre of the room. Three people sat there at work, two men of my own age and an older woman. They looked up as Horn and I entered and simply nodded when I was introduced. All three were German speakers. The men were not fit for military service and had been given civilian posts. Judging by her dialect, the woman was from Vienna. One of the men acted as group leader.

Horn familiarised me with my first duties. It wasn't demanding. I was to slit open envelopes. A basket full of letters was placed before me — my job was to open the letters with a pair of scissors and then place the opened letters in another basket. Closely following Horn's instructions, I managed it after the second try. Obviously a quick learner.

When the basket was full, a trusted employee was called to take it to another room, where the letters were read. He would return with a basket of censored letters ready for resealing. I had to stick tape over the opening, and stamp the tape with 'Censored by German Military Intelligence'.

The work was monotonous and tedious. I was bored after a few days and complained to Tor. This was not what I had expected. I had thought I would be making myself useful. A child of ten could open letters. Tor comforted me; I would definitely be promoted as long as I kept my nose clean.

I must have been good because after a week I was moved to another room. I was promoted ahead of my letter-opening colleagues for obvious reasons. They only spoke German, whereas I spoke both German and Norwegian. Major Schacke realised that I could be of greater use as a censor.

Tor had already told me about the workings of the post censor. That is why I knew which jobs I would do as I rose in rank. Every morning a basket of opened letters was brought in and I began to read. The work took place in several large rooms, where small groups of censors sat at their tables. Every group had a leader, an *Oberprüfer*, who would watch over the work from the head of the table.

Tor and I were in separate rooms. Tor had been chosen to check the foreign correspondence from Norwegian companies and I was reading the personal letters. A

Captain Romer watched over the foreign section; above myself and those with whom I shared my table, was Horn, who had his own room which nobody was allowed inside. When we had finished a letter we had to write a short summary detailing the mood of the letter. It was called *Stimmungsbericht*. We filled in the name of the sender and receiver, the date and in which part of the country it had been posted. We wrote a short *resumé* of the contents in German.

Tor had explained that the Germans were, first and foremost, interested in gauging the morale in Norway; how the Norwegians viewed the occupation. How did they feel about this new situation? I recorded what would be seen as positive views about the Germans. These were sent on to the propaganda sections for use in the press and radio broadcasts to display national feeling.

We had orders to make a note of the anti-establishment material. This we did, but on a much smaller scale. Sometimes I placed these hate letters in the 'out' basket without completing the forms. At the same time I tried to memorise their names, so that Åge Berg could get the message to them through his contacts.

Tor scribbled down names on scraps of paper which he hid beneath his watch or secreted in a pocket. He wrote microscopically and when we had returned home I would sometimes need a magnifying glass to decipher his writing. I simply tried to remember the names so that I could make a note of them when I was in the toilet. Sometimes I seemed to spend an unnatural amount of time there, but it went unnoticed.

We had orders to set aside suspicious post for special investigation. I would have liked to have hidden them but it was impossible; we were subject to spot checks and closely observed. Horn often patrolled up and down behind us, studying our work. He was a pest, always complaining, and he appeared to have it in for me. He was stupid, but it was perhaps his stupidity which had made him suspect me from the very start. I knew he didn't trust me.

I had managed to win over Major Schacke with a logical argument. Horn could not grasp subtleties like that. To him, every Norwegian was a potential enemy. He saw it as his duty to watch us closely and to pester us at every opportunity.

One day Horn approached me and laid several postcards on the table. I looked at them. They were photographs of Hitler: the Führer pinching a little girl's cheek; the Führer sitting on the balustrade at Berchtesgarten; the Führer receiving flowers from small children. 'How would you like to buy a picture of the Führer, Moe?' Horn asked, showing his brown teeth.

I was annoyed. He had been breathing down my neck for a whole hour, just watching me. I didn't think twice. 'No, I'm not interested.'

Horn stiffened; I had let my hatred of him cloud my judgement. I had set myself up as the faithful Nazi, and that was the role I had to play. 'I already have them all,' I said quickly. 'I collect them.'

Horn stared at me. I know he didn't believe me, but there was nothing he could say; he didn't even think of asking me to bring them along to show him. Instead, he gathered up his cards, turned round, and stormed out of the room, slamming the door behind him.

Tor warned me about Horn on the way home. He was also aware that the old Nazi had taken a dislike to me. 'He charges a mark for every postcard,' he said. 'He makes fifty pfennig on each one.'

I promised not to show my feelings in front of Horn and to keep a cool head in future. When he spoke to me I answered politely and did whatever I was told, without question. I think he eventually began to trust me. Well, he could hardly find any cause for criticism. I worked quickly, wrote my reports in correct German and squeezed out as many complimentary comments about his countrymen as I possibly could. My accounts of Norwegian morale probably got the propagandists rubbing their hands with glee.

Tor had been living at home with his parents, but after a few weeks we decided to rent a couple of rooms together and share the cost. We found some furnished rooms on Svoldersgatan with a lady who had recently lost her husband. We could feel independent there, and if we wanted to invite girls back, as was often the case, we could do so without offending anyone.

We became good friends with one of our workmates at the post office. His name was Wilfried Redelien, a lawyer and also a good pianist. His Scandinavian was pretty good, thanks to several years touring around Norway and Sweden playing concerts.

Redelien often came home with us in the evenings. We enjoyed each other's company. He was German and so we kept our real motives to ourselves. But he wasn't a Nazi. 'I don't like the Nazis,' he said. 'And I don't think much of their war. But what can I do? Fortunately, I could speak a little Norwegian and that's why I was put into the Civil Service. In Hitler's Germany you're grateful for what you can get.'

Tor got to know Gerd, one of the girls working at the censor's office. They started going out, and the three of us spent many evenings together. As employees of the German military authorities we were sometimes invited to parties and *soirées* at the German Embassy. We reluctantly went along a couple of times because we had to keep up appearances.

The rumour slowly spread round Oslo that I was working for the Germans. I noticed that some of my old friends had stopped calling on me and were generally avoiding me. It felt awful, but I couldn't tell them my secret. They had to believe that I was a puppet in the hands of our occupiers.

One evening at Regnbuen, the popular dance-restaurant at Tivolihallen, I caught sight of an old friend. I hadn't seen him for a long time but we had met now and again; he had once rented a room in my father's flat. He was with a girl. He leant across the table and I stretched out my hand to shake his. He ignored it. Instead he spat in my face and then strode out of the restaurant, the girl running at his side.

'Take it easy,' said Redelien, who was with me at the time. 'It's best to ignore people like that.'

I knew he was right. It would seem as if I really had chosen sides and as such I would have to bear the consequences.

Work was tiring and often boring. The art of writing witty letters had not advanced too far. Dutifully, I read my post, wrote my reports on morale, and turned a blind eye to the indiscretions and anti-German comments. I made a note of those I felt were treading dangerously, and in the evenings I put my notes together with Tor's microscopic contributions and made up a list for Åge Berg.

If there was anything unfavourable about Quisling or the National Assembly I usually noted it in my reports, but emphasised that it was not directed against the Germans. I knew that they couldn't care what people thought of the Quisling puppet government. Redelien had told us that. A traitor gains no respect from either side.

One day I was given a letter that hadn't been opened during the usual routine. 'Has anyone got a pair of scissors?' I asked. No one did. I knocked at Horn's door and entered at his command. I asked to borrow a pair of scissors. He pointed to a table in front of a cupboard. I found the scissors and at the same time got a good look in the cupboard. It was divided into small compartments and above each one was a named label stuck on with a pin. I presumed that letters reserved for special inspection were kept in these drawers. Everyone under observation had their own pigeon-hole.

I didn't dare examine the cupboard, but I managed to sneak a look at it. When I was reading the labels I noticed that one of them was headed 'Field Marshal Mannerheim'. It held a solitary letter. Without thinking, without really realising what I was doing, I took the letter and looked at it. What was a letter from the Finnish Field Marshal doing at the German censor in Oslo?

I heard Horn's voice shout from the other end of the room. 'Moe, what are you doing?' He threw down the papers he was holding and rushed across the room. 'What's this all about, Moe? What are you up to?'

'Nothing,' I said as calmly as I could. 'I caught sight of Mannerheim's name and was curious. It isn't every day you get to hold a letter from him in your hand.'

He grabbed the letter and put it back in its pigeon-hole. 'Get out!' he yelled. His breath stank of stale beer and cheap cigars. I hurried to the door, but just as I reached it he called me. 'Moe! Take the basket with you.' He pointed to baskets of letters which stood at the end of the table. They were full of censored, ready-sealed letters. Obviously another spot-check. Horn put the one basket on top of the other.

I turned back for them and, with my arms full, I opened the door with my elbows. I took them out and left them to be collected for posting. I returned to my seat, annoyed at my carelessness. I should never have touched that letter. I should have been satisfied with just looking at the names and trying to memorise one or two of them.

I visited Åge Berg in the evening. I suggested to him that we needed to find out who had been set aside for closer investigation. Redelien had mentioned some type of secret file. It would be risky but we could but try. Åge Berg told me to be careful. It was more advisable to carry on just as before. Under no circumstances were the Germans to discover the leak.

The following day I was a few minutes late. My workmates were already in their seats and had received their first basket of letters. I pulled on my grey working clothes. Major Schacke suddenly burst into the room. He was agitated, the sweat pouring down his bloated face, and he breathed heavily. Horn looked in a similar state of panic when he marched into the room close behind. Something had happened. I realised that it had to be important when a second later a guard came through the door followed by two men in civilian clothes. They looked like the Gestapo.

They all vanished into Horn's room, slamming the door after them. Raised voices could soon be heard; something was shouted, and another voice replied in a much quieter tone.

An hour passed. I tried to work but didn't achieve much. I was disturbed by the raised voices; it was a long-drawn-out interrogation which occasionally turned into a violent argument.

Suddenly the door was wrenched open and Horn rushed out. He was deathly pale, his dirty hair stood on end and his half-open mouth gave him the appearance of a mangy rat trapped in a blind alley, preparing for a last desperate attack.

Horn went for the throat — my throat. 'It's him!' he yelled. 'It's Moe. He's taken it!'

I stared blankly at him. Taken what?

The officer and two other men came out with Major Schacke in tow. They ignored Horn's bellowing and disappeared.

'It's you, Moe,' shrieked Horn. 'I'll make sure you go to prison for this, you damned little shit! How the hell could you dare!'

'What's this all about?' I asked as he struggled for breath.

'You know damned well!' he screamed.

I shook my head. I knew nothing and remained calm. Surely my little indiscretion with Mannerheim's letter couldn't have caused such a rumpus, necessitating the presence of the Gestapo.

The guard re-entered the office and marched towards me. 'Major Schacke would like a word with you, Moe,' he said.

I got up and followed him. Horn stayed where he was and thumped the table so hard with his fist that the letter trays jumped into the air.

Schacke was alone. He looked serious. He wiped his face with a large handkerchief, folded it and tucked it away in his trouser pocket. 'It's about the list,' he said.

'List?' I looked at him quizzically.

'The list that's gone missing. Horn thinks you've taken it.'

'What list?'

Schacke didn't answer. He just shrugged his shoulders and without raising his voice he said, 'The Gestapo want to talk to you, right away, at their headquarters.'

'The Gestapo?'

'You're expected at Victoria Terrace. It would be best if you left now.'

'What do they want?' I asked.

'Now!'

I realised there was nothing more to say. Schacke had simply been given his orders and he was just passing them on to me. I had to follow his command.

I went back and told Tor and the others I had been summoned by the Gestapo. I was suspected of having taken some sort of list. No one knew what exactly, but I could see that Tor had an idea what it might have been. 'Take it easy, John,' he said. 'I shouldn't think it's anything serious. If it had been, they'd have picked you up.'

I took off my working jacket, put on my own sporting the swastika badge, and, draping my raincoat over my shoulders, I left.

The Gestapo were waiting at Victoria Terrace.

8

I was received by two Gestapo men in an interrogation room. I recognised them as the two who had been at the office earlier on in the day questioning Horn and Schacke. One was thin with a long, narrow face and large, protruding ears. The other was broad-shouldered, his black hair slicked down on either side of his middle parting. The first thing that occurred to me was which hair cream he used. I didn't dare ask him. This was serious.

The thin one did the talking. He wanted to know my name, address and place of birth, all the routine questions. The one with the centre parting took notes. Why? I didn't know. A pile of papers lay on the table in front of him. I was convinced that they were mine, and that all the answers were there.

'You're a member of the Labour Party, Mr Moe?' the thin one said suddenly.

'No,' I replied.

He looked at his colleague who rummaged through my papers and who then nodded. 'That's what it says in our documents,' he said. 'Surely you're not suggesting that we've got it wrong, Mr Moe?'

'I'm a member of NNSAP, Norway's National Socialist Labour Party.'

'Right. The Labour Party,' said the thin man. 'So it's true.'

'The National Socialist Party,' I said. 'It's completely different.' I leaned forward to show them my badge. Then I took out my membership card which I always carried in my inside pocket. I handed it to the thinner one who glanced at it briefly and passed it to his partner.

'It says "Labour Party" here,' he said, having studied it carefully.

'It says Norwegian National Socialist Labour Party,' I said. 'The NNSAP. My subscriptions were signed for by the leader himself.'

'Quisling?'

'Quisling is the leader of the National Assembly.'

The interrogation took place in German. It was clear that both Gestapo officers had been ill-informed as to the situation in Norway. They had probably only just moved across to Oslo. I decided to try and capitalise on this fact and began a detailed account of the differences between the various parties. The NNSAP was the small, and only genuine National Socialist Party of which I was a member. 'The swastika is our party emblem,' I continued, showing my badge once again. The thin man nodded; he had obviously got the parties confused. He accepted my explanation. True or otherwise it could always be looked into afterwards.

He changed the subject. 'Do you know why you were asked here, Mr Moe?'

'Major Schacke said a list had disappeared. It seems I'm suspected of having taken it.'

'Where's the list?'

'I don't know what list you're talking about,' I said. 'So it follows that I don't know where it is.'

'Were you in Mr Horn's room yesterday?'

'Yes.'

'What were you doing there?'

They knew very well what had happened during my short visit. Horn had certainly given them all the details.

'I went to fetch a pair of scissors,' I said. 'I asked Mr Horn if he had a pair and, if so, could I borrow them. He pointed to a table and I went to get them.'

'And then?' The man with the centre parting looked interested.

'I happened to catch sight of a cupboard by the short

wall. I saw Mannerheim's name and was curious.'

'You took a letter?'

'Without thinking, I looked at the envelope. Mr Horn took it away immediately and put it back in the pigeon-hole.'

The thin man smiled. I didn't like the way he grinned, so I launched into the attack.

'I was just curious,' I said. 'I don't understand why the Gestapo are wasting their time in interrogating a loyal servant of the military censor about something like this.'

He stopped smiling. 'Then what did you do, Mr Moe?'

'I immediately left the room,' I replied. 'Mr Horn ordered me to remove two baskets of letters, which I did.'

'Where did you take these baskets?'

'I went straight into the other room and put them down on a table.'

'Then what?'

'I went back to work. What list am I meant to have taken?'

'A paper has disappeared,' said the other. 'Mr Horn swears that you took it.'

'When and how? And why? Mr Horn was watching me the whole time. I've no idea where his list is.'

I began to feel on safer ground. I was telling the truth. I was accused of something I hadn't done. Tor and I had nothing to do with this.

'Who did you give the stolen list to, Mr Moe?'

I realised it was a last attempt. Despite himself, he had begun to believe in my innocence. Perhaps he disliked Horn too and trusted my version of the story. 'I joined the post censor because I wanted to contribute to the New Society that we are trying to build with your help. And I'm subjected to this!'

I opened my arms in a gesture I hoped would be taken for despair. 'I am very disappointed,' I continued. 'First Mr Horn's unjust accusation, and now this. I'm being treated like a hardened criminal.'

The thin man stood up, but I carried on regardless. I

spoke of my hatred of English society, of the shock I had received when I heard about the English and the mine incident; I explained just how long before the Germans' arrival in Oslo I had actively worked for a Norway, a National Socialist Norway, with the Führer's Germany as its guiding light.

Both officers listened, the thin man grew impatient. Maybe I was laying it on a bit thick. He finally moved towards me and interrupted my outburst. 'Thank you, Mr Moe. You can go now.'

I hadn't finished yet, but I realised that the best thing to do was get out as quickly as possible. So I got up, bowed, and left the room, furious.

When I reached the street outside I felt exhilarated. I knew what list they had to be talking about. It was the file detailing all those who were to be specially investigated by the censor. Someone had managed to smuggle it out. It wasn't myself, Gerd or Tor, but the list had vanished, that was the main thing. The people would be forewarned.

Upon my return to the office I went directly to Major Schacke's office, knocked on his door and stood in front of his desk. I felt both relieved and proud. The charges had been dropped.

'Did you go to the Gestapo, Moe?' Schacke asked.

'Yes, Major,' I replied. 'I told them the truth. I have nothing to do with the disappearance.'

Schacke waved a piece of paper. It looked like a telegram. 'I have just received orders from Berlin,' he said. 'You have to be out of here in fifteen minutes, Moe.'

I stared at him.

'Did you hear me, Moe? Fifteen minutes.'

'Am I . . .?'

'You're fired, Moe!'

'But I haven't done anything.'

'Didn't you hear me, Moe? It's an order from Berlin.' He showed no emotion, he simply verified Berlin's command. John Moe, post censor, was to be fired, immediately. The decision had been taken. It couldn't be changed, nor could I appeal. I had fifteen minutes to pack my belongings. When I realised that I could do nothing, that I was irrevocably dismissed, I grew frightened. I was filled with uncertainty.

I left Schacke without another word. He offered no comment. He did not thank me for the work I had done there, nor did he say he was sorry that things had turned out this way.

'How did it go?' asked Tor when I went to collect my things.

'I've been fired. I've got to go.'

'I don't understand,' said Redelien.

'I've got to go,' I said, shoving some pencils in my pocket. 'I'll see you tonight.'

It was drizzling outside. I hadn't noticed as I was making my way back from the Gestapo. Now I felt the cool rain on my face and, sweeping my coat around my shoulders, I made my way slowly up to the Atheneum. I passed by the Government buildings as several German officers came through the main doors. The German flag fluttered from the pole on the roof of the building guarded by armed soldiers. Reichkommissar Josef Terboven resided here. I had just been thanklessly dismissed by his subordinates.

It was autumn. There was a slight breeze, the trees had turned yellow and the flowers drooped, withering along the borders. I had lost my job. I could put up with the fact that the German Military Intelligence would no longer be paying my keep. It was not as if I relied on the income, but I was very scared. There had to be a reason for my dismissal. What would happen now? Would they carry on looking for the list? Would anyone discover what Tor and I had been up to? Would the Germans find a lead to Åge Berg?

I went to Tivolihallen and paused outside, looking at the sign over the salon door. 'Helge K. Moe & Son'. That was me. I belonged here. Maybe it was foolish to have started working at the censor? I didn't even know if we had accomplished anything. Had we managed to save anyone from internment or imprisonment? What had Åge Berg done with our lists? We had no idea, nor did we particularly want to know. Our job was to supply the information. But had we achieved anything?

Father was surprised to see me.

'I'm no longer working at the censor,' I said.

He squeezed my hand. 'I'm glad. I've been worried,' he said. 'I never liked the idea. You shouldn't have stuck your neck out like that.'

'I shouldn't, and what about you?' I replied.

'That's completely different,' said father. 'I hope you'll be carrying on here now. There's so much to do.'

'Tomorrow,' I said.

I took the tram home to Skillebekk and waited for Tor. He arrived just after five, panting hard — he had run all the way from the tram stop. Redelien was with him.

'What a day,' said Tor. 'I thought it would never end.'

'What's happened?' I asked.

'Tor blew up,' Redelien explained, 'and he gave Captain Römer a piece of his mind.'

'He's got nothing to do with it,' I explained.

'Attack is the best form of defence,' said Tor. 'I was scared they might suspect me. After all, I recommended you, so I went up to Romer and slammed my fist down on his desk.'

'You could hear it echo through the building,' said Redelien.

'What did you say?' I asked.

'That it was a disgrace to have fired you, and that I'd be next in line for a hard time. Römer understood and apologised, but there was nothing he could do. The orders had come from Berlin. I said that my loyalty was in doubt, but Römer tried to calm me down, saying that nobody doubted my trustworthiness for a second.'

'And the list?' I asked. 'What has happened to it?'

'It's disappeared without trace.'

'Why did they accuse me?'

'It was Horn,' said Redelien. 'He was accused of misplacing it and he in turned blamed you. He got a severe talking to from Schacke, though.

Redelien told us that Horn had been asked to account for

his actions the previous day. He admitted having the list with him in the afternoon. In the evening he noticed it had gone. During the interrogation he had remembered my visit. He had clearly chosen me as a scapegoat. I was Norwegian and I had refused to buy his pictures of Hitler. This was his revenge.

I hadn't taken the list, that was a fact. Or had I? Perhaps I had, without realising. I recalled that when he had seen me with Mannerheim's letter he had been reading over some papers. He had then cast them aside and rushed over to me. It could have been the list he was reading. It may well have landed in one of the baskets I had taken with me; it could have gone down to the sorting office — they were all Norwegian down there.

I decided not to mention it while Redelien was there. For the time being I was still under suspicion. Even if the Gestapo had let me go I had still been fired. 'What'll happen?' I asked. 'Will they carry on with the investigation?'

'Probably,' said Redelien. 'You had best prepare for it. Once you're on file they don't let go.'

'Should I try to get to Sweden?'

Redelien shook his head. 'That's about the worst thing you could do,' he said. 'It would show guilt. Then Tor would get into trouble, not to mention your parents.'

'So I'm supposed to sit it out in Oslo and wait for the Gestapo to come knocking at my door?' I asked.

There was nothing else I could do. There was no alternative; I was terrified.

Redelien went out into the hall and returned with a bottle of brandy which he had hidden in his coat. I fetched some glasses and he poured it out. It was a means of ridding ourselves of the worry we all shared. We sat up chatting for ages. Redelien was concerned about me. He was a lawyer and knew how the German authorities worked.

'The danger is that you could end up on one of their lists. You could be taken hostage. Law and order is almost non-existent in Germany. In an occupied country the Gestapo will carry on regardless if they see fit.'

'All I can do is sit and wait,' I said.

'Try to look at it from the Gestapo's point of view,' said Redelien. 'You're a Norwegian with a dubious background. Sure, you have proof that prior to occupation you were a member of NNSAP, but that doesn't account for everything. And you were in the room the afternoon the list disappeared.'

'What about John's point of view, then?' Tor interrupted. 'He wanted to make himself useful. He has shown his willingness. He's innocent, he's lost his job, and he's now totally confused by the way he's been treated.'

'I'll write and complain,' I said. 'I'll demand that justice be done.'

'Write to Schacke,' said Tor.

'I will write to the Reichkommissar himself, Josef Terboven.'

We all laughed; it relieved the tension. We drank a toast, emptying our glasses. Redelien refilled them and we carried on joking. Redelien suddenly grew more serious. 'It's a brilliant idea.'

'What is?'

'Writing to Terboven.'

'I meant it as a joke,' I said. 'There's no way I can write to him.'

'Anyone can,' retorted Redelien.

'You don't think for one minute that he'll read a letter from John Moe, ex-post censor? I'm a nobody.'

'He won't read your letter, you're right about that,' continued Redelien. 'He probably won't even get to see it, but somebody will, and it'll be recorded.'

I had mentioned writing to Terboven in jest; the alcohol had given me Dutch courage. It was only meant to relax the atmosphere — a way of overcoming my fears. I could see that Redelien meant it. If I composed a letter of complaint to the highest German official in Norway, the letter would arouse the curiosity of some official; after all, who would dare address a letter of complaint to Terboven? Where would it end up?

'Sooner or later the Gestapo will hear about it,' said Redelien.

'In that case it isn't a particularly good idea,' I said.

'Don't you see how they will react? They suspect you. They have a file on you. Then a letter arrives, addressed to Terboven, a letter in which you complain of your recent treatment. The question they'll ask themselves is this — would a guilty man turn to the Reichkommissar? Of course not. The Gestapo will swallow it hook, line and sinker. Believe me.'

Redelien was enthusiastic and persuaded me. I would play the innocent victim who had felt so degraded that, in sheer desperation, he had written to the highest possible authority in search of justice. We finished off the bottle and decided to write the letter together the following evening. That is if I hadn't changed my mind by then.

I didn't. In the morning I bought several sheets of top quality, handmade writing paper; and in the evening we sat down to compose the letter. It was to be in German, but we decided to include a few deliberate errors for effect. After all, it was supposed to be written by a wronged young Norwegian. We worked on it for hours, considering every word and phrase and, once we were happy with it, I wrote it out neatly in blue ink.

I had been suspected of something I had not done. Deeply hurt, I was now seeking to clear my name. Not even the Gestapo, who had been quite fair with me, had found evidence of my guilt. Despite this, I had been rudely dismissed from my post. I was requesting that Josef Terboven right the wrong that had been done to me. We re-read the letter several times. I was pleased with it. Having placed it into a large envelope, I wrote the address: Reichkommissar Josef Terboven, Stortinget, Oslo.

The following day I travelled to his headquarters and left the letter with the guard at the main entrance. He took the letter, looked at it and read the address on the envelope; he looked up again and re-read Terboven's name.

Then he saluted and marched up the steps.

9

All I could do was wait. I didn't expect any reaction from Terboven or the authorities who received the letter. As far as I was concerned there was no question of reinstatement.

All the same I looked forward to the post arriving. When the phone rang I would jump up to answer it expectantly. However, I heard nothing. I carried on working at the salon and every morning Tor left for work at the censor. Now and again he would arrive back with a new list which I would pass on to Åge Berg.

We began to accept the situation after a couple of weeks; I had been totally banned from the censor's office. But at least Tor could continue collecting whatever names he came across. I fell back into my old routine. The excitement and worry subsided, and once again my life felt meaningless. What was I doing perming ministers' wives' hair while a war raged on in Europe? When every day that passed saw the Germans tighten their hold on Norway; while rumours of terror and torture grew ever more common.

I arrived home one evening to discover something had happened. It was written all over Tor's face. He sat in the living-room, in an armchair, his head stuck in a newspaper. He did not even look up when I said hello.

At first I paid no attention. It was up to him if he would rather not say anything. We didn't owe each other any explanations.

He put the paper down. 'I've got something to tell you,' he said. 'I've been offered a new job.'

'Congratulations!' I said. 'Doing what?'

'A while back I met the German secretary of legation. I told him that I knew about the people who travelled over to England in fishing boats, and that I was interested in that type of work, to be sent over to England on a mission for the Germans.'

'England.' I said. 'You're mad; why England?'

Tor continued without answering my question. 'This morning I received a phone-call from Major Öelsner of counter-espionage. He wanted to arrange a meeting today, after lunch.'

'What did he say?'

'He asked if I was really interested in travelling to England. If so, he might be able to do something for me. A South American was being sent over and there was the possibility that I could go with him.'

'By fishing boat?'

'By plane. We'll be dropped off along the coast with a dinghy; we'll have to row to shore.'

'What would you be doing?'

'I don't know. Major Öelsner simply asked if I'd be willing to take the job.'

'So what did you say?'

'I asked if I could have time to think it over.'

'You realise they want you to spy, don't you?'

Tor nodded. Of course he understood. Even if it was not advertised everyone knew that they sent people out to spy for them. This was a wonderful opportunity to double-cross the Germans. If Tor was sent along he would be able to relay false information.

'You've got to go,' I said. 'You'll have to.'

'I cast the bait and they swallowed it whole. Now it's just a question of reeling them in.' Tor smiled and I could see that this hadn't been the first time he had given it some thought. It was a brilliant idea.

We started making plans straight away. 'As soon as I get there I'll hand myself over to the English police,' said Tor.

'I'll write you a letter for grandfather to take with you,' I said. 'He'll vouch for you. And then . . .'

What would Tor do next? My imagination began running away with me.

'Who's this South American?' I asked.

'A radio-operator,' said Tor. 'That was all I was told.'

'Then they'll give you a transmitter,' I said. 'You'll be able to fool the Germans. Tell the English police who you are and then act the spy and relay falsified information.'

I knew it sounded naïve. This wasn't a boy's adventure story. This was war. Tor had been asked to become a German spy and go across to England. What would happen? How did the British counterspy network operate? What does a special agent do anyway? What information was he meant to obtain? I didn't know, and Tor didn't know. It was highly dangerous, of course. Tor could get hurt.

He realised that too. He was taking a risk. If he didn't manage to persuade the English of his real intentions he could be shot as a spy. But I felt that fresh opportunities and avenues were opening up before us. If Tor played his cards right he could achieve a great deal. However, a trip to England meant we would have to part. We couldn't make any more plans together. I realised my life would feel empty without him.

'Just think if the two of us could go,' I said. 'I know England better than anyone else. We'd be able to do so much.'

'They've already asked the South American,' said Tor. 'All the Germans need is someone to help him, someone whose English is passable. He'll be doing the work. I don't know what I'll be doing, but I can guess.'

'You'll be in charge of sabotage whilst he looks after communications,' I said.

Tor started pacing up and down the room. 'Should I say yes?' he asked.

'For the time being; you can always back out at a later date.'

'We're the advance guard,' Tor explained. 'The major used precisely those words, "advance guard". The

Germans will be marching into London in a few months. We're to be there when it happens, to meet them.'

'The Germans will never manage to invade England. You can go across with every confidence and hand yourself over.'

Tor nodded. 'That's exactly what I thought,' he said. 'And that's why I felt I should make the most of the opportunity.'

We talked about the offer for a long time. I wasn't the one who had been asked but I was the more enthusiastic. I could see myself doing it; the rubber boat arriving on a rocky beach; security men welcoming me and giving me the false information to give to the Germans.

My mind was certainly made up: Tor had to take the chance. He knew the mission wasn't going to be easy. A lot could happen. Perhaps his travelling companion was a committed Nazi and would insist on their doing the task they had been sent for. Maybe he would be forced to kill him.

Tor was frozen stiff at the realisation of what he was letting himself in for. He wanted to go. It had been his intention from the start. I would help him. Together we would plan his strategy. We would carefully rehearse a plan he could implement on his arrival, but first we needed more details. Who was this South American? Where would they land? What tasks would they be set? What sort of information did the Germans want them to get hold of? How were they going to communicate?

Tor told the major from counter-espionage of his decision. He was informed that the head of operations would contact him. Until that happened he was to stay calm and bide his time.

Tor waited. A week passed. Then a man called Andersen phoned him. He told Tor that he had been okayed for the job and that they would soon start work.

Tor met his new boss, but received no orders to leave, simply to prepare himself.

Several more days passed. Winter had begun. Cold

winds swept over Oslo and the first snows fell. I continued at the salon, paid the wages, saw to the accounts and worked in the lab. One day, when I was in the middle of perming a customer's hair, our cashier, Edith, came up to me and told me I was wanted on the phone. I excused myself and went into the office.

It was Tor. 'Can you get back home?' he asked.

'I've got a customer,' I said. 'I'll be finished in half an hour. Is it important?'

'Something's happened,' said Tor. 'Can't you come now?'

I could tell by the tone of his voice that something was on his mind. He was clearly agitated. 'I'm coming,' I said and put down the receiver. One of the assistants took over from me. I excused myself, saying I had forgotten I was meant to be at the dentist, and rushed off.

Tor met me in the hallway. 'He's bottled out,' he said. 'It's all off.'

'Who's bottled out?'

'The South American. He didn't want to go. The project has been postponed. They don't want me to go alone.'

That was it. Tor should have felt relieved. For the time being he would not have to make his journey into the unknown. He didn't look relieved, though. He was disappointed but excited at the same time.

He looked at me, thoughtful. I suddenly realised what he had in mind. 'Do you think it's possible? . . . The two of us?' I said.

'I don't know,' said Tor, 'but I could suggest that you replace him. It'll be difficult, but I've already started bluffing them, so I might as well continue.'

My enthusiasm was bubbling up inside me. This was it, this was what we had talked about ever since Tor had been contacted. We could travel to England together as German spies, only to become British double agents.

'Who's better qualified for the job than I am?' I said. 'English is my second language. I can move about the country freely, just like a native.'

'I know,' said Tor. 'That's what I'll tell them.'

'Tell them my previous hopes to work for them have been dashed, that I tried more than once. Tell them about the letter to Terboven. That should impress them.'

'They'll be able to read that in your papers; they won't need me to tell them.'

I continued to provide Tor with sound reasons. We would succeed if we were cheeky enough. 'And don't forget to tell them about my membership of the National Socialist Party, and that I prided myself in the swastika on my lapel.' Well, I hadn't worn it since my dismissal from the post censor, but Schacke and the others could verify the fact if they were asked. 'Besides,' I said, 'I've got an English bicycle. A genuine one with rubber tyres. We can take it with us, what could be more English?'

I don't know if the bicycle eventually persuaded Tor that the Germans would accept me. He promised to put forward the proposal. He could do no more than that. Then it was up to them to decide whether or not I could be trusted. My overall qualifications were good. The language, my knowledge of the country, and grandfather. They surely weren't so stupid not to realise what a find I was.

'We can use grandfather's address as a point of communication,' I said. 'That's important. His position gives us a perfect cover for our operation. What more could the Germans ask for?'

'That's enough! I'll put it to them tomorrow,' said Tor.

'You could try today,' I said.

'Tomorrow. It has to look as if I've thought about it. They mustn't think that this is a flash-in-the-pan idea I came up with just because the South American couldn't go.'

He was right. Tomorrow.

I returned to the salon. I was in such a good mood — humming to myself, laughing and joking with the customers.

Tor succeeded in arousing Andersen's interest in me, but the reaction wasn't exactly what he had expected.

Andersen asked if he could buy the bicycle. He offered fifty kroner for it; it was a good price.

'What'll I do?' I asked.

'Sell it to him,' said Tor.

'The cycle must be worth more to Andersen. Imagine being able to equip a German agent with a genuine English cycle.'

'Let him have it for the price he offered. That way you'll be showing your goodwill. We might be grateful for it later on.'

'So you haven't given up hope?'

'Of course not,' said Tor. 'This business of the cycle was Andersen's idea, totally off the cuff. He'll be looking through your papers now.'

I agreed, and the next day the cycle changed hands. We immediately wasted most of the fifty kroner on a good meal out.

Tor paid another visit to Andersen. It was a success. I don't know how, but he had managed to perfect the art of outwitting the Germans. One day he appeared unexpectedly at the salon and told me that we were both to go for an interview in Stortingsgaten.

I knew that the Germans wanted to meet me in person, to make sure I was right for the job. Naturally Tor had already given them all the information they needed. He had assured them of my loyalty and emphasised my 'virtues'. However, they still had to look into my background. Someone would take my file from the Gestapo archives and study the details. How much attention had they paid to the missing list and their subsequent suspicions? Would the letter to Terboven have any effect?

Obviously their investigations had turned out well for me, because when Tor and I got there I was asked the usual questions by a polite man in civilian clothing. Name, date of birth, address and qualifications. I told the story about Mitchell for the third time. I showed my membership card for the NNSAP, and expressed my disdain over the British planting of mines. I was learning fast.

Then we left. Tor and I would be contacted when it was time to start our training. We were to be instructed in Morse telegraphy and code. We would learn how to use a transmitter and the skills of sabotage.

I tried to conceal my excitement back at work, but I couldn't help myself. Father was curious and asked me if anything was the matter. 'Nothing,' I said. 'Everything is just fine.'

'Is it a girl?' father asked. 'If so, I'll leave you in peace.'

I let him believe that my high spirits were due to a new love affair.

After a few days we were told to be at Akers hospital. At the reception we were to ask for Andersen. We took the bus to the hospital. The driver apologised for the lack of heating. We shivered with the cold, and when we got off the bus, half-frozen, we were met by an icy wind. The snow crunched in time with our steps. We hurried into the warmth, found the reception and asked to see a Mr Andersen. A nurse showed us to a private room. We knocked and entered. A man in his fifties was lying in the bed. His face was ash-grey, his hands were shaking and he had difficulty looking directly at me. 'Hello, Mr Andersen,' said Tor.

'Welcome,' said Andersen in a hoarse voice. He turned his head in order to see me better. I noticed his ears were large and stuck out. He paused: 'So this is Mr Moe,' he said. 'I hear you want to join our organisation. Mr Glad has recommended you.'

I said that I was indeed Moe, and that I was interested in the job I had been offered.

'So, Mr Moe, you are willing to make a contribution for Germany?' he hissed.

'It's been my greatest wish for a long time,' I said.

He tried to smile but he could hardly move his lips. He looked seriously ill. 'We've discussed your offer,' he whispered, 'and we've acccepted you both. As from now, as from this minute, you're a special unit within Abwehr, under my command.'

Andersen was German; it was certainly not his real name. He had a heart condition and was an alcoholic; Tor had told me. However, he was the top man in the department, responsible for recruiting spies in Norway; he trained them all and sent them to England. Tor suspected that he received a bonus for every agent he managed to recruit. He looked as if he was dying, but he was a man with influence. And he might get better.

'I'm glad you have confidence in us,' I said. 'We'll do our best. I hope we'll live up to your expectations.'

He tried to nod, but couldn't manage. Then, with great effort, he turned in his bed, stretched out his arm and fumbled about with the bedside table. He groped for the catch and pulled out the drawer, put his hand inside and pulled out a pistol.

'Come here,' he said to Tor. Tor went over to him. 'Mr Glad, you're to carry this,' he said and handed him the weapon. Tor took it.

Just as slowly, and with just as much effort, he pulled out another pistol. This one he gave to me. Then he shut the drawer and sank back into the bed, completely exhausted.

Tor took a quick glance at the weapon. I could tell he wasn't too happy. The pistols were Spanish and of very poor quality. We stood there looking at Andersen, our pistols in our hands, contemplating the sick man. Was this some sort of test, I wondered? Was he testing to see if we would use the weapons on him?

Of course not. When I looked at his satisfied expression, I understood. Giving us the weapons was a sign of acceptance. As from that moment we were a part of German counter-intelligence. We were employed by Abwehr, with the right to carry firearms.

'We'll shoot our way to victory,' Tor said solemnly.

Andersen tried to smile.

Then we bowed, wished him a speedy recovery and left the room.

As we made our way slowly and silently to the bus stop, I could feel the cold weapon as it thumped against my thigh.

10

So Abwehr had found two new recruits: Tor Glad and John Moe. We had been accepted by the Germans; our papers had been checked and our background found to be faultless. We were in a position of trust. We had entered the organisation and were to be sent to England on a secret mission. It was amazing how easy it had all been. Next we were to be trained as spies. Even if the selection was carried out on such a slack basis, the training no doubt would be thorough. The Germans spared no expense on providing resources even if it was a crash course.

The first of these arrived in the form of a petty officer. A week after our official appointment by the dying Andersen, we were contacted by a young man who introduced himself as Pavlowski; he had received orders to instruct us in telegraphy. We arranged to meet him on a Sunday. Our tuition would take place at home. We went to work as usual during the day — Tor at the post censor, and myself at the salon. Our tuition was therefore relegated to evenings and weekends.

Winter had set in. In the park the snow lay a metre deep and the temperature stuck stubbornly around minus twenty-five centigrade.

Our tutor rang at the door on the Sunday morning. He was tall, blond and his cheeks were red with the cold. We invited him in, gave him a cup of hot tea and chatted about the weather for a while. It looked as if it was going to be an unusually severe winter. It would cause a great deal of hardship to many. Most things were rationed, and coke and coal were practically impossible to get hold of.

For the first lesson he brought a pair of Morse keys with him. We sat in the living-room and he started by carefully going over the code with us, teaching us how to operate the small device.

After a few weeks we got to know our teacher quite well. He wasn't a Nazi, but a patriot. He had completed his military service in the navy and after the occupation he had received orders to go to Norway. He enjoyed his special duties. For a while he stuck to the usual routine and took great pains to teach us what he'd been sent to do. He was a skilful teacher who took his job seriously. He knew who we were and the reasons for our training. To him, we weren't just ordinary pupils. We were important people, meaningful links in the continuing battle against Great Britain, a battle that we would win. He realised that our mission was both tough and dangerous. He was responsible for us. We were relying on him to train us sufficiently for us to be able to carry out our mission.

We learned quickly. After just a few lessons we had mastered Morse code and were quite fast and competent on the keys. But we were highly motivated, realising that we would not be sent away until we had passed the last test. We sat practising by ourselves every evening, tapping out short and long at a great rate, often late into the night.

Whilst we were working with our telegraphy keys one afternoon, the doorbell rang. I opened the door. Redelien stood there. I was really happy to see him. After I had been forced to give up my job at the post censor we had met only a couple of times.

'How's it going?' I asked. 'Are you managing without me?'

'With difficulty,' said Redelien, laughing.

I invited him in and we sat down on the sofa. Tor fetched a couple of Solos which was all we had left in the way of drink.

'Has anything been said about the letter to Terboven?' I asked.

'Not a word,' said Redelien. 'But then I didn't expect

anything. The letter is probably buried in some archive somewhere. You'll never get a reply.'

'I know,' I said. 'I was just curious.'

Redelien got up and went to the big table in the middle of the room. Tor had managed to hide our papers, but one of the Morse keys was still there.

'Are you learning telegraphy?' he asked.

I looked at Tor. He nodded. We could trust Redelien. He wouldn't pass on the information. Besides, we were doing this for the Germans. 'We've got another job,' I said. 'We're now employed by Abwehr. We're going to be flown to England in a few months' time.'

Redelien picked up the Morse key, holding it in his hand a while as if feeling its weight. Then he put it back on the table. 'How can you do it?' he asked.

'We know there are risks,' I said.

'I wouldn't do it if I were in your shoes,' said Redelien.

'The job at the post censor could end any day,' said Tor, 'and I don't want to be left doing nothing. It does more to wear you down than anything else I know. I want to do something.'

Redelien looked at him and shook his head. 'I don't want to know anything,' he said. He went back and sat down. He didn't touch on the subject again that evening. He didn't mention the subject at all; even when we all went to the Ritz a week later.

I think he suspected our intentions. He knew us well enough to realise that we weren't loyal to the Nazis. He himself had told us what he thought of them, and as a lawyer he took care not to ask us any indiscreet questions. He realised that to know too much could be dangerous. However, he kept his doubts to himself; he never tried to hamper our progress in the intelligence service.

Our teacher, the petty officer, was very pleased with us. He gave us more advanced tests. We had to learn the international Q-code and eventually we got our own code system and started putting messages together. The codebook consisted of a little paperback volume of crosswords which we used to build up the combinations of messages that we wanted to relay. It was a simple but ingenious system, although it meant that our reports would be difficult to decode. We had a couple of dozen crosswords to choose from. Without the decipher it was impossible to make any sense of our messages.

Those days were hard. We worked intensively every evening. In our breaks we drank tea and ate 'fyrstekake' which we bought at the 'Bon Mot', a bakery in the neighbourhood. Our petty officer fell in love with the marzipan pastries.

Andersen kept in touch with us throughout. He had in fact recovered and been discharged from the hospital a couple of weeks after we had started our training. We were called to his office at Stortingsgaten now and again; every so often we met in town and went to a bakery together. Once or twice we went to a restaurant.

Andersen was part of Abwehr and was directly responsible for us as well as the other agents who were being trained. We never found out who the other recruits were, but we realised that it was far from easy for the Germans to find suitable candidates. If the number of volunteers had been large they certainly wouldn't have chosen us. My background must have made them suspicious from the very start but I suppose they had carefully weighed the risks against the advantages. There were lots of advantages. I could play a convincing Englishman, I spoke the language fluently and grandfather gave me the perfect cover. Besides, it was only a temporary commitment. England would soon be defeated and then our services would no longer be required.

'Anyway, I'll arrange work for you in London with *Gauleitern*,' said Andersen, 'if you behave.' He laughed, clasped his chest, grimaced and took a deep breath. He had a bad heart.

Andersen gave us the benefit of his advice. He explained what we were to do once we had landed. We should try to be as discreet as possible; the first few weeks we should lie low and do absolutely nothing. All we had to do was blend in with the refugees who were pouring out of the bombed cities. Once we had settled ourselves in, then we could begin our real work.

'What's that?' I asked. 'What are we going to be doing?'

Andersen smiled. First of all we would set up radio contact, he said. We were to find somewhere safe where our signals could be picked up and where we could receive replies. We did not discover what we were meant to be looking out for, or what information we were expected to collect and pass on. All our orders would be given via the radio. We understood why. Nobody could be sure that we would manage to land safely. We could be captured by the English, we could fail; in that case it would be far better that we knew nothing.

They were taking no chances. Perhaps they had no plans for a mission at all? Sometimes Tor and I discussed the possibility. Maybe we were just a sacrificial unit, sent out to see if the British coastal defence was on its guard? To see if this method of landing was an alternative to landing by parachute? That question was not answered and we had to keep on playing the game. We were a small advance spy unit; we would be there when the Germans invaded the Isles.

'Don't worry, boys,' said Andersen. 'We'll soon be seeing each other in London.'

Major Müller repeated Andersen's words when we were introduced one afternoon: 'If your mission is a success, we'll all meet in London.' Major Müller was the head of Abwehr and had infiltrated Norway prior to its invasion; his base had been in Hamburg. He had a mouth packed with gold and whenever he smiled his fillings sparkled and glinted. I stared at him, fascinated.

'The codename for this operation is Hummer Nord III, Glad's codename is Tege, yours, Moe, is Ja,' said Müller. 'Mr Andersen will be responsible for your equipment. The date of your departure has not yet been decided, but your mission is high priority. I expect that we'll be sending you in March.'

It wasn't far off, but time still seemed to pass very slowly. It was still winter, the cold weather refused to lift and the fjord was covered in thick ice.

I knew that the English would be interested in any information about the Abwehr in Norway. If they could identify Müller, Andersen and the others, they could be kept under surveillance, as could those Norwegians with whom they made contact; it might even be possible to discover the identities of other recruits undergoing training.

Everyone in Abwehr wore civilian clothes. Andersen himself lumbered around in a heavy, green cloth coat; it was the only one in Oslo. We knew his real name was not Andersen but we never discovered his true identity. His office was small and cramped. From the outside it looked like a base for an export company.

A picture of Andersen would make it easier for the English. We really ought to make sure that we had photographs of the most important people in the German spy network. I bought a motion picture camera in Tivolihallen. It cost a thousand kroner, on hire-purchase. I showed the camera to Andersen, saying it could come in useful over in England. We might find something of interest. The films could then be given to a contact who could send them on to Germany. That we should get involved in such advanced techniques had hardly been touched on during the planning. At first Andersen was not interested in my idea, but after a few days he changed his mind. My initiative was excellent, he said, and well worth trying.

'I'll learn how to use it,' I said.

We went out into the street outside his office. I focused and started photographing passers-by. Andersen was in a few of them without his noticing. Now it was just a matter of getting the others in front of my lens and somehow smuggling the films over to England.

'We'll find a way,' said Tor.

Slowly the days grew lighter. Spring was on the way.

During the day the snow melted on the south-facing slopes, the streets became slushy and then icy when at night it all refroze.

We now had a sound knowledge of every conceivable code and had reached a considerable speed with our telegraphy keys. It was time to set about learning the next skill.

A different teacher was sent to us. His name was Korsewitz, an explosives expert and teacher of sabotage techniques. The first lessons were purely theoretical. Korsewitz went through the process of making an incendiary device, using chemicals that could be picked up at any chemist or even at the grocer's. We made a note of the different proportions of sulphur, potassium nitrate, weedkiller and sugar necessary to obtain the best results. Korsewitz had brought along some fuses; we had to time the burning rate and then work out the requisite length of fuse needed to give us a chance to take cover. We were shown how to detonate dynamite — we would be provided with detonators and fuses, but we would either have to steal the explosives or make them ourselves.

Tor had learnt something of explosives in the forces. It was understood that he would take the lead role in our sabotage manoeuvres.

One day we were sent out to find the required chemicals. Korsewitz had given us the money to buy the sugar, sulphur and other components necessary to make an effective incendiary bomb. We loaded it all in the car which he had at his disposal and he drove us out to Fornebu. The tests were to take place at one of the tightly guarded aerodromes.

Korsewitz had selected a small section of forest well away from the hangars. We climbed out, unloaded the equipment and laid the ingredients on the ground. 'Off you go, gentlemen,' said Korsewitz. 'I want to see an incendiary bomb just over there.' He pointed amongst the trees at a pile of stones. The stones represented a house. That was to be our target. Korsewitz strolled back and forth, sneaking a glance at our work, but did not interfere. He had done his part, it was now up to his protégés to show how much they had understood.

Tor and I began measuring the chemicals. We mixed the powders in one of the bowls we had brought with us. We judged the mixture carefully, gently stirring and blending, according to our instructions. We adjusted the fuse and trimmed it to the right length. The wick was slightly longer than necessary, but it was best to be on the safe side. I carried the bowl in amongst the trees, treading deliberately, like a bridegroom on his way to the altar. Tor followed close behind me, ready to catch me should I slip or stumble.

I placed the bomb on top of the highest stone, standing on tiptoe to slide the bowl on to the rough boulder. Then, making sure it was steady, I nodded to Tor. We said nothing to each other — it was not necessary. We had learned the routine in detail. The next step was to light the fuse, then run and take cover.

Tor lit a match to the fuse which was hanging over the rock. It started to spark, the flame crackling upwards. We studied it. According to the instructions we were to make sure that everything was going to plan. Then we rushed out of the wood towards the car, taking shelter behind it. I threw myself down on the ground, watching the stone which could only just be seen between the trees. Tor and Korsewitz stood between myself and the bomb. 'Get down!' I yelled. 'Take cover, the bomb will explode any minute now.'

They remained where they were. Nonchalantly, Korsewitz lit a cigarette, took a deep draw, and blew a couple of smoke-rings.

'The bomb's about to explode!' I screamed.

'An incendiary bomb doesn't explode,' said Tor.

Some gulls glided over the clump of trees. A cool breeze blew in from the fjord. Spring was in the air, but it was not yet warm. The snow still lay deep on the northern slopes. The gulls floated on the wind. I lay pressed against the ground behind the car and noticed that I had thrown myself into a rivulet of melted snow which ran over the road. Korsewitz and Tor still stood between myself and the bomb. It would explode soon.

'Don't you understand what I'm saying?' I said.

'The fuse is too long,' said Tor.

The seconds ticked by but neither man made a move for cover. I knew that the fuse was far too long. Or had it gone out? I tried again: 'Ten seconds to go!' I yelled.

Korsewitz stood with his legs apart, calmly watching the rock. He took a puff of his cigarette. I could see him from my hiding place, with the tree trunks in front of him and the contour of the stone on which the bomb lay.

Suddenly a spout of flame rose up from amongst the trees. A blazing puff of fire and smoke was cast half a metre into the air, sank down casting a few embers, and then died out.

'Excellent,' said Korsewitz. He threw his cigarette butt away and walked over to me. I got up slowly and felt my trouser-leg, soaking wet, thanks to the melted snow. 'Congratulations,' Korsewitz continued. 'Your first incendiary bomb worked perfectly. An unnecessarily long fuse perhaps, but that doesn't matter. The main thing is that you've tried it out.'

We went back to the stone. It was black with soot. Our homemade bomb had had no other effect. But at least the bomb had gone off. We were qualified saboteurs. We had passed the test.

We lit three more devices that afternoon. We placed the first one in the grass by one of the runway extensions. This was stronger: the puff of smoke spouted up almost a metre high and a wide circle of last year's grass had been burnt away. Then our audience arrived. A car pulled up and Müller and Andersen climbed out together with a man I had never seen before. Before they came into earshot, Korsewitz whispered out of the corner of his mouth that the third man had just arrived from Berlin to check on our progress. 'He's fairly high up the ladder,' Korsewitz informed before the man reached us.

'Don't let us disturb you,' said Müller. 'Carry on with the exercise as planned.'

We gathered the chemicals for another bomb, making the mixture as powerful as the last one, and carried it out on to the grass. I wasn't as worried as I had been previously, but I was surprised at their arrival. Were we really so important that a German commander thought it was worth paying us a visit, all the way from Berlin?

I left Tor to light the fuse himself. I had an idea. I went over to the car and got my camera. It was loaded. I focused and checked the exposure. 'I'll see what this thing can do,' I said. 'I've not learnt how to use it yet.'

I took pictures of Tor lighting the fuse, and then as he ran back to take cover and the bomb flared up, I took several dramatic photographs. Then I turned round and focused on the small group of laughing supervisors who were clearly delighted with our performance. I snapped a photograph of all four of them together.

'What are you going to do with the film, Mr Moe?' asked Müller.

'Nothing,' I said. 'I'm just practising.'

'You'll have to show us the results when we meet in London,' Müller said, giving me his golden smile. He said it jokingly. We would soon be enjoying an evening together in the English capital once Britain had been taken.

It never occurred to him that Tor and I would be going there long before them, and he certainly had no idea that I had every intention of showing the photographs in London — but to a completely different audience.

11

Our training was drawing to a close. We had learned all that
the Germans had required of us. We could send telegrams
with relative speed, we could decode messages using our
crosswords with no trouble at all; and we had learned to
make bombs. Tor had given up his job at the post censor;
Andersen wanted him to devote all his time to our
preparations. My visits to the salon in Tivolihallen also
became less frequent.

One evening at the beginning of March we took our first
test. We met outside Andersen's office. Korsewitz arrived
in one of those civilian city cars owned by Abwehr. A heavy
case was placed in the boot and we all got in the car.
Andersen, Tor and I in the back; Müller sat in the front
passenger seat.

Korsewitz drove south towards Drammen. We passed
Hövik where my mother's salon was situated. I'd worked
there for a while, 'blacklegging'. A year ago the salon had
been blacklisted; mother did not belong to any employers'
association and none of her employees were trade
unionists. She didn't want to close the salon and had asked
me to help her, which I did, albeit reluctantly. I didn't
enjoy it there but all the customers were optimistic — they
were the diehards who strongly condemned the action
being taken against mother.

I pointed out the salon as Korsewitz drove us past. He
just nodded. It was only when we reached Blommenholm
that he slowed down, swung off the main road and drove up
to a large house.

It was evening and already dark. In the glare of the car's

headlights we could see an outhouse resembling a garage. Korsewitz swore and braked heavily in front of the house, turned off the headlights and told us we had arrived.

We clambered out. Andersen asked us to open the boot and carry the case into the outhouse. It was heavy so we took it together.

The house consisted of a single room; a solitary table in the very centre. The curtains were drawn; Andersen locked the door behind him. We were told to lift the case up on to the table and open it. Inside was a radio transmitter. It was German, run by battery, and both heavy and awkward. However, it closely resembled the sets we had practised on before.

Tor and I helped set it up. We rigged up the aerial, fastening it to the ceiling, then fixed it up with the transmitter. We were to use the equipment to send a couple of messages. This was a practical test under realistic conditions. For the first time we would be transmitting on the airwaves. Our task was to contact Oslo and Abwehr's radio station on the top floor of the house in Klingenbergsgaten. Someone was there ready to pick up our signals and reply to them.

Tor began the exercise. He called, waited, and called again. He was nervous, calling again and again. Müller noticed his nervousness. 'Take it easy,' he said. 'It's your old instructor at the other end. He has the Morse key at the ready and will do all he can to help you.'

Suddenly the reply signal came over the speaker. Tor had managed to make contact. Relieved, he began to laugh and the Abwehr men applauded.

Later I took over from him. I was to transmit a few lines of nonsense, first coding, and then relaying the message. The answer came back in code. I deciphered the reply and read it out. Pavlowski congratulated us. Tege and Ja had passed the test.

Müller and Andersen were pleased. We had proved to them that we had mastered every detail. We could handle the radio equipment without the slightest difficulty. Having packed away the set, Korsewitz drove us back to Oslo.

The following day we were called in to see Major Müller.

'Congratulations,' he said. 'I was very pleased with last night's results. Now all we have to do is wait for the date of your departure.'

'Well, we're ready,' I said. 'When do you think we'll go?'

'That's for Berlin to decide. We need an aeroplane and then it will just depend on the weather. We need to wait for the right conditions. We will just have to be patient. The instructions will come from the flying division. They'll be taking care of your flight and so on.'

Müller pulled open a drawer and took out two toiletry cases and belts. He put them on the table. 'Presents,' he said, smiling.

I certainly needed a belt for my trousers and a bag for my toothbrush and shaving kit would come in handy. However, both the belts and the cases looked well used. Besides, the belt was wide and bulky, definitely not the latest model. I reached for one of the belts and lifted it up, feeling its unusual weight.

'Thanks,' I said. 'I'm sure it'll come in useful.'

'I hope so,' said Müller, revealing his gold teeth. 'I certainly hope so. The belts were, in fact, specially made for your benefit.' He picked up Tor's belt and turned it over to reveal the back. I looked at it quizzically.

'I expect you can see what it is, gentlemen?' said Müller. We didn't see at all. 'It's fuse-wire,' said Müller. 'Secreted between the bands of leather are four wires.'

He opened the desk drawer again. This time he took out a cross-section of a similar belt. Between the thin leather strips lay the black wires neatly concealed. 'Try them on and see if they fit,' he said.

We fastened our sabotage belts round our waists. They fitted, but were very long. However, the longer they were the more fuse-wire they concealed. We would certainly be well equipped.

'What's in the cases?' I asked. 'More fuse-wire?'

'No,' said Müller. 'Detonators.' He opened one of them

and took out a clothes brush. It was made from polished wood with light-coloured hard bristles. It looked fairly ordinary to me.

'Hollow,' he said and tapped the wood. 'I'll show you.' He unscrewed the top of his fountain pen and drew a sketch of the brush. It held four detonators in small compartments which had been hollowed out at both ends. Detonators had also been placed in the shaving brushes which were later given to us. They were also secreted in small niches in the handle and were easily picked out with a knife.

I felt a sudden elation. This was really something to show the British. At the same time, however, a sudden fear passed through me. It was a feeling I had experienced before. It all seemed like a sinister game. Müller, Andersen and Korsewitz had been given their orders; they had an objective. We were to be trained, equipped, prepared and advised for a dangerous and critical mission. As it stood we were willing to learn. We listened carefully and showed our dedication and loyalty. What else could we do?

Yet, at the same time, we were fully aware that our goal was not theirs. Quite simply, we had to make sure that we reached Britain at their expense. We would immediately hand ourselves over to the British authorities and reveal all that we had seen of German Intelligence. That was our first priority. The belts and clothes brushes were but minor details to us, objects to show our friends on the other side of the North Sea. We were not interested in the length of fuse-wire hidden in the belts, nor did we care how many detonators were concealed in the brushes. We had no intention of using the fuses and we would never have to pick out our detonators.

We had to keep up appearances. We had to pretend, posing interested questions when Müller gave us our instructions and advised us on our forthcoming trip to England.

'You'll be flown over at night,' he said. 'At dawn the plane will land just off the coast. Naturally enough it's a seaplane. You'll have to paddle to shore in a rubber dinghy. Once you have reached dry land your first priority is to destroy the dinghy.'

'We'll need knives,' I said, trying to look as if I was soaking up every word he said.

'There will be knives and spades in the dinghy,' he continued. 'The first thing to do is bury it. There must be no visible signs on the beach by the time it's light. Dig a long, narrow hole about a metre deep. When that's done, puncture the boat and squeeze all the air out, roll it up lengthwise, put it in the hole and place a couple of rocks on top. Finally, fill the hole with earth and level off the ground to make sure it's well hidden.'

We nodded and tried to appear interested. We had no intention of digging any hole. Neither would we puncture the rubber dinghy nor roll it up. The first thing we would do once on land would be to report to the nearest police station or military camp, or whatever authority we came across. The dinghy would remain fully visible on the beach so that the British could see what type of craft the Germans used to equip their spies.

'We reckon it'll take you a couple of weeks to acclimatise,' said Müller.

'A couple of weeks?' said Tor.

'We think it'll take a certain amount of time before you get the opportunity to make your first contact. You'll need somewhere to stay and you'll also have to get acquainted with the area. During this time you must hide the radio equipment in a safe place.'

It hadn't occurred to us to hide it, but it was best to take it all in. He continued with our instructions. We should try and find a wooded grove to conceal the radio under shrubs and branches. If possible, we were to avoid burying it. The moisture in the soil might damage the more sensitive components. Then he explained how to find a suitable site from where we could relay messages; a hill preferably, as high as possible, and covered in trees; it would be easier to mount the aerial. It had to be isolated; we could not take the risk of being seen whilst we were trying to contact our colleagues.

We nodded, pretending to commit his words to memory. He was aware of our deep concentration. We could tell he was pleased with his recruits. Then we discussed what we should do if our equipment needed replacing.

'If it's urgent and absolutely necessary, it can be arranged,' said Müller. 'We can fly the equipment in and drop it by parachute.' We nodded. It was a wise precaution and good to know that the possibility was there, even if we would never use it. 'Only if it is vital for an extremely important job. Otherwise, no chance,' he continued.

We promised to avoid any unnecessary complications, but we needed to know that if a problem arose we were not completely alone.

Müller carried on. If, for some unforeseen reason, we were to receive equipment via a parachute, we would need a safe dropping zone, well out of sight. It would need sufficient surrounding landmarks by which the plane could navigate, and signals would be given with a torch or firelight.

We memorised the details. The British might just be interested.

'Don't worry,' said Müller, 'it won't be for long. England will soon be a beaten nation.'

'We'll meet in London,' I said.

We smiled at one another. It was a stock phrase. We would all gather in the English capital. We were preparing the way and would soon be redundant.

'Britain is already in a state of chaos,' Müller added. 'The roads are packed with refugees. It'll make things easier for you. All you'll need to do is blend in with the refugees. No one will have the time to wonder who you are.'

I looked at him. He wasn't joking. He was perfectly serious. Didn't he realise that was pure propaganda? We had heard it all on the news and read it in the papers. Britain was already beaten: people fled in panic away from the bomb-threatened cities; the roads were jam-packed; hundreds of thousands of people were desperately seeking shelter; communications were at a complete standstill.

The German propaganda machine laid it on thick. Not many Norwegians had the strength to listen, even less to believe it.

We were better informed. We made a point of listening to the BBC. True, the Germans had confiscated all radios in Oslo. Every household had been told to exchange their old radio for a new one that could only receive a couple of German radio stations. Even father had obeyed, but he had an ancient set that had been stored away in the loft. The new radio which had been bought just before the occupation was hidden. We took it out in the evenings and listened to the British foreign news. The BBC never mentioned a thing about chaos and evacuations. They openly declared that the situation was a serious one, that German bombings had caused serious damage to factories and housing estates. However, Britain was not beaten. We knew that these tales of masses of refugees out on the roads was quite untrue. What surprised me was Müller's belief in the propaganda. Wasn't the German Intelligence Service better informed?

However, neither Tor nor I questioned Müller's version of the situation. We just nodded and agreed that such circumstances would definitely make our forthcoming operation a lot easier.

Then the conversation came to an end for the time being. We took up our belts and cases, leaving Andersen's office where all of our meetings with Abwehr had taken place.

Now it was simply a question of waiting and preparing both ourselves and our equipment. The days became long and uneventful. We talked to alleviate the boredom. We chatted non-stop about our forthcoming mission, planning our strategy, discussing our plans for our arrival, and how we would approach the British authorities. We imagined the reception we would be given. It would be a heroes' welcome. After all, we had double-crossed the Germans.

We met Andersen almost every day. Now and again Müller would put in an appearance. On one occasion we were each given one hundred English pounds and twenty dollars; to us it was a lot of money. We could survive a couple of months on it.

'We didn't really have any other use for the money,' said Müller. In a mere six months the Germans would be occupying London. The money was quite genuine, obviously taken from British soldiers who had been captured somewhere on the Continent. They were well-used notes. Müller suggested that they would help avoid any suspicion. We were also given a collection of incendiary bombs that looked just like ordinary ink pens. Müller showed us how they worked. All you had to do was break off the nib and then hide the pen somewhere. In an office, a waste-paper basket, a bus stop or in a factory. 'A couple of these bombs placed in different locations will be enough to create utter panic throughout the whole of London,' he said.

We nodded and I wondered if he truly believed what he said.

Andersen gave us two bicycles; a Norwegian-made one for Tor and an English one for me. I recognised it. It was my own, the one I had sold to Andersen for fifty kroner. He did not ask for the money back, nor did I offer to buy it back. The cycle was part of our equipment and the Germans were paying for that. Andersen gave us seven hundred and fifty Norwegian kroner. Earlier on he had given us something to keep us going, but never as much as this at any one time. He told us we were to buy clothes with the money. Warm clothes that looked English. It was important not to look too different from the refugees that we were to blend in with.

We bought ski-suits. They were practical garments; the Germans approved of them. Andersen clearly felt that we ought to be prepared to spend at least the first few nights out in the open. It was still cool out, so we had to take sufficient clothing to keep us warm during the damp nights. The clothes did not look English. I knew enough about English fashion to realise that our uniform-like ski-jackets would arouse suspicion. When we put on our peaked ski-hats we really looked the part, but we would never be taken for Englishmen.

Neither Andersen nor Müller reacted. Their knowledge of conditions in the country we were going to was minimal. Maybe they were happy with our choice? Our ski-suits were similar to the clothes that the National Assembly henchmen wore.

When we had first been engaged by Abwehr we had received strict orders not to tell anyone what we were doing, not even those closest to us. We had kept our promise. We had told no one of our mission, with one exception — Tor's fiancée Gerd knew everything.

During this time we often spent the evening at Gerd's. It was safe there, and as she was the only one present we could talk quite openly, no longer having to disguise everything. It was a welcome break — we needed it. Even after the short time we had been in Abwehr, we felt the strain. It was not physically difficult, our training was not physically arduous, but we were continuously under psychological pressure.

While we were with the Germans we had to watch our every word. We could not allow Müller and his men to suspect that our eagerness to learn was not for the German victory they so frequently talked of. They were never to suspect that we had joined their unit in order to be in a position to help their enemies. At the same time we could not reveal our special engagement to our friends and families. If the Resistance group had ever got wind of the news, it would have put an immediate end to everything.

We were in a very complicated position. Our friends were not to be told that we were now German agents, and our colleagues were not to suspect that we had other ideas. Each time we met a new acquaintance, be they German or Norwegian, we had to think twice and play our roles convincingly. Except at Gerd's home, where we could relax. Gerd became our greatest support. It was partly thanks to her that we managed to withstand the pressures and continually appear beyond suspicion.

The day of departure drew closer. Our thoughts turned more and more to what might happen when we had gone. Our friends would surely wonder about our sudden disappearance. Mother and father would be worried if they did not see me at least a couple of times a week.

We discussed this with Andersen. He eased our minds. The Germans had considered this detail. Once we had left Oslo the Germans would spread the rumour through their contacts that we had been chosen to serve on board a weather ship in the Norwegian sea. That would explain our absence and we were to tell our parents and friends the same story, otherwise they were bound to be worried if we disappeared from the city. No one would be surprised that we had been sent to a weather ship with a secret destination.

One day at the end of March, Müller summoned us. By that time our long wait had made us irritable and impatient, and we didn't greet him with the usual reserved respect. The Abwehr major noticed this but pretended not to. Instead, he threw a bundle of British ration cards and identity papers on to the table. I picked up the papers that were written in my name. At least I would not have to change my identity.

'You've now got everything you need,' said Müller. 'The wireless is ready and you already have your equipment. Now, your departure.'

'When?' asked Tor and I in the same breath.

Müller smiled his golden smile. 'The 30th of March,' he said. 'Six days from now. You'll be taking the night train to Stavanger.'

12

I was overjoyed by Müller's announcement. At last something was going to happen. In a few days' time we would be on our way to England.

'Don't get nervous, Mr Moe,' said Andersen. He had noticed how excited I had become, but he did not know why. I was not nervous about the journey, I just felt intensely happy that we were so close to our goal.

'I think you gentlemen ought to go home and start packing,' said Müller. 'I'll be in Stavanger too, so we'll be able to go over the final details together.'

I calmed myself and we said goodbye. We made a controlled and dignified exit through the corridor and down the stairs. We reached the road still expressionless, and turned off homewards. We walked along the pavement side by side. Our pace quickened, and when we turned the corner of the block we broke into a run. Then I yelled out loud and we started laughing. We hugged each other, shouting and laughing. We had reached our goal.

People turned to look at us. The spring sunshine had made life in Oslo a lot more pleasant, but it was not so pleasant and agreeable that it warranted shouts of joy through the streets and in the middle of the afternoon! We noticed the looks of surprise.

We didn't calm down until we got home. We decided to go out and celebrate our departure, but first I wanted a rest. I felt so tired.

No wonder I was worn out. The tension of the past few weeks had suddenly eased. Understandably I was physically drained.

Tor promised to wake me in time for our big celebration. I fell asleep immediately and woke up when he shook me. I felt hot and had a splitting headache.

'Your face is all yellow,' said Tor. 'Surely you haven't got jaundice?'

I got off the sofa shakily and staggered over to the mirror. It was true. My face was yellow and when I felt my forehead I could tell I had a fever. Tor had had jaundice a while ago and I might have caught it off him.

'I can't go out tonight,' I said. All I wanted to do was go back to the sofa and sleep.

I slept badly that night, dreaming and delirious. In the morning I still felt feverish. I managed to get up and phone Doctor von Krogh, the family physician who had looked after me ever since I was a young child. He asked me to go to his surgery where he would see me straight away.

I managed to order a taxi, and quarter of an hour later it pulled up outside the door of the corner house where von Krogh lived and worked. The house lay in the crossing between Hegdehaugsveien, Parkveien and Wergelandsveien; it was a focal point through which an endless stream of trams, buses and cars passed every day.

Doctor von Krogh diagnosed jaundice.

'How long will it take me to recover?' I whispered.

'A week. Maybe longer.'

My illness would ruin our plans. What would the Germans say once they discovered that their agent could not make his first mission?

'I have to be better in a couple of days,' I said. 'I'm going away and I can't change the date.' I said it in such a way that he must have been persuaded that this journey was more important than anything else.

He took out his stethoscope, listened to my heart and said, 'Then we'll have to give you a quick cure.'

'Will I be better soon?' I asked.

'If this journey is so important to you I'll have to make sure that you don't have the fever by the time you leave.'

He showed me into the bathroom, which was large and

old-fashioned; an old water-heater sat perched on the wall. 'Take your clothes off and lie in the bath,' he said.

I did what he told me, quickly removing my clothes and climbing into the tepid water. He fetched a large glass cylinder, filled it with water from the heater and gave me a half-hour's enema. Afterwards he congratulated me on having put up with the treatment so patiently. Then he gave me some medicine and told me to spend the rest of the day in bed.

I felt weak and shaky, and decided to visit my mother. Someone had to look after me. It only took a couple of minutes to get to Wergelandsveien. Luckily the lift was working and I pressed the button for the eighth floor. Mother was in. She let me have her own double bed and I fell asleep and slept until late in the evening. When I woke up I felt better, and when she came in with some dinner I thought I must tell her about the journey. I decided to stick to the truth as closely as possible.

'I'm going over to England in a few days' time,' I said. She stared at me. 'That's all,' I continued. 'I'm travelling to England. I hope to be able to visit grandfather.'

'What will you be doing there?'

'I don't know yet. Tor and I are off to the west coast the day after tomorrow. Then we'll have to see. As far as you're concerned, we're serving on board a weather ship. That's what you've got to say if anyone asks.'

It wasn't exactly the truth, but it wasn't a total lie either.

'I hope you know what you're doing,' said mother.

'You mustn't worry,' I said. 'Everything will be fine. I have to go, and that's that. Let's not talk about it any more.'

I stayed in her flat overnight, slept peacefully and did not wake up until late morning. I still had not completely recovered but I felt much better. I had to get ready for the journey.

'I'll help you pack,' said mother. I had planned to pack myself but I could not refuse her offer.

Two days later I collected my belongings from our flat.

Tor was there and we helped each other to load it all into a taxi. Back at my mother's house we started packing my things in a large rucksack. Socks, shirts, two double-breasted suits, an extra pair of trousers and a hat, a genuine borsalino which could be folded without being damaged.

The doorbell rang and mother went to open it. It was a friend of hers — a neighbour. I had met the lady before and called her Aunt Tilly.

She looked at the half-packed case. 'Are you going somewhere?' she asked.

Mother answered for me. 'John's going to England,' she said. She had already forgotten about the weather ship.

'Are you escaping from the Germans?' wondered Aunt Tilly. I nodded. 'How exciting. By boat?'

'I don't know yet,' I said.

'I've got a present for you,' said Aunt Tilly, rushing off.

A few minutes later she was back. In her arms she was carrying a flag, a Norwegian flag, over two square metres of it. 'You're to take this with you. You shouldn't forget your home country during this awful time.'

I stared at the flag and at Aunt Tilly. Her joyful expression told me that I could not refuse it. I had to accept her gift, but when she had left I would hide it in a wardrobe. I couldn't see myself taking a Norwegian flag with me in a German aeroplane over the North Sea. Our luggage might be searched by Andersen before our departure. How would he react if he found an enormous flag in my bag?

'That's wonderful,' I said. 'Thank you for the thought. Norway will always be in my mind no matter where I am.' I tried to put it as well as I could. She was not to think that her present would never be unfurled on British soil.

We folded up the flag. It was made of a light crease-proof material. Despite its size it did not weigh much. I managed to find a space for it in my rucksack. Why not! It could be doubly useful. If Müller or Andersen found it I could always say that it would make us look more genuine to the British. They would like that. It showed initiative. If the British doubted us, I could show them the flag; they would never foresee the Germans equipping their spies with Norwegian national flags. It would stay where it was. Aunt Tilly looked pleased. She had made her patriotic contribution.

It's much the same for a lot of us these days, I thought. We want so much, but don't know how to go about it. What could we do to help our country and cause the greatest possible problems for our captors? We all wanted to do something; the difficulty was how. Tor and I felt that we had found a way. The gift was Aunt Tilly's way of showing where she stood. She had managed to conceal it, locked in a linen closet. At last it would be of use. It was a simple gesture, but to her it was as meaningful as the decision which Tor and I had taken. For a fleeting moment I was not sure which of us was the more naïve. Her attempt to protect her flag from discovery, or our ludicrous ideas of playing at German agents.

'Aunt Tilly was so pleased that you wanted to take the flag,' said mother once her friend had left.

We finished packing. It was a large rucksack, so I would have no trouble taking what was left at our flat in Svoldergaten: the camera, the rolls of film, the belt, toiletry bag, clothes brushes and a few other things.

'I hope everything goes well,' said mother. 'Give my love to grandmother and grandfather, and Trygve Lie, if you meet him.'

Uncle Trygve was the Norwegian Minister for Foreign Affairs, presently in exile in London. We had heard him speak in several BBC broadcasts. He would be somebody to contact once we arrived. We had already discussed it. He could vouch for us if something went wrong; if the authorities did not believe us we would refer to him. I had an idea.

'Maybe you could write a few lines to him. Just a quick note, an introduction, if you like; just to be on the safe side?'

Mother obliged. I've no idea what she wrote; it was sealed when she handed it to me. I put it in my pocket. Here was I, a German spy soon to be dropped off the English coast equipped with both a Norwegian flag and a letter addressed to the Norwegian Foreign Minister. I felt well prepared.

On the day of departure I felt almost well again. I went to see father in the morning. As usual he was at the salon. I asked if we could speak in private. I had not seen him for a week, not even to see how he was. Now I had come to say goodbye. He was thinner and looked tired. Several years ago he had suffered from angina pectoris. Obviously he was having trouble with his heart again because his box of nitroglycerine tablets were there in his waistcoat pocket. I decided to tread carefully.

'I'm off travelling,' I said. 'I came to say goodbye.'

'Will you be away long?' he asked.

'I don't know. A while, but I promise I'll get in touch if possible.'

'So, you're off abroad?'

'I'd thought of going to England.'

He nodded. It did not seem to come as a surprise. Either that or he was disguising his feelings particularly well. 'Take care,' he said.

I had expected more questions. When are you going? How are you getting there? What are you going to be doing in England? Are you going to visit grandfather? Are you going to study? Are you going to join the Norwegian troops? I had even prepared myself for them. I had rehearsed the answers I hoped would satisfy him, but he did not ask.

'I'm travelling to the west coast tonight,' I said.

He laid his hands on my shoulders and looked directly at me. 'Don't say anything, John,' he said quietly. 'I don't want to know. If you say nothing I'll have nothing to pass on.'

I could see what he meant. If he were threatened or tortured into revealing information it was better to know nothing. 'Thanks, dad,' I said.

'I trust you, John. I know you're doing what you think is

right. What'll I say if any of your friends ask after you?'

'Just say that I'm working at a weather station,' I said.

'I'll remember.'

He held me a short while, then he walked quickly towards the door. Before he closed it he said, 'Sorry, John; I've got a customer waiting.'

'I've got one more thing to ask,' I said. 'I've bought a camera on HP. Could you make sure it's paid off?'

'Of course,' he said and disappeared into the salon. He was disappointed. I was the only son, meant to follow in his footsteps. He had planned to leave the salon to me. He had built it up lovingly through years of hard work.

I had been on the verge of leaving him once before. Some years before the occupation grandfather had asked me to stay in England. He wanted to put me through medical school. I was going to study in Manchester. It was a tempting offer. England was my second home, I liked it there and I had often considered becoming a doctor. When I returned to Oslo after the summer holidays I discussed the matter with father. I noticed how distressed he seemed. I suppose I had dashed all his expectations. He was divorced from mother and now even his son was leaving him.

So I wrote to grandfather turning down his offer. Father reacted in exactly the same way when I had left the salon to go and work in the post censor. But this time it was different. He understood me better now. I had wanted to do something for my country for some time and he could accept that. It was only a question of a few months. The Germans were soon to suffer defeat. Then I would return and everything would be back to normal.

He was clearly pleased at my dismissal from the post censor, which allowed me to return to the salon, although he must have wondered why I was away so often. Now, totally out of the blue, I had announced my leaving Oslo. It was definite. If I was to go to England I might not return for some time, not until the Germans had withdrawn.

He must have had a lot of questions on his mind. How long would it be before he saw me again? Why was I going?

Did grandfather's offer still hold? Would I stay for good? Would I forget that I was to inherit one of Oslo's leading salons?

I gave some thought to this after I had left. I could still get out of it, make some excuse and go underground. Whatever. However, I knew that I had made the right decision. First the war had to be won. So it was important that Tor and I get to England.

It occurred to me that Trygve Lie really ought to be expecting us and be informed of our mission if something happened to go wrong. Father didn't want to know a thing, perhaps somebody else could help? I decided to go to Erling Jörgensen. I looked at my watch and realised that I had barely an hour left before meeting Müller.

I knew that Erling Jörgensen was likely to be at the Travellers Club, which had moved to Stortorvet. I was lucky, he was there and I told him about the situation. Tor and I were going on a mission for the Germans to England; could he get the information to Trygve Lie? If he could, it would make things far easier for us once we had contacted the British authorities. It was a further precaution. Erling Jörgensen asked no questions, but he promised to make sure the message got through. He had the right contacts. I had nothing to worry about. Trygve Lie would be informed.

I caught the tram from Stortorvet and then walked the rest of the way to Andersen's office. Everything was packed and ready. The rucksacks were in our flat. The bicycles had been checked, the tyres pumped up and the chains oiled. We had paid the rent. The things we were to leave behind us had already been moved. New tenants would soon be moving in.

I had difficulty catching my breath even though I was walking slowly. Beads of sweat formed on my forehead. I still had a slight fever and in truth I really needed a few more days' rest.

Tor was already there. Andersen and Korsewitz too.

'One small detail,' said Müller. 'It's about your

financing. You've already been given some British currency. That will last a while, but not for ever. If you need more then contact us by radio.'

'How would we receive the money?' I asked. 'By parachute?'

'There are other methods,' said Andersen.

'Then there are your wages,' said Müller. We hadn't thought much about actually receiving a salary. Our position with Abwehr would cease as soon as we landed. We had never expected that we would be on the payroll. 'We've opened an account in your names at the Christiana Bank og Kreditkasse,' said Müller. 'Every month a sum of money will be paid in. When you've completed your mission and returned, then you're free to do as you please with it.'

We thanked him. It was generous. However, I was convinced that when we did return there would be no Germans left in Oslo. Our accounts at the Christiana Bank og Kreditkasse would be worthless.

'That's all,' said Müller. 'We've covered everything. We'll collect you tonight, but you'll have to make your own way on to the train. No one must see us together. Our men will take care of the bicycles.'

A car stopped outside an hour before the train was due to leave. Korsewitz started the engine and drove us along Munkedammsveien to Vestbanestasjonen.

Tor and I had a sleeping compartment to ourselves. I climbed into the top bunk. Tor took the middle one and we put the radio case and rucksacks on the bottom. We left the blind down. Someone on the platform might recognise us and wonder what we were up to. Just the fact that we had a sleeping compartment might arouse suspicion. It was a luxury that was now almost totally reserved for the Germans and their henchmen.

The train shuddered forward. The first stage of our journey to Britain had begun.

13

The train pulled into Stavanger early in the morning. We collected our luggage. Korsewitz, who had been travelling in another compartment, got our bicycles which had been put on board in Oslo; and then we clambered into a large staff car that had been sent to collect us. We did not cause any commotion. Tor and I looked very Norwegian in our ski-suits. The Abwehr men were dressed in civilian clothes as usual.

We had rooms reserved at the Victoria Hotel where the foyer was full of Germans. It looked like the occupation forces had taken control of the whole building. We were now serving the powers that be, and were welcomed by the receptionist. A couple of porters took our luggage and Korsewitz made sure that they went to the right rooms.

Then we had breakfast. Müller and Andersen appeared, and all five of us sat at a round table in the dining-room.

'We're here in plenty of time,' said Müller. 'I'm not expecting the aeroplane until tomorrow evening.'

'You can go and explore Stavanger,' said Andersen. I could see the two incredibly long, boring days that lay ahead. Explore Stavanger! The city sights could be viewed in half an hour. What were we going to do after that?

When breakfast was over Tor and I went up to our room. The radio case and rucksacks had been placed in a neat pile on the floor, the bicycles had also been taken up and stood against the wall. We lay down on top of the beds and stared at the ceiling. The sound of the train and the thudding noise as it passed over the points still echoed in my head. The ceiling was a dirty yellow colour. The cornice was adorned with simple stucco work. In one corner I could see the moisture stains left after a leakage.

I was excited. I did not want to wait any longer. I wanted to get away. I wanted the waiting out of the way.

So far everything had gone well. We had convinced the Germans that we were Nazi idealists, determined to fight for the cause. We had to play the part for just another two days. I did not know if I would manage. Suddenly, I felt frightened. Had we overlooked anything? Had the Germans taken us to Stavanger just to see how we would react when the moment of truth arrived? Maybe the whole journey was merely a test, the idea being that we might drop our guard and reveal our true plans?

I thought about Doctor von Krogh. Several months ago he had written out a prescription that entitled me to a special bread ration. It stated that I had a bad stomach and could not take the coarse bread which was all that could be bought with normal ration cards. On medicinal grounds I had to eat white bread, the pre-war kind made from wheat-flour. Had the Germans discovered the truth? Could they send a sick man on such a mission?

My membership of Yngvar Fyhn's party was yet another weak spot. Had they pressurised the disillusioned ex-party leader and made him confess that my card was postdated? They must have carried out a thorough personal examination before deciding to take me on and put me through the training. Would they search our luggage before we left? Did I have anything that might arouse suspicion? I went over in my mind all that I had packed. I had prepared excuses for the flag and the letter to Trygve Lie, which was just as well, should they be spotted. What German spy could reveal a letter for the exiled Government's Foreign Minister? Those details did not worry me, the Germans would believe my motives.

What about the rolls of film? Did I dare carry out my original plan? In my case I had packed the camera, five unexposed rolls of film, and those five that I had not taken to be developed. Korsewitz knew he was in at least two of the films. I had photographed Andersen more often, and I had got a whole sequence of pictures of Müller relieving himself in a ditch. What would I say if someone asked me why I had packed the films? That I had made a mistake? That I had not been thinking? Or should I say that I had taken them with me so that we could look at the pictures when we met in London?

'What'll I do with the films?' I asked Tor.

'Take them with you,' said Tor. 'The English will definitely be interested in them.'

'What if Andersen looks in the case?'

'Why would he want to do that? Hide them somewhere.'

'They might find them.'

It would be wise and more sensible to give the films to Andersen and say that I had forgotten about them in my excitement over the journey. He would probably believe me. The films were not essential. We could give the English other details about Abwehr. We knew where their office was in Oslo; we could describe the people working there; we knew what cars they drove. A British agent in Oslo would have no difficulty in identifying them.

I felt calmer having made my decision. I fell asleep for a while, waking up in time for lunch. Tor and I managed to finish our meal before the Germans arrived. I could not have managed to make small talk with them there and then.

We went out, strolling slowly up and down the streets, ending up outside the city boundary. It was cloudy and cold, but we were warm, thanks to our thick overcoats. Then we returned to the city. I needed a drink.

'There's only light lager in Stavanger,' said Tor. 'Rogaland County is dry.'

'I wouldn't think the Germans give a damn about prohibition,' I said. 'There has to be a German bar somewhere. We're working with them. Let's make the most of it for once.'

We had not made use of our official position before. Naturally, we had not used our pistols, which we viewed as a necessary evil. Neither had we needed the identity cards

Müller had supplied us with. It was not intended that we should use them, other than in an extreme situation. However, we should have them handy if for any reason the German military police arrested us or if we were subjected to a body search by a patrol. Then we were to show our cards — but only then, in an extreme emergency.

Right now my need for a drink was an emergency. We passed by a large house. Outside stood a row of German military cars and inside a few uniformed bodies could be seen. We realised that it had been commandeered by the Germans; a mess or a staff headquarters.

'Let's go in and try,' I said.

Tor hesitated, but not for long. When I went through the gate he followed.

In the hall a soldier stood behind a table. He asked us what we wanted. 'We're part of Abwehr,' I said. 'We were just passing by.'

'Who are you looking for?'

'We want some brandy,' I said. 'Could we buy a bottle?'

He laughed, then studied our identity cards. 'Wait a minute,' he said. He disappeared into a nearby room. An officer came out into the hall and looked us up and down. We clicked our heels.

'Good afternoon, Captain,' I said, standing to attention.

'Heil Hitler!' he replied.

It sounded slightly odd. He stared at us a while then he carried on out of the front door.

Now and again during our training period we had been reprimanded for not answering this greeting with outstretched arm. A couple of times we had felt obliged to salute, but not very often. We tried not to, but at the same time we had to play the game.

The guard returned. In one hand he held a bottle which he handed to Tor.

'How much do we owe you?' I asked.

'Compliments of the Wehrmacht,' said the soldier, sitting down behind the table.

We thanked him. Tor slid the bottle into the inside

pocket of his ski jacket and we marched off. Our evening was made.

On the way back to the hotel we passed a café. We decided to go inside. We only had an hour or so to kill before eating dinner with the Germans, so we had decided not to open our newly acquired bottle until afterwards. We were not about to risk losing our heads while we were together with Müller and his men.

There were a few round wooden tables in the café, surrounded by brown-stained, squeaky stools with round seats. There were not many customers. A young couple were sitting at the window, and a German captain in uniform at the table next to them.

We took off our coats, hanging them up on a stand in the corner. Whilst removing one arm from my coat, I felt the pistol brush against my hip. I did not want to leave it in my coat while we were drinking our coffee, so I took it out and put it in my trouser pocket. The German captain saw the weapon and rushed over to me. He grabbed my right arm, holding it tightly, his hand ready by his pistol which hung from his belt.

'What are you doing with that pistol?' he asked.

'I don't want to leave it in my jacket,' I said.

'Give it here!' shrieked the captain and held my arm tighter. I glanced at Tor. For a moment he seemed at a loss as to what to do, but then he collected himself. Quickly he pulled out his identity card and held it in front of the German.

'Let him go!' he then said loudly.

It sounded like an order and I felt him release the grip on my arm.

'Everything's under control,' Tor continued. 'You can go back to your seat.'

Tor was firm. The German let me go and shrugged his shoulders.

'I didn't realise,' he said.

'No harm done,' said Tor waving him away. The German slunk back to his table. I sank into my seat.

'Thanks,' I said. 'You just saved my neck. You sounded just like an officer.'

'A non-commissioned officer,' said Tor. 'I didn't get any higher, but I did learn to give orders.'

The German drank his coffee and left. He did not look over in our direction; the girl by the window laughed at him. He must have heard her but chose to ignore it.

We ordered. The coffee tasted awful, as usual. I still had not got used to the substitute they served.

'What would have happened if he hadn't believed us?' I said.

'Nothing probably,' said Tor. 'The military police would have been called in. The Gestapo might have turned up, but all you would've had to do was refer to Müller and it would have been settled.'

I wonder if it would have been settled quite so easily. Would Müller have let us go ahead after an episode like that? If I could not even act discreetly in Stavanger, how would I cope with spying in Britain?

'You look tense,' said Müller when we had gathered for dinner. 'Don't be nervous. Everything will be fine.'

We were convinced of that too. We were not at all apprehensive about what would happen over there. We were worried about what could happen now, before we had even left.

'If you're captured and interrogated you must stick to the cover story,' Müller continued. 'You escaped from Norway in a fishing boat.'

He had been over this with us several times before. There was a definite risk of being discovered. Not so great a risk as we both spoke perfect English. I had a good Lancashire accent and Tor spoke with a slight foreign lilt. But no one would bother about that. We would blend into the new surroundings without much trouble at all. However, something could always go wrong, and that's why we had to have a cover story should someone become too curious.

We were to say that we were refugees. We had come to Britain in a boat under cover of darkness and put ashore.

Now we were trying to contact other Norwegian refugees. Our aim was to join the Norwegian Resistance unit that was being organised in England. We listened to Müller's plans absentmindedly. We would never tell this story to the British anyway. Besides, we thought it was naïve. Didn't Müller realise that there would be more questions? What was the fishing boat called? Where were you dropped? How many were on board? Why hadn't we registered as refugees straight away? What was the skipper's name? Where was the boat from? How long had the crossing taken? We would never survive an interrogation. Müller ought to have realised that.

Once again I started to wonder why exactly we were being sent. Of course we knew what we were doing, we had proven that, but so much had been badly prepared. We were convinced that we would never survive more than a day or two as genuine spies.

We had got to know the three Germans quite well during our training period and they were not exactly intellectual giants. Still. . . . Too much had been badly planned and badly thought out, or was it purely left to chance? It did not make any difference to us. We knew what we wanted and what to do, but we were definitely not the only spies trained to serve in Britain.

We did not know exactly what Abwehr did in Oslo except in connection with ourselves. We took it for granted that other spies were struggling with Morse keys and codebooks throughout the city. Trainees who were 'genuine', who would loyally carry out their mission with the best intentions. They did not stand a chance; well, not if they had received the same advice and preparation that we had.

As soon as dinner was over we left the Germans and went up to our room. We made sure that the door was properly locked. Then we opened the bottle, poured the brandy into our toothbrush glasses and drank a toast. After two glasses I felt the tension easing. So far everything had gone well. There was only one day left to go. I slept soundly and peacefully, and woke up late. Tor had already got up and was crouched over the hand-basin. He splashed water over his face again and again, then he dried himself carefully.

'I've got a splitting headache,' he said.

I sat up in bed. It suddenly struck me that I still had the rolls of film. I had not given them a second thought, but I knew exactly what to do. 'I'll leave the five that aren't exposed and take the other five with me,' I said.

'What?' asked Tor, massaging his neck with the hand towel.

'The films.' I scrambled out of bed and found the ten rolls in my case. I laid them on the bed. I had written 'exposed' on five of the cartons so that I would not mix them up.

'I'll just swap them over,' I said. 'I'll put the unused films in the used cartons and give them to Andersen.'

'He'll see that the films aren't exposed. And then he'll realise you've taken the films of him and Müller,' said Tor.

It was a bad idea. For it to succeed the films I left had to be exposed. The Germans knew that I had been taking photographs — they had seen me. They knew that they were on the films.

'What if I expose them to the light?' I said.

'When?' asked Tor.

'Now. Here. I'll load the camera and let it run. Over-expose the films. Then it'll look as if they've been used; but when they're developed there'll be no pictures.'

'What'll they say then?'

'That I'm a hopeless photographer. I hadn't managed to get one decent picture.'

The idea seemed a good one. I carefully opened the unused cartons and exchanged the exposed films, found a bag, put them into it and then put them in my rucksack. Then I loaded the camera, put the aperture to its minimum and pointed it towards the clear blue sky. When they were developed Andersen would laugh at my amateurish lack of skill. I tripped the shutter again and again. When the first film had finished I put a new one in and continued until all the rolls had run through the camera.

Afterwards I put the films in the used cartons and made

up a small parcel. I would give it to Andersen just before we left. It was important that he did not get a chance to develop the films before we were safely on the other side of the North Sea.

In the afternoon Tor and I took a long walk. We did not stop at any cafés, we did nothing to arouse suspicion. We just wandered around Stavanger's streets, quietly waiting.

When we arrived back at the hotel we met Andersen in the foyer. 'The transport's here,' he said. 'We're having dinner with the captain. We'll meet in the dining-room in an hour's time.'

We hurried up to our room and I put on a suit and tie. I looked extremely elegant in my double-breasted suit. Very English.

14

We had to wait a while before the flight captain arrived along with one of his crew, a sergeant in a Luftwaffe uniform. The first thing I noticed was that the two of them responded to Müller's 'Heil Hitler' with a salute, and also that they were not actually party members but soldiers.

The flight captain's name was Hoelenbaum. He was tall and thin with a pointed face. He radiated confidence and I trusted him immediately. We were relying on him for a safe journey over to England, and I had no doubt that he would complete his mission successfully.

Hoelenbaum spoke with a distinctive upper-class German accent. He did not say much about himself but I hoped that he was an experienced pilot for Tor's sake and mine. His father had been a pilot and his grandfather had been one of those flying pioneers during the years before the First World War. 'Grandfather was too old for active air service when war broke out,' he said. 'He never got over being grounded while the younger ones took to the air.'

During the meal our flight was not mentioned at all. In Hoelenbaum's company one clearly did not discuss business at the dinner table. When we had finished, we moved into a lounge adjoining the dining-room. We found a table in the corner, the waiter set out coffee cups and Hoelenbaum asked him to bring some glasses. Then he lifted up his briefcase, opened it and took out a bottle of Johnnie Walker. 'I thought this would be appropriate in view of our destination,' he said.

'Where did you get the whisky?' I asked.

'There's still a bottle or two left in France,' said

Hoelenbaum. 'I've just returned from there. I have my contacts.' He poured it out, we raised our glasses and the Germans wished us good luck.

'We're flying a twin-engined seaplane,' said Hoelenbaum. 'It's specially equipped for missions like this. Its top speed is 370 kilometres per hour, but we'll be cruising at about 280, which means a flight of almost two hours.'

'Where will we be put ashore?' I asked.

Hoelenbaum looked at Müller. The Abwehr major nodded. It could now be revealed. Hoelenbaum took out a map and spread it out on the table. I wondered why we had not been told this before. Tor and I had asked several times, but Müller had not given us an answer. There was time enough for us to know. Maybe Müller had told the truth, maybe he didn't know. Maybe it was Hoelenbaum and the air division who decided on the exact spot. The pilot was certainly much more familiar with the whereabouts of suitable landing places. Or had it all been decided in Berlin? Müller always used to refer to Berlin. He received all his orders from there.

Hoelenbaum pointed at the map, placed his finger on Stavanger and guided it across the sea to Scotland. He stopped north of Aberdeen by the Moray Firth, the large inlet which cuts into the very north of Scotland. So, we were not going to England! This was yet another poor piece of planning by the Germans. As spies, it would be even more difficult to mix with the Scots in a sparsely populated area than with the English in one of the large cities. We could not speak the dialect and I was unfamiliar with the area. Müller ought to have realised.

It did not matter to us, though. We simply wanted to get away and to hell with the problems. It mattered little whether we found a police station in Scotland or England.

I studied the map and tried to memorise a few place names. Furthest out on the point lay the port of Fraserburgh. A couple of miles to the west lay a place called Banff, which I had never heard of before.

'That's all you need to know about the flight,' said Hoelenbaum, folding up the map. 'Now all we need is the right weather.'

'When are we off?' I asked.

'We should be ready an hour after midnight.'

'Tonight?' asked Tor.

'Tomorrow night. Or the day after. That's all I can say. The weather will be the deciding factor.'

We realised that. If the plane was to land on the waters off the Scottish coastline we would not want it too windy, or too rough. If it was, it would be impossible to land let alone get our rubber dinghy out. I still felt disappointed. Tomorrow or the day after. That meant another one or two days of waiting. Still more hours in which to worry and think. Just one false step and the trip would be called off. Or something even worse could happen to us.

'Is the dinghy on board?' I asked. Hoelenbaum nodded.

'They have orders to destroy it and bury it as soon as they land,' said Müller.

Hoelenbaum smiled. 'We usually advise filling the boat with stones and sinking it in deep water. It's quicker and doesn't require so much work.'

Müller became noticeably annoyed. 'Do what you want,' he said. 'As long as the boat disappears.'

Nothing else was said about the flight. Hoelenbaum had given us the information he thought we ought to have. We had been told where we were being dropped and at what time of day the departure would take place. That was all we needed to know. We stayed there a while, chatting. The whisky bottle was soon empty. The waiter took away the glasses and filled our cups with coffee.

The following day we went for more walks. By this time we had wandered along every street in Stavanger, walked on every pavement and looked in every shop window. A woman said hello. Obviously she had seen the 'ski-suited' wanderers on several occasions and felt that she knew us.

Late in the afternoon we sat in the foyer flicking through the German papers that had been laid out for the hotel guests. Müller came rushing down the stairs and ran up to us. 'I've been looking for you,' he said. 'Where have you been?'

'Out walking,' I said. 'We've become permanent fixtures in town. We'll soon be Stavanger's biggest tourist attraction.'

'It's tonight,' said Müller. 'We'll be leaving the hotel at twelve o'clock. Are you ready?'

We had been ready for a week. Our rucksacks were packed, we had checked the equipment every day, the bicycles stood ready in our room.

'We're ready,' said Tor.

'Make sure you don't forget anything,' said Müller.

We promised.

The hours passed even more slowly than before. We had dinner and then went back to our room and tried to rest. We would not get much sleep that night, and perhaps not the next night either.

'Have you decided what to do with the films?' asked Tor.

'I'm taking them with me,' I said. 'I'll give Andersen the over-exposed ones to develop.'

'I hope you're doing the right thing.'

So did I. I still had time to change my mind. I could give all ten of them to the Germans. Then we would not be running any risks. Andersen might check our luggage at the last minute. If he searched my rucksack he would find the films and understand. Then I would come really unstuck. I would be in serious trouble.

Suddenly there was a knock at the door. We did not answer. Then there was another knock. 'Come in,' I said finally in a hoarse croak. The door opened. It was Andersen. Everything would be revealed now.

'You've pumped up the tyres I trust?' said Andersen. He went up to them, bent down and pinched the tyres. They were hard. I started giggling. Then Tor started, and we burst into hysterical laughter.

'What's so funny?' asked Andersen. We tried to answer him but we could not. Our laughter echoed out through the half-open door into the corridor. Andersen stared at us. 'It must be the excitement,' he said. 'They've been difficult days for you lads. Just a few more hours and you're off.' He walked up to me and put his arm round my shoulder. I managed to calm down, sniggering a couple of times, but then forced myself to be serious.

'Sorry,' I said. 'I couldn't help it.'

'I understand,' said Andersen.

Tor tried to smooth things over. 'Here we are, worrying about the journey,' he said. 'It's a matter of life or death to us. What if we're captured? And then you arrive, Mr Andersen, and ask if we've pumped the tyres up.'

Andersen smiled. 'Count yourselves lucky that someone thinks about these details,' he said. 'You'd better rest now. I'll send Korsewitz up just before midnight to help you with your luggage and the bicycles.'

'Thanks,' said Tor.

Andersen turned and went to the door. I remembered the films. 'Just a minute,' I said. 'I'd forgotten this.' I handed him the packet. He took it and asked what was inside. 'The photographs that I took of you and of Major Müller when he was, em, relieving himself.'

Andersen grinned. He knew what I was talking about.

'The films haven't been developed,' I said.

'I'll take care of it,' said Andersen. 'Then we can have a good look at Müller's armoury.'

'That I'd like to see,' I said. 'Don't forget to bring the photos to London.'

Andersen started laughing. Not a nervous bawling like ours had been, but wholeheartedly just the same. Then he left and Tor locked the door behind him. I sank down on to the bed. I was worn out. We had to leave now. Nothing could stand in our way. I would last another couple of hours but not more. If, despite everything, the flight was cancelled tonight I would back out, saying that I had changed my mind, that I wanted to return to Oslo and start working at the hair salon. It was decidedly quieter there.

'I'm surprised that Andersen didn't say something about

your little outburst,' said Tor. 'He must have asked himself if you were up to it, if you couldn't even act normally for a few hours before departure?'

'You laughed too,' I said.

'Hang on in there,' he said. 'In two hours Korsewitz will arrive and tell us it's time.'

Two hours later we let Korsewitz in. We had been dressed and ready for half an hour. The rucksacks were by the door and the bicycles stood against the wall. We carried the luggage downstairs. Korsewitz hauled the heavy radio case. Tor and I managed the rest on the bicycles.

It was twelve o'clock when we left the hotel. It was cold but it was a clear, starry night. We got into the car that Korsewitz had arranged for the journey to the seaplane. He drove slowly and very carefully. Nothing was to go wrong during these final stages. We arrived at the quay and saw the aeroplane moored to the dock by its tailfin. It was painted black and was larger than I expected.

Korsewitz helped us to unload the car. A couple of crew members in Luftwaffe uniforms took care of the bicycles and rucksacks and lifted our equipment up through a hole on the underside of the plane's body.

Müller gave his final speech to Tege and Ja. We stood attentively in front of him, trying to listen. 'The first thing you've got to do is get rid of the rubber dinghy,' he said. 'Then as soon as possible make sure that you've hidden everything that should be hidden. Be careful with the radio. It's the most important thing you've got. Without it you've got no chance of establishing contact.'

We knew all of this. We would forget about it as soon as we got there.

'If you're interrogated you must stick to the same story,' Müller harped on. 'You'll definitely be questioned separately. It's important that you both tell the same story.'

We promised we would tell the same story. We had practised it. We knew exactly what we would say.

'In that case we're ready,' said Müller, putting out his hand.

Tor was the first to shake it. Then our chief shook my hand at length, saying nothing, but showing his rows of gold fillings. This is the last time I will ever see your gold teeth, I thought.

Then it was Andersen's turn. 'Good luck, lads,' he said. 'You've been good students. Make sure your training is of some use to us.'

'We'll do our best,' said Tor.

Korsewitz did not say a word, but put out his callused hand. I thought he looked moved. We did not have anything against him; he was a kind man and we had spent pleasant times in his company. Maybe he would miss us.

We walked down some stone steps and over the gangplank which led to one of the floats. The seaplane rocked with our weight but soon stabilised itself.

It was a very cold night. The moon was shining. It was the first night in April. It was almost wind-free; ideal flying conditions. We climbed up a ladder and then into the plane. Onc of the crew helped us up and showed us where we were to sit. Then he pulled up the ladder and closed the hatch.

We had been seated in the middle of the seaplane on a bench. It was uncomfortable, but it did not worry me. I could manage to put up with a two-hour flight.

I looked around. Hoelenbaum was sitting in the very front. A couple of steps led down to his pilot seat. He turned round, raised his hand in greeting and nodded to us. Then he returned to his check list. Beside him sat the sergeant whom we had met the night before and, behind him, a third crew member. He was the radio officer; he had a pair of earphones on and was sitting in front of his panel of knobs and dials. The two crew members who had lifted our rucksacks on board had fastened themselves into the rear of the plane.

There was a large, black rubber cover on the floor in front of them. I realised it was our deflated rubber dinghy. The bicycles had been secured to the shell, with our luggage in a coarse meshed sack in front of them. Everything was ready for take-off.

There were no windows by our seats but we could see out through the front. We saw the water and the pale moonlight reflecting off the soft ripples of the water's surface. We could not see the quay. We did not know if Müller and his subordinates were still there, but they probably wanted to wait to watch the plane disappear over the North Sea.

One of the crew gave us some chocolate; round macaroons wrapped in plain paper. I took a bite. The chocolate tasted bitter.

'Not yet,' said the crew member. 'There's caffeine in it. It's just for when you need to stay awake.' I put them in my jacket pocket. I might need them later on.

Hoelenbaum started up one of the engines. It spluttered for a few seconds, then it caught and started running smoothly and evenly. Hoelenbaum revved it up, the plane shook and the cabin was filled with a deafening noise. Then the second engine started up. The noise increased.

'We're on our way!' I shouted to Tor. He did not hear me, but he laughed and I joined in.

The plane started to move and swing round. I tried to look out of the front window: the quay and jetty could be seen momentarily but I could not tell if the Germans were still there. Hoelenbaum opened up the throttle and the plane accelerated over the water. It bounced a couple of times, then it rose and started to climb upwards.

In two hours' time we would be in Scotland.

15

It was not the first time I had flown. I had once been up in a Junkers, on a five kroner round trip over Oslo, and again in England when I had been allowed in a sightseeing plane for just a short trip. On these occasions I had been able to view the scenery quite easily. The whole point of the exercise was to allow the customers to look down on the city and spot the landmarks.

Right now I was unable to get my bearings other than through the cockpit. From where I was sitting I couldn't see much, but I caught sight of the waves glinting in the pale moonlight. I realised that we were flying very low when we passed a ship which suddenly appeared like a shadow just below the nose of the aircraft.

Conversation was impossible. We couldn't make ourselves heard above the engines. Tor tried shouting to me and although I caught a couple of words I couldn't understand what he was trying to say.

Once we reached cruising speed the two crew members at the rear of the plane began to inflate the dinghy with small hand pumps. It looked like hard work. After half an hour the shell had still shown no signs of swelling with the air. The plane began to heave and sway, and halfway across the water it sank down into an air-pocket and was buffeted around for some time. It was most unpleasant. I had had very little flying experience and was not exactly sure what was happening. I tried to calm myself down. Hoelenbaum knew what he was doing.

The rubber shell began to take shape, the two men pumping frantically, sweat pouring from their faces. They had a deadline to meet.

I peered out of the cockpit and sat a while looking at the waves beneath. The dimly lit waters looked cold and unwelcoming. The monotonous engine noise made me feel sleepy. I glanced at the two men as they continued to battle with the dinghy. Tor and I had long given up trying to talk to one another, but when I caught sight of land I couldn't help myself from shouting to him. He smiled and nodded. We were approaching the Scottish coastline.

We appeared to follow the coast northwards. There was land to the left and sea to the right. Hoelenbaum soon changed course again and the land disappeared. At the same time he eased down the throttle; the engine revs dropped as the plane began to sink down. We were preparing to come in.

I said a quick prayer and my mind turned to our mission. Tor and I would soon be sitting in our dinghy, quite alone, off a foreign shore. Would we make it to the coast? Would we be spotted? I thought of mother and father. There was no turning back now. We had to go on. When would I see them again? How much longer would the war go on?

The nose of the plane tilted downwards, the engine pitch dropped, and with it the noise, but it was still impossible to talk. We stared outside as we slowly approached the dark waters. Then Hoelenbaum levelled off, still flying low, so low we felt we could almost touch the waves. The foam was so close now. A minute passed by. He seemed to be searching for a suitable place to bring the plane down. Or perhaps he was trying to edge nearer to the coast to save our arms. He suddenly opened the throttle and the plane began to rise. We turned to the left. He did not straighten up until we had turned a full 180 degrees. We continued to climb ever upwards. I could see that he was talking with someone through his receiver. Perhaps he was chatting to the radio officer who, I could see, was playing with his dials.

Then I realised what was happening. We had turned off and were on our way back. Something was wrong. The radio officer had received a message — Hoelenbaum had given up his search for a place to land, lifted the nose and set course for Norway. We were on our way back to Stavanger.

I glanced at Tor, who had turned very pale. He was about to speak but cut himself short. I tried questioning one of the crew members. They shrugged and shook their heads. They knew nothing; it didn't matter to them anyway. We were the ones to go ashore.

I grew frightened. Müller and Andersen must have got wind of something. They wouldn't call us back for nothing. New orders had been sent through. We were to return to Stavanger. But why? Had Andersen had the time to develop the films and realise what I had done? Had they received fresh information about myself and Tor? Perhaps something had happened to mother? Or father had been arrested? The Gestapo might have interrogated Gerd. We might even have been spotted earlier by British agents who had relayed the message that two foreign spies were to land in Scotland. It could have been any number of things. The possibilities were endless. Whatever it was, it had to be important. We had come so far for Müller to call us back. Something must have gone wrong. Had he realised his mistake in sending us off? Had he stopped us at the last minute to get his own back?

I breathed heavily and my heart pounded inside me. Nobody took any notice of us, or told us what was happening. We just sat there. It was as if we no longer existed. I began to pray once again, but this time I wasn't concerned with the mission. This prayer was far more desperate. I begged for help. It wasn't something I did very often. I begged that the Germans hadn't found us out; please God, don't let them arrest us and turn us over to the Gestapo. Perhaps He heard my prayer. If He did, He gave no answer.

I was bathing in sweat when two hours later we came in to land. I was terrified. The films were still in the case. I kicked myself for not having got rid of them. Our luggage would certainly be searched once we reached the ground. Everything would be checked out meticulously.

What would I say? That I had got them confused? For some inexplicable reason they had been swapped over? Would they believe me? I was prepared to say anything. Blame it on my pre-journey nerves. That was why I had confused the packages. I could give them a million excuses. I would explain everything. My conscience was clear.

The plane landed and cruised to the jetty. The engines were switched off. I heard someone outside yell that the moorings were secure. I glanced at Tor. He sat there pale and glazed. He was as terrified as I was and was clearly suffering the same anguish.

The hatch opened up, I was beckoned down the ladder. It was dawn. The early morning light had begun to brighten the darkness. The sky was a dull grey and it was drizzling. I jumped down on to one of the floats and looked up towards the jetty where I spotted Müller, grave-faced, at the head of a small group of Germans. He was flanked by armed soldiers. I could see their guns, bayonets fixed, silhouetted against the grey sky. Andersen and Korsewitz stood beside them. They looked equally serious, staring at the aircraft which had brought back their two deceitful colleagues.

We had clearly been expected. Abwehr had asked for the help of the military to take us in. There was no escaping it. I had to walk across the gangplank to the jetty, climb the stone steps to the scaffold, to be met by my executioner with his golden fangs.

I took my time. As nonchalantly as I could manage I sauntered over to the steps which had been made slippery with the rain. I would have to try and look normal. I couldn't approach Müller for his forgiveness. I had to appear as I had always been, if anything annoyed by our forced return, whatever the reason.

Walking up the steps I caught sight of the soldiers' heavy boots. Müller was wearing overshoes. Once I reached the jetty I stood directly in front of Müller and looked him straight in the eye to receive the verdict.

'It's the wretched weather,' he sniggered, baring his

gold teeth. It took a while for it to sink in. I had noticed that the sea was rough, but hadn't given it much thought. So that was it. Hoelenbaum hadn't been able to take us in. They had radioed Stavanger to say that we were coming back. That was all. It was nothing to do with the films, just the weather.

'It's disappointing,' I said, trying to disguise my relief. I tried not to reveal how glad I was that the weather was the reason that we found ourselves in the harbour once again. I could hardly burst out laughing or show the horror I had felt earlier on.

'I'm afraid we can't help the weather,' said Müller.

'I thought the British had got wind of us,' said Tor.

'Not at all. You must have noticed the conditions.' We replied that we had and were pleased that the pilot had not wanted to take any risks. But it was still a bitter blow. We had come so close. Müller was disappointed too.

Our luggage was brought ashore while the dinghy and cycles remained on board. It was taken to a car sent to collect us. I spotted Korsewitz struggling with my rucksack. The films! My heart skipped a beat. Why had he picked up my rucksack? We walked over to the cars. Müller climbed into the first car and beckoned me inside. Korsewitz squeezed in behind the wheel. The damp morning air had made the seats cold and clammy. I looked at Müller who was staring straight ahead. Korsewitz turned the key and put the car into first gear.

'Isn't Tor coming? I asked as the car pulled away.

'Glad is going with Andersen,' Müller grunted, dismissing my question. I wanted to ask why we had been separated but I didn't dare. Fear struck once again. Could I really trust Müller? Had it really been just the weather which had forced our return?

The harbour road linked up with the main route to Stavanger. I saw the sign to the city. Leaning forward, I asked Korsewitz how much further we had to go. He didn't reply but drove straight past the sign. The road to Stavanger disappeared behind us.

'Where are we going?' I asked. 'Shouldn't you have turned off further back?'

'We're not going to Stavanger,' said Müller. He looked at me through half-shut eyes. Just as I had feared. Something had gone wrong and Operation Hummer Nord III had been called off. We couldn't be trusted. Tor and I had never been kept apart before. It could mean only one thing. We were heading for interrogation. We had been found out and caught. The evidence was lying there in my rucksack. All they needed was a confession. I could always say that I was operating by myself, that Tor knew nothing.

'We can't risk taking you back to Stavanger,' said Müller. 'Someone might recognise you.'

'Why not?'

'It's just too risky.'

'So, our mission's been called off?'

Müller laughed. 'You've had a rough night,' he replied. 'We'll soon be there.'

'And Tor?' I asked.

'Andersen's gone to get you something to drink. He just wanted a bit of company. We thought you could do with something strong after tonight's episode.'

'Where are we going?'

'To a place called Hummeren. We thought it might be safer there. You can relax while we wait for better weather.'

The tension eased off and I began to laugh. Korsewitz couldn't help himself joining in. Not long after we slowed down, turned down a side road and wound our way through the barren hills. We soon arrived at a house.

'Here we are,' he said.

A few moments later Andersen pulled in beside us. Tor and I got out. I ran over and hugged him. He looked at me in surprise.

'Hummeren,' said Müller. We went in together.

Hummeren was a summer-season restaurant. It had been closed for the season but Müller had taken over the place and forced the owner to open.

We made a tour of the premises, brandy in hand. There was a hole in the floor of the square-shaped restaurant. It was a small pool, meshed with chicken wire, full of huge lobsters.

'You can gorge yourselves as much as you like,' said Andersen. 'You're the only guests. I hope you like shellfish.'

I remembered the parties mother used to have. I would always set off in the tram down to Sörensen's, the fishmonger at Piperviken, to buy the food. We would all sit round the table; white wine, toast, mayonnaise, lemon slices, and in the middle an enormous plate of lobsters. I would sit at the head of the table listening to mother's theatre friends with their wild stories.

The staff had obviously been sent for during the night. The restaurant was freezing cold but Tor and I were given a couple of warm rooms that had been specially prepared. The rooms were small and the beds hard. We settled in and dropped off to sleep, waking at lunchtime.

We were served lobster, lager and coarse toasted bread. It tasted like straw but we didn't complain. It would only be a short stay. We could be given orders to leave at any moment.

However, the order wasn't to come that afternoon, nor the following day. We sat shivering in Hummeren for six whole days. We played cards to help pass the time. Andersen gave us some books, but we spent most of the time wandering about aimlessly, staring out of the window. We refused to eat the lobster they insisted on serving and chose fish. Cod was not rationed like everything else. If you were early enough, you could buy it fresh from the fishmarket. I had a particular liking for cod's head. The meals were our only amusement. Foul coffee, eggs that tasted of fish, that coarse bread which I was beginning to loathe intensely, and watery beer; that was the sum total of it.

The Germans realised we were not too happy. Once or twice Müller gave us some brandy to cheer us up. I was surprised not to experience the same irritation that I had felt earlier. Perhaps it was because I was now less tense, I no longer feared for our safety. They had accepted us. Perhaps we had never been mistrusted; it was the first time it had occurred to me. It was thanks to the weather that we sat here feeling very uncomfortable. I didn't even find it funny. Tege and Ja were bored stiff.

Our three Abwehr colleagues tried to make our wait as pleasant as they could, visiting us every day, doing their best to liven us up, sorry that we were shut up indoors. We had to be patient. We were to remain out of sight, just in case we were recognised.

Müller went over our schedule almost every day. I noticed that he now avoided mentioning the dinghy. He just told us to get rid of it. We were not interested in his lectures but simply interested in the weather forecast. An area of high pressure replaced the depression eventually. We would leave on 7 April.

The evening before departure we were smuggled into the Victoria Hotel where Müller had rented a room. We had been invited to a farewell party. We were kept well out of sight, even from the waiters, who left everything outside the door leaving Korsewitz to bring it inside.

It was soon time to leave. We had drunk a reasonable amount and were somewhat unsteadier than usual, but we would manage. The procedure was exactly the same as before. We arrived at the plane just after midnight. Our luggage was placed on board. We said goodbye to Müller and his men once again and turned to shake hands with Hoelenbaum, who was sorry that we had had such a long wait. He had probably spent a pleasant weekend at the Victoria.

The hatch slammed shut. Hoelenbaum started up the engine, steered out of the harbour, opened the throttle and we lifted off the water.

We sat in our now familiar places. The noise was just as loud as before, and the view equally limited. The flight was calm and uneventful. There was no sign of British fighters. After the two-hour journey we began to descend.

The dinghy had remained inflated since our last flight; the bicycles, too, were just as we had left them. We had forgotten nothing. We had all that we might need. Once we had landed the plane slowed down to a halt, bobbing on the water, rising and falling with the movement of the waves. The weather was poor. Although there was little wind the waves were almost a metre high.

One of the crew opened the hatch and climbed down. The other man passed him the dinghy, which he then tied to one of the floats. The small craft tossed about like a feather. The dinghy grew more stable once the rucksacks and bicycles had been strapped inside, but it still seemed rather frail. It was oblong, like an elongated circle in shape, the bottom constructed from strips of wood which were surrounded by the inflated rubber cushion. Tor sat himself at one end of the craft and I took the oars. They were made of aluminium and secured to a loop to prevent their loss. Before we set off Tor took his compass out and set our course south. We would need that compass if we were to keep our bearings. It was hazy, making visibility very poor. The drizzle did little to help. We could have put up with it all if it hadn't been for the violent rocking of the boat. We rose up and down on the waves like a rollercoaster. I was sure that we would capsize. However, we were determined not to fly back. We might not get a third chance.

When we gave the signal, one of the crew loosened the line and then climbed back into the aircraft. He pulled up the ladder and shut the hatch. The engine pitch rose and the seaplane circled our dinghy. Hoelenbaum waved; we waved back. Then he swung away from us and accelerated against the waves. The noise of the water beating against the floats grew louder and more frequent and then disappeared. We watched the plane rise into the darkness until we lost sight of the sparks coming out of the exhaust pipes. The sound of its engine remained for a short while as we sat listening. It faded, slowly, until all we could hear was the slapping of the waves. We were totally alone in our small dinghy just off the Scottish coast.

16

It was cold and wet. There was just the strong roar of the sea and the boat rocking. The swelling waves lifted the small rubber dinghy up and down. We sat in silence for a while and listened. We were not totally convinced that Hoelenbaum would not return and spot us as we were trying to make our presence known.

We had discussed how we would go about it many times. Every detail had been covered; we knew exactly what to do. Our first step was to try and get ourselves spotted. We wanted to be discovered as soon as possible, preferably whilst we were still in the boat. Tor studied the compass and pointed me in the right direction. Then he took out the flashlamp which had been packed with our equipment. He pointed it into the haze in the direction of the coast and started signalling. We had agreed that he should flash the Morse signal for 'Can we land?'. It was a perfectly standard signal which anyone could be using. We did not want to risk being shot.

Tor started flashing, repeating the question over and over again, but no one answered it. We did not know our distance from the coast, nor did we know how far the signal would reach. However, Tor continued to signal and I started rowing. I realised that I had overlooked an important piece of equipment. I had not packed a pair of warm gloves. There was only a pair of thin cotton gloves in my jacket pocket. I pulled them on, but they got wet straight away and after just a few minutes my hands were cold and stiff. There was nothing I could do about it. We did not dare swap places in the unsteady dinghy; but perhaps we were close to land, perhaps the boat would soon scrape against the rocks of shallow waters.

Tor continued signalling. He repeated his question and now and again I stopped rowing so that we could listen for a reply. There was nothing to be heard. We received no answer to our signals. Tor peered into the dark, but he saw no flashing light.

The boat was swaying rhythmically now. Wide swells lifted us up slowly just to bring us back down into the troughs. The wind had dropped slightly but the slow movements made Tor feel ill.

'I feel sick,' he whispered after a while.

'We're almost there,' I said.

I increased the pace, heaving myself backwards with every stroke. My hands were icy-cold. I squeezed the oar handles and worked at it as hard as I could. I didn't notice the boat moving forward at all. Tor put down the signal lamp, leaned over the soft, rounded side of the boat and threw up. He was quite sick with the rising swell of the sea. I stopped rowing, thinking that I should try to help him, but I didn't dare get up to crawl over to him. He would have to take care of himself. It was better that he put up with a passing sickness than the boat capsizing and the two of us being thrown into the water.

'It'll pass,' I said.

Tor lay prostrate over the side of the boat and I saw his body convulse as he was sick once again. I continued rowing, pushing the shapeless form of the dinghy through the water. The haze hung damp around us; it seemed to be drizzling harder now.

Tor straightened up.

'Keep at it,' I said. 'We'll soon be there. Keep on signalling.'

I thought it might take his mind off his seasickness. Perhaps it helped. He lifted the lamp and began to flash the code. I thought he looked slightly better. We still received no reply to his signals. Even when I lifted the oars from the water for a few seconds I could hear nothing.

Tor was sick again, but only briefly. There was probably nothing left in his stomach. I struggled on rowing. My hands were totally numb, but I still had some strength left in my arms. Tor signalled; I rowed. From time to time Tor checked our bearings. We were headed in the right direction, south, towards the coast, but I could not tell how fast or slow we were moving.

After half an hour, I thought I detected a sound change; waves hitting the shore, the smashing of breakers, crests of waves falling and frothing into foam. I turned to look into the haze but I spotted nothing. No coastline could be seen but the sound of the sea had definitely changed.

Tor worked at the flashlight. If there were any signs of life on the shore we surely could not go unnoticed. But there was still no reply; not a sound, neither man nor engine. If there was land ahead, it lay very still and quiet.

Some time later I thought I heard some sort of echo. The noise of the oars beating against the water was booming back to us, faint, but still it was there. I rowed on. The wind was now barely noticeable, but it was still drizzling. The echo grew more distinct. Tor shouted, pointing behind me. I dropped the oars into the water and pivoted round. Out of the darkness appeared a high wall, rising up from the sea ahead of us. The waves exploded against its face and as we came closer, I saw its concrete texture. I rested on the oars as the dinghy slowly drifted towards the wall.

'It must be some sort of fortification,' I said. 'A sort of defence wall. We'd better watch out for mines.'

The wall appeared to stretch several metres high. There was no way we could scale it from the boat. We would have to row alongside it and hope to find an opening somewhere. If it were part of a defence line there would certainly be guards along its length. We started shouting, our heads tilted upwards, Tor working with the flashlight. No one answered. I rowed alongside the wall, carefully dipping the oars into the water. The concrete slowly slid by.

'I don't think mines could be triggered off by this dinghy,' said Tor. It seemed to make sense. I hoped he was right. The wall seemed endless. I carried on rowing while Tor called out and flashed Morse with the lamp. We saw no sign of life. The wall was there, dark and silent, but we saw no one. Then the dinghy caught a rock.

Tor pointed, 'Over there. I think I can see the shoreline. It looks like a gap, a sort of opening.'

I changed direction and rowed a bit further, turned and saw a thin strip of beach made of smooth pebbles. I grew excited. The dinghy sped along once again and glided into the shallow waters. Again it scraped the bottom and we found ourselves lodged on a large rock. Tor scrambled up and jumped from the boat. The water came to just over his knees and seeped into his boots; he didn't notice.

'We're here,' he shouted and began to pull the boat on to land.

It was still dark but the first feeble signs of daylight were breaking through the haze. I looked back to the wall; it was clearly not as I had suspected. It was simply a jetty, built to protect a small harbour. We had followed its outer edge and landed on the strip of shore beside the inlet. The jetty had appeared so high because of the low tide.

'Jump ashore!' cried Tor. 'We've got to get the boat up.'

I couldn't. My hands had frozen stiff to the oars. I had lost all feeling and couldn't move my fingers. 'You'll have to help me,' I said.

Tor massaged my hands and I finally managed to prise my fingers from their grip. I knelt in the dinghy and dipped my hands into the water to get some movement back in them. Then Tor peeled off the flimsy soaking gloves and I put my hands beneath my jacket to warm them up.

Tor dragged the dinghy over the slippery stones as far up the shore as he could manage. The tide would soon be in and the water level would rise; we needed to haul it up far enough to ensure its safety. We could then hand it over to the British in a reasonable condition.

I was not much help. Tor had to unload our equipment by himself. He untied the rope that had fastened down the bicycles and then lifted them on to dry land. He then carried the rucksacks and wireless up some narrow, slippery steps and laid our gear on the jetty. He clambered up and down several times to fetch everything. I watched him, calling out occasionally in the hope that someone nearby might hear. There was no reply. The harbour lay silent.

Dawn broke, bringing more light. The coastline took shape. The sea slowly stretched further out and turning round I could see a steep slope upon which clung some grey, wet houses. A small fishing village. There had to be people here.

When Tor had gathered together all of our equipment, he dragged the much lighter dinghy further up the slope. 'Put a few stones in it to keep it weighted down,' I said. Captain Hoelenbaum would have been proud of me, although his advice was not being channelled in the way he would have expected.

We stood on the jetty and started shouting towards the houses perched on the slope. Tor tried signalling but realised that it was pointless. No one would be able to read his message in the dawn light anyway.

'We'll have to find someone,' I said.

'We'll just have to knock at one of the houses,' replied Tor. 'People will still be asleep at this time of the morning. We'll have to wake someone up.'

Leaving our rucksacks and bicycles behind us, we walked towards the cliff. Broad stone steps led us upwards, forking into two paths halfway up the slope. A small path weaved its way towards the first house.

'We'll try there,' I said.

We made our way up the steep steps and saw the house far up above, built of stone and nestled into the rock face.

'You can do all the talking,' said Tor.

I was quite happy to take the lead. This was my second home and I felt perfectly at ease. I went up to the door, as the rainwater dropped from the side roof, and knocked weakly. I still had not got the strength back in my hands. I tried again but the door was solid timber and my light tapping was barely audible. Drawing the pistol from my jacket pocket, I held it by the muzzle and hit the door with the butt. That did the trick. I thumped several times, listened for any movements inside and carried on tapping at the door.

Then I heard somebody inside. As they came to the door, I felt elated; at last we had reached our goal. I thumped again and the door opened. In the doorway stood a small, sturdy man dressed in long woollen pants and a thick grey jumper. He looked half-asleep and had obviously been woken from his bed. He rubbed his eyes and stared at me, slowly taking in my appearance, from my face and ski-hat with its peak pulled down over my forehead to the uniform-like skiing-jacket and the pistol in my hand. He seemed confused. Having been rudely awakened in the middle of the night by a loud knocking, he had answered the door to find a man, pistol in hand, just standing there. I realised I needed to set his mind at ease, to reassure him that I was not posing a threat.

'Sorry to wake you so early in the morning,' I said, trying to smile, 'but we've just been landed here by a German aircraft.'

He drew back and slammed the door. I heard him turn the key twice.

'What did you say to him?' asked Tor as he came towards me.

'That we had just been landed here by the Germans. Just the plain, simple truth.'

'No wonder he looked terrified,' said Tor. 'Put that pistol away and try again. And don't mention the Germans.'

I hid my pistol in my jacket pocket and Tor knocked at the door. After a little while the key was turned again and the man in the woollen pants opened the door once more, only much more carefully. He opened it slowly, a couple of inches, stuck out his head and stood ready to slam it shut if he were threatened again.

'We just want to find the nearest police station,' I said, 'or the nearest military camp.'

The man nodded. I saw that he had understood me. He understood the word 'police' despite the fact that he was not used to the Lancashire accent. It seemed as though he believed me. He opened the door another couple of inches. 'Police?' he asked.

'Yes, or the military,' I said. 'We've got to get in touch with someone in authority immediately.'

Perhaps he realised that someone asking for the nearest police station could surely not be dangerous. Even if they were armed and had arrived by an enemy plane. He opened the door wide, took a step out on to the front step and pointed. 'Go up the hill,' he said. 'There's a path over there. And steps.' I looked in the direction he was pointing. A narrow path could be seen, a low garden wall. 'When you get to the top, turn right,' he continued. 'Then you'll come to the road.'

'Thanks,' I said.

He nodded again and drew back quickly, shutting the door. It did not matter now we knew which way we were headed. We went back to our bicycles.

'We'll take the boat too,' said Tor. He removed the stones and pulled out the air valves. The air, which had so laboriously been pumped in, hissed out, and the dinghy lost its shape. Then he rolled it up and fixed it into the carrier. I took the radio equipment. I lifted up the case and fastened it on. It was going to be difficult balancing it on the cycle. Then we heaved our rucksacks on to our backs and started pushing our equipment up the steep path. When we reached the steps we had to help each other, taking one cycle up and then the other. My hands felt better, the blood was circulating again, but they were still very sore.

We eventually reached the top, tired and weak, and sat down for a rest. We saw a narrow road winding its way through the hills. Below us the slope inclined steeply down to the shore and the harbour. On the hillside lay the tiny village. I desperately needed to go behind the bushes, so I tore out several pages of *Hjemmet*, a magazine that Andersen had given me at Hummeren and which, for some reason, I had put in my rucksack.

The sun had not risen yet but it was light. People would

soon be up and we would be able to ask our way to the police station. We still did not know where we were. It struck me that the Germans had not provided us with a map. I had not thought about it as we would hardly have any use for a map if we intended to hand ourselves over immediately. Müller had reckoned on our hiding somewhere first, giving us the opportunity to establish ourselves before carrying out the work which was the whole point of our mission. He ought to have given us a detailed map of the area, but he had not. Was this yet further proof that he viewed us as guinea-pigs?

We rested a while before we felt ready to continue. We climbed up on to our bicycles and pedalled off. Since they were so heavily laden they were quite unstable. The case carrying the radio equipment weighed a good deal. It was just as well Andersen had checked that my tyres were pumped up.

We passed by a field. A little way into the newly ploughed land we caught sight of a man standing with his back to us. He was dressed in an old trenchcoat. I stopped and called to him. He turned round and came over to us. His expression was vacant and green snot ran down his chin.

'We're looking for a police station,' I said.

He flapped about and then ran across the field making croaking noises. I looked at Tor and we shook our heads. First a frightened man in woollen pants, then a poor village idiot. Who would we meet next?

We continued battling our way up the hill. Pasture land lay on either side of the road, the grass green and fresh. Then we heard the sound of an engine as a lorry appeared just at the bend of the road, making its way towards us. We stopped. It worked its way slowly up the hill, the exhaust fumes forming a black cloud behind it. The open-sided wagon was full of women in overalls, equipped with hoes and spades. I realised that they were a voluntary labour force unit on their way to their farm work, replacing the farmer who had been called up for military service. I was aware that the British had organised these units at the beginning of the war. They had occasionally mentioned them in the BBC reports. We waved and shouted as the lorry disappeared behind the next hilltop.

Was there no single sane person to help us and show us the way to the police station?

'Müller would be pleased,' said Tor.

'How come?'

'So far no one's thought us especially odd. We would have made perfect agents.'

We struggled back on to our bicycles and pedalled on. We did not know if we were going in the right direction, but sooner or later the road had to reach some town or village. We had to find someone. After quarter of an hour we heard the sound of another engine. This time it was a car. We spotted it in the distance. It was black and as it drew closer we saw the two policemen sitting side by side. I cycled up to meet it, raising my arm to stop them. We had been cycling on the right-hand side of the road. It was simply habit. I had not given a second thought to the fact that the British drove on the left.

'We're on the wrong side of the road,' I said to Tor.

'Bet you we'll be fined,' said Tor. He was thinking of our zealous police officers in Oslo. We hopped off our bicycles. The car stopped. The policemen climbed out and saluted. Tor, who was nearest, put his cycle down in the ditch and walked over to them.

'Can I be of assistance?' asked one of them. He took out a small notebook and pencil.

'I'd like to surrender this,' said Tor, and eased the pistol out of his jacket pocket.

The policeman took the weapon and noted the details. 'Is there ammunition for this?' he asked.

Tor pointed at his rucksack. 'In there,' he said.

The policeman noted it down. I took a step towards him, handed him my pistol, and said as calmly as I could, 'We were put ashore as German spies.'

The policeman wet his pencil.

17

It had stopped raining. We stood at the side of the road; our cycles lay in the ditch, the two policemen standing in front of us, one of whom was armed with our pistols, holding them somewhat uncomfortably in the one hand. The other scribbled in his black notepad, looked at his watch and continued writing.

'What are you writing?' I asked.

'The outline of my report,' he replied. 'I've just made a note of the landing of two German spies along with the precise time.'

'We're not spies,' said Tor.

'But the gentleman here just said so.' He looked at me with his blue Scots eyes.

'Could you take us to the police station?' I asked. 'We'll explain everything when we get there.'

'As the gentleman wishes.'

'What about our rucksacks and the case?' I pointed to our cumbersome equipment.

'I think there'll be enough room in the car,' said the blue-eyed policeman. 'The cycles will have to stay behind. I'll collect them later.'

We loaded up the car. One of the policemen struggled with the radio pack as he tried to lift it into the boot, straining beneath its weight. 'It's a transmitter,' I explained. 'I'll show it to you later. It's all part of our equipment.'

Tor kept a low profile; we had decided that I would do all the talking. I spoke English well and could act the part of a native. Tor, however, stepped towards the blue-eyed policeman as he was putting away his notebook. 'We need to get in touch with the Norwegian Government officials in London.'

'We'll see about that once we get to the station,' came the reply.

Tor and I climbed into the rear seat. The man with our pistols sat himself at the wheel. Having driven a short distance we turned into a side road and were then taken to a village a few kilometres away. I asked the name of the place.

'Banff,' said blue eyes. I recalled the name from Hoelenbaum's map. So, we had landed exactly where the pilot had pointed out.

Banff was not a large community, but it at least had a police station and, nearby, a public house. The police station was in fact a small, red-brick house. The car pulled up at the main entrance. We stepped on to the pavement and were shown into the office.

The room was divided in half by a small partition. The officer in charge, a sergeant, sat on the other side reading the morning paper. As we came in he looked up from his paper and, rising from his chair, moved towards the partition. He leaned towards us, his gaze fixed upon us. 'So, our gentlemen have arrived.'

'We came across them along the road,' said his colleague with the blue eyes. 'They were cycling.'

The patrol car had obviously been sent to search for us. Of course, our friend with the woollen long-johns must have called to tell them. We should have realised. As soon as we had left the village he would have rushed to the nearest telephone box to warn the police at Banff that he had been visited by two German spies. It could only be in our favour, I thought. The police would clearly understand that we had done everything in our power to make our presence known from the very outset.

'A cup of tea?' asked the duty sergeant. We accepted the offer and moved to the open fire which breathed a pleasant warmth from one of the room's long walls. The sergeant called out and a constable clomped into the office from an adjoining room. He was given his orders and soon returned with two mugs of sweet, steaming-hot tea.

'Where do you come from?' asked the sergeant.

'Norway,' I replied. 'We were flown in overnight from Stavanger.'

'Did you parachute down?'

'It was a seaplane. We were put down on the sea and then rowed ashore in a rubber dinghy.'

'We brought the boat with us,' explained Tor, pointing to our luggage which had been carried in from the car. The sergeant seemed curious. He quizzed us about the conditions in Norway, why we had gone to work for the Germans and about our flight across the North Sea. It was far from an interrogation; there were no notes taken, but Tor and I answered his questions in detail. I could see that the sergeant was very interested. After all, it was not every day that two German spies appeared in Banff.

'I would like to make a phone call,' I said. 'To my grandfather in Manchester. He can verify our identities.'

'Interesting,' said the sergeant, 'but I'm afraid you'll have to wait.'

The door opened and two uniformed men entered the room. They were obviously from the Home Guard, here simply to satisfy their curiosity. The news of our arrival had already spread through the village.

We huddled in front of the coal fire glowing in the grate. The constable offered more tea. We explained why we had come to Scotland. I told them about grandfather, and that I was hoping to visit him. We described Müller and Andersen, and Tor passed a few remarks about our work at the censor.

'It's all perfectly true,' I explained. 'We were sent by the Germans to spy for them.' Of course, it was sensational news to them. Two German spies handing themselves over, of their own free will, changing sides. We felt that at least this tiny gathering in Banff police station believed we were not genuine agents. Our sole intention had been to dupe the Germans and we had succeeded.

Then the chief constable marched in. The constables and the sergeant stood to attention.

He stroked his military moustache and hung his uniform hat on a peg at the far end of the partition. Bending down, he removed the bicycle clips which protected his trousers from the oily chain of his cycle. He héld out his hand and introduced himself. He welcomed us to Banff, and the station, hoping that we had been well taken care of. Indeed we had. We were amazed at their friendliness.

With a mug of tea in his hand he began to question us. The same questions we had answered several times before. We endeavoured to give precisely the same detailed responses as before but were surprised that, once again, nobody took our remarks down on paper. Perhaps it was the small gathering which rendered the questioning informal and unofficial. An interrogation proper would be held in a private room. The interrogator and interrogated face to face alone.

The telephone rang. It was answered by the sergeant, who paused and then cupped his hand over the mouthpiece. It was for the chief inspector. 'Aberdeen,' he added.

The inspector walked to the other side of the partition and took the phone. He said very little other than 'yes' and 'no' and 'I'll see to it', but his complexion visibly changed and as he put the receiver down his cheeks were glowing a bright red. 'Get the room cleared,' he said to the duty sergeant. Then, grasping the railing, he stood on tiptoe and bellowed, 'Leave the office!' A few constables dawdled behind. 'You too!' he shouted. They shuffled into an adjoining room.

Our room was now empty bar the chief inspector, the duty sergeant and ourselves, the two German spies.

'I'm sorry,' explained the inspector. 'But I have my orders, from Aberdeen, to keep you in isolation. You are to talk to no one.'

Someone should have thought of that before. As captured enemy agents we should not have been questioned in public until we had been subjected to interrogation by Military Intelligence or some other security unit. Even Tor and I realised that. We had always presumed that our relaying messages and false information to the Germans would naturally take place under the supervision of British Intelligence. If we were to succeed at all, we could not risk the publicity of news items describing how two enemy agents had now freely offered their services to Britain. If the Germans were to get wind of that our messages would be rendered worthless and impotent.

'What's going to happen to us?' I asked.

'We're expecting somebody soon. Until then I must ask you to stay calm.'

'May I phone grandfather while we wait?'

'I'm sorry,' replied the inspector. 'No phone calls. And I'm afraid I will also have to separate you.' He beckoned to the duty sergeant who led Tor by the arm into another room. I was to remain in the office.

At lunchtime the landlord of the public house, a small, bald-headed old man was allowed inside the station. He looked frightened, and carefully avoided looking at me. He served us with a type of pudding and pints of beer. I hungrily gulped down the beer and pudding. Tor, who ate with me, was more cautious. He still had not fully recovered from his bout of seasickness.

The hours passed. We waited. I had sat myself in front of the coal fire in a somewhat uncomfortable chair, occasionally standing up to walk about the room. The duty sergeant was not as talkative now, but once the inspector went into his office we passed a few pleasantries about the weather, a safely neutral, almost inexhaustible, topic.

The inspector returned regularly, telling us to be patient. They would soon be here. He didn't know when exactly, the roads to Banff were by no means the best, but someone would arrive soon. That was what he had been told.

'There's no rush,' I said. 'We've nothing else to do. No train to catch. No one's expecting us.'

'Somebody is coming up from Edinburgh,' said the

inspector. 'He's a security man. They usually handle this sort of case.'

The gentleman did not arrive until after six. By that time the trembling landlord had paid us another visit, bringing our dinner, a barely edible Scottish dish apparently made from cow's stomach, barley grain and swede.

The man from Edinburgh was a Major Peter Perfect. He introduced himself as a security officer and showed us into the inspector's office. He sat down behind the desk and apologised for having made us wait so long but said he simply couldn't have got here any faster.

'There's no need to apologise,' I said. 'We've been made to feel quite welcome. We've had several charming visitors. The time passed quickly.'

'Several?' asked the major.

'The police station was full of people trying to satisfy their curiosity this morning,' replied Tor.

'And you spoke to them?'

'Of course,' I replied.

'What about?'

'They only wanted to know where we were from and how we had got here. So we told them.'

The major stood up violently, his chair scraping loudly across the floor, almost tipping over. He hurried into the room which the inspector had made his office for the time being. We overheard very little of their conversation but understood enough to realise that the man from security was far from happy. Before he left the chief inspector I thought I heard him demand a list of all those people who had spoken to us that morning. 'I'll come back to you about this,' he said as he opened the door.

'I'm sorry for the interruption,' he explained, 'but this matter demands the highest security.'

The interrogation began. He wanted our names, where we were from, our Oslo addresses and, of course, what the purpose of our mission was. He made notes and asked more searching questions. I explained to him about my work at father's salon, mother's whist friends and my grandfather; but I was still not allowed to telephone him.

It was all quite relaxed and informal. Major Perfect was extremely polite and even jovial at times. Tor and I had a clear conscience; we were no longer forced to play out a role and could talk of our plans in detail — our double-crossing the Germans at the office of the post censor, and during our training as saboteurs. I showed him the letter addressed to Trygve Lie; we demonstrated the use of the radio equipment, and I handed over my rolls of film, describing the Abwehr men stationed in Oslo. We pulled out the hairbrushes which concealed the detonators and the fuse-wire belts. He studied our equipment very carefully and probed us about our training.

The minutes soon passed. The major was meticulous in his questioning, posing the same questions, and often returning to certain details, but from a slightly different angle. He was clearly good at his job. If we had dared to pass off a feeble cover story such as the one Müller had dreamt up, he wouldn't have missed it. He was testing us. All we could tell him was the truth. I began to feel tired.

'We barely slept last night,' I said. 'Could we possibly rest for a few hours?'

Peter Perfect looked at his watch. It was late, midnight already. We had been questioned over a period of six hours.

'Is there a hotel nearby?' asked Tor.

'I would dearly like to accompany you there,' replied the major as he rose from his seat. He walked round the table, leaned towards us and smiled. 'However, not in view of present circumstances,' he continued. 'Look at it this way. You have just landed in Scotland as enemy agents and we don't want to attract too much attention. In other words, I have already arranged your accommodation, gentlemen. I hope you won't mind spending the night in our local prison cells?'

'Prison?' I asked in disbelief.

'I'm afraid so,' replied Peter Perfect, his smile broadening. 'You would be spotted at the hotel. People might begin to ask questions.'

We certainly hadn't come all the way to Scotland to be put in jail. Our imprisonment at Hummeren had been quite enough. However, I realised that we had to follow his wishes. He had asked us very pleasantly, but it was an order just the same.

'All we want is a bed,' I said. 'It doesn't really matter where.'

'Thank you,' replied the major. 'I knew you would understand. I promise to arrange for more comfortable accommodation in the future.'

We gathered our personal belongings together — our other equipment would have to remain there. We were then driven to the local prison. They were expecting us. The doors were opened by the prison warder himself, who was perfectly friendly; we were thankfully not treated as other prisoners. They had prepared two separate cells for us, their doors left open and the lights on. The doors were steelplate, safely secured by both a strong lock and a heavy bar which slotted into a niche in the wall.

My cell was very cramped. The warder's wife brought us some beer. I sat on the edge of the bunk and drained the glass. The cell was dimly lit by a naked bulb and equipped with a small hand-basin and a latrine bucket in one corner. A small barred window sat high up into the wall. I was totally exhausted. I had a whole night's sleep to catch up. I politely declined the offer of another glass of beer. All I wanted was to sleep.

The cell door was slammed shut. All I remember before I slipped into a deep unconscious sleep was the sound of the key as it turned and the bar drawn heavily across the door. Did they suspect us?

18

I awoke to find somebody standing by my bed. It took some time before I realised where I was and that it was the warder's wife come to wake me. She stood in the centre of the small cell holding a cup of tea and a biscuit.

'Good morning,' she said as I gradually came to. 'It's seven o'clock. Time to get up.' I hadn't had enough sleep. Barely six hours had passed from when I had been shut in my cell. I closed my eyes. 'There will soon be somebody to fetch you,' continued my hostess. 'Breakfast will be in the kitchen.'

She placed the teacup on a stool and left the cell. I heard the rattle of keys outside Tor's cell. There was nothing I could do but get up. I clambered out of bed, washed and dressed, occasionally taking a sip of tea. They trusted us sufficiently to leave the doors open, even if we were in prison. I understood why. The major didn't want us to feel like criminals. But at the same time I was nagged by a constant doubt. Did we now find ourselves in prison because Major Perfect mistrusted us? Did he suspect us of being genuine Nazi spies, captured attempting to escape? The next step was an obvious one. As a captured enemy agent it was all I could expect. If only I had managed to contact grandfather. The word of a colonel carries considerable weight.

As I entered the kitchen my fears and worries left me. The room was large with whitewashed walls, a solid-looking table in the centre and a huge blazing coal fire. Two windows looked out on to the garden, where I noticed the outside toilet. A clock hung from one of the longer walls and a brass kettle of water hissed on the stove, its hinged lid clattering nervously.

I was greeted by the smell of bacon and freshly baked bread. Tor was already sitting at the table. The warder's wife drew up a chair and I sat down. It was only then I noticed the little girl in the corner. I nodded to her. She was about twelve years old, with dark hair and large brown eyes.

'My daughter,' said the warder as he sat himself down beside us. We were not treated as prisoners, but guests. It certainly helped us feel a lot more comfortable. Nothing could go wrong now; just a touch more red tape and we could then start work.

The girl asked us where we came from and how we had come to Scotland. We had nothing to hide but were markedly more cautious about what we said than we had been the day before. Our host reached towards a shelf and took down a jug, offering what I presumed to be milk. But as I poured I recognised the brown, tea-coloured liquid.

'Whisky,' said the warder. 'I work at the village distillery as well.' I passed the jug to Tor who poured himself a drop and then the warder took the jug. Raising our cups in a toast, the warder officially welcomed us to Scotland. We drank to victory and then helped ourselves to more of our host's refreshment. I felt that we should show our appreciation in some way, a little something to remind them of our first night in Scotland. Neither Müller nor myself had given much thought to that, however. I remembered the Norwegian pendant which I was wearing in the collar of my blue ski-jacket. I had found it at mother's. Andersen had liked the idea. Removing the tiny flag I stood and walked over to the daughter and pinned it to her blouse. Embarrassed, she curtsied, blushing slightly. Once again the whisky jar was passed round the table.

We were in good spirits by the time the police car arrived to collect us. We had been well fed and were touched by the kindness shown to us. We fetched our rucksacks and went outside to the car. The chief inspector from Banff and another officer, the driver, were to be our escort. I looked for the rest of our equipment but could see neither the radio nor the dinghy. I asked where they were.

'Don't worry,' came the reply. 'They're in safe keeping.' Perhaps the major had taken charge of them? British Intelligence were bound to be interested in them. It made no difference to us. We didn't need them.

'Where are we going?' I asked.

'To Aberdeen,' said the inspector.

We drove through Banff on to a narrow winding road. It was a dull, cloudy day, but at least it wasn't raining. The road was dry and the driver made haste. The inspector was not especially talkative. He clearly wanted to hand us over as quickly as possible.

We sat admiring the scenery: the hilly landscape, tiny villages, people passing by on foot, cyclists, villagers chatting on street corners, the occasional car, and even some horse-drawn carriages and an old milk cart. Nearing Aberdeen, we saw the simple granite houses lying on the outskirts of the city and then the paved streets, shops, and the tall, elegant buildings of the city centre.

The car slowed down alongside a large building on one of the main streets. Aberdeen police station, we were informed by the inspector. We continued through the gates and drew to a halt in the high-walled yard. We were then escorted up a wide stairway and handed into the custody of the Aberdeen police. Our escorts appeared relieved to bid us farewell. We were then taken to an older, pipe-smoking officer who introduced himself as McConnought. He asked a few friendly questions along the same lines as those we had answered before. I asked if I could phone my grandfather but the request was turned down once again.

'Perhaps later,' said McConnought, billowing a cloud of smoke. Instead he arranged for us to have lunch and then returned to questioning us. Later he ordered dinner and eventually informed us that we would be travelling down to London on the night train accompanied by Inspector Slatter and a police sergeant.

Slatter and his colleague arrived to collect us with plenty of time to spare. We were driven by car to the railway station, where a group of policemen dressed in civilian clothing met us. Half of them formed a small group ahead of Tor and me, and the other half followed half a step behind us together with our two escorts, thus cutting off any possible means of escape. Slatter told us that we were to talk to no one. Our escort was not simply there to prevent us making any contacts, however. I fully realised that. They were keeping a very close watch, waiting for the gentle nod to a passer-by. They were clearly taking no risks at all.

We reached the platform. The train was waiting; travellers rushed past laden with cases; a couple shared a final embrace as another solitary figure waved sadly with a handkerchief.

Our companions discreetly led us to a carriage situated at the front of the train. It appeared to be empty. There were no passengers leaning from carriage windows for the last goodbye. I heard the guard's whistle. Slatter opened the carriage door and just as we climbed aboard the train slowly began to pull out from the station. It was just like the scene that always seems to appear in old crime films, I thought. The fugitive desperately leaps on to the train as it accelerates from the station, his dejected pursuers left stranded on the platform once again.

Our particular compartment had been reserved in advance; there was a small reservation slip on the door. The curtains were drawn, the corridor empty. We would neither see nor be seen. We had aroused a great deal of interest in security circles and were to be handled carefully. But protected from what?

Inspector Slatter was not a particularly tall figure, in his late thirties, dark, and with a thin, gaunt face. His suit was visibly crumpled. The sergeant was younger but of similar stature. He sat by the door, presumably to prevent other passengers from entering the compartment. During the rickety journey through Scotland we chatted to our chaperones. Once again it was not an interrogation, but we were happy to answer their questions, retelling our tale for the umpteenth time.

'You're to reveal none of this to outsiders, you understand?' the inspector said suddenly.

'We realise that now,' replied Tor. 'But we did talk with a few people at Banff.'

'I know,' said Slatter. 'Our security people had their work cut out there.'

'Why is that?' we both asked.

'They had to track down everybody you had been in contact with and guarantee their secrecy. That meant even those who had simply seen or heard of you.'

'Sorry,' I apologised.

'The young girl was asked to hand over that Norwegian pendant as well,' Slatter continued.

'Oh, surely not,' said Tor. 'It was simply a small gift, a harmless gesture. She liked it.'

'Her friends at school wanted to know what it was. Do you know what she told them?'

We had no idea.

'"I got it from two German spies."'

Slatter chuckled, lit a cigarette and loosened his tie. 'Fortunately I missed out on that occasion. Fancy having to give a talk to a group of schoolchildren on how important it is that the Germans don't find out that we have captured two of their best agents.'

'We seem to have caused a great deal of uproar in Banff,' said Tor.

'It's of the utmost importance that nothing gets any further,' Slatter continued. 'The press are to know nothing.'

I was amazed at the amount of work that had been done in order to cover our tracks. Security had obviously taken us very seriously. Perhaps Major Perfect had already proposed that we be allowed to carry out our intentions as planned and co-operate with British Intelligence. It would explain their earlier actions. A column in the local paper, however small, and Abwehr could easily get hold of the news. They probably had their people filtering information from all the national and local newspapers.

Our journey to London could not have been arranged in total secrecy. That became obvious when the guard suddenly entered the compartment and asked for our autographs. We both looked at Slatter. He nodded, smiling, and I took the pen and paper which the guard had held towards me.

'May your chicken never die,' I wrote, and signed my name. Tor added, 'Greetings from Norway' and the guard bowed, thanked us and left.

We dozed off for just a couple of hours; the seat was quite soft but not especially comfortable. It had been a whole year-and-a-half since I had last travelled in a British train. I remembered the journey, a crowded, desperate affair, and then the hordes of people anxiously searching for a place on board any boat, rumours buzzing, and strangers conversing with strangers to help dampen their fear.

I had still experienced little of the war. There had been no sign of it in Banff, which remained a sleepy pastoral village, apart from the curious presence of the Home Guard. Even Aberdeen had not been scarred by the war. We saw no derelict buildings, no refugees, and witnessed no signs of panic. German propaganda was sadly misleading; I had now seen the proof of that with my own eyes. Of course, we had merely caught fleeting glimpses from a car window and experienced brief meetings with the native people whilst at the police stations in Banff and Aberdeen. Our impressions of the country and its people were admittedly very skeletal.

We arrived in London in the early morning, collected our rucksacks and climbed down on to the platform. Slatter and the sergeant led us to the guards' room where two men were unloading cases and boxes. We watched them unload the radio pack, the dinghy and a bag in which Major Perfect had packed our pistols, ammunition and other sabotage equipment.

'Wait here,' said Slatter, turning on his heels and walking

towards the exit, closely followed by his sergeant. So we waited. The platform slowly emptied and the men finished unloading and pulled the luggage trolleys away. We were left alone, still waiting.

Ten minutes passed. Fifteen minutes, and Slatter had still not returned to take charge of his two spies, who stood in the middle of an empty station waiting.

'Where's he gone?' asked Tor.

'I've no idea.'

'Do you think they're testing us? Just to see if we try to escape? I mean, we have the radio and pistols, we could easily slip away.'

Tor was probably right. It was a test of our honesty and reliability. They clearly still had their doubts and were probably watching our every move. We must have passed with flying colours because Slatter returned. 'Sorry to have kept you waiting. I thought we'd never get hold of a taxi.'

He helped us carry the luggage to the cab. There was no lack of taxis at the rank; there must have been a dozen of them waiting outside the station. We said nothing as we climbed into the cab and left Slatter to give his instructions to the driver. We were on our way to New Scotland Yard. Here I was in London once again. It had been twenty-two years since my birth, here, and I felt exhilarated to be back. However it was clear that a great deal had changed. Banff lay unblemished by the war, but London was in the very heart of it.

Sandbags lay in piles along the pavements and windows had been taped to prevent their shattering. The streets were full of soldiers and policemen in hard hats, metal truncheons swinging from their belts. In the distance we could see an enormous bomb crater surrounded by derelict houses. The road had been blocked off, so we turned down an alley and on to another main road.

It was business as usual at one department store we passed, even with the sandbags stacked in front of the display windows. It all seemed so unreal. Norway seemed so far away, and Oslo was overrun by Germans, but here we were, Tor and I, sitting in a London taxi. Only three days ago we had been in Stavanger.

We arrived at the entrance to the police headquarters. Slatter paid the fare and Tor and I were sent up the stairs. It seemed almost as if Slatter feared that we might try to escape at the very last moment.

The entrance was vast with a marble floor, at the end of which sat an elderly policeman behind a reception desk. He caught sight of us and stood up. 'Good morning, gentlemen,' he said. 'What can I do for you?'

'We've just arrived from Aberdeen,' I said.

They were clearly expecting us. The Scottish police would have phoned ahead. 'I know,' he said. 'I was told you would be arriving this morning.' He pointed towards Slatter and the sergeant who stood behind us and asked, 'Are these the prisoners?'

I burst out laughing.

Slatter approached the desk, 'No,' he explained authoritatively. 'I am Inspector Slatter from Aberdeen.'

'I beg your pardon, sir,' said the policeman at the desk, blushing. 'I'll send for someone to collect you. Or would you rather have a cup of tea in the canteen first? I can phone and tell them you're on your way.'

We decided to have a cup of tea and were shown to the canteen on the second floor. It was a very plain room, with just a few tables and a counter on the far side next to the kitchen. Two policemen sat drinking their early morning tea and a solid-looking woman with straggly hair stood guarding the counter.

'Four teas, please,' said Slatter. 'I believe we're expected.'

The woman simply glowered at him, and putting her hands on her hips she hissed, 'I'll not serve spies!'

'I'm Inspector Slatter from Aberdeen. I asked for four teas.' The woman didn't move, but stood, legs astride, staring at him angrily.

She must have served plenty of suspects over the years. Suspected thieves, rapists, murderers and their escorts have to be fed. We are all human, after all. It appeared, however, that spies were not. Captured German agents did not even warrant a cup of tea. I was not annoyed by her refusing to serve us as I neither was, nor felt like, a German spy. I could understand her feelings, her profound hatred for the Nazis who had destroyed the city. The Luftwaffe raids had not instilled any desperate panic, simply a deep hatred and solid resistance which was now manifesting itself against four thirsty visitors to Scotland Yard. Slatter tried to explain that we had been sent over by the Germans as spies, but that our sole intention was to work for the British. It didn't seem to help. As far as she was concerned reception had said 'German spies', and German spies we were. She would serve Slatter and the sergeant, but definitely not the spies.

Slatter's patience was running out. Pushing aside the woman, he reached for the telephone on the counter and demanded the reception's extension number from the telephonist. He dialled the number and asked the policeman to come up right away. A minute later his panting figure arrived and he began to explain things to the canteen manageress, confessing that he had possibly not expressed himself correctly. We were to be treated as normal visitors, and besides, it was up to the courts to decide whether we were genuine spies or otherwise. Canteen staff had no right to pass such judgements.

By this time a long queue had formed behind us. Perhaps the rumours of our arrival had spread along the corridors; either that or Slatter's raised voice had aroused a considerable amount of curiosity.

'Where are you from?' asked a policeman behind me.

'No questions, please,' demanded Slatter.

I shrugged my shoulders, took the teacup that the woman had reluctantly offered me and sat down. The new arrivals sat themselves at the next table. They toyed with their cups and stared at us as they would at celebrities or monkeys at the zoo.

Our guard arrived shortly after, glaring towards our

neighbours. 'Your transport has been seen to,' he said. 'It should arrive very soon now.'

We said goodbye to Slatter and the sergeant. They had done their job and would now return to Aberdeen. Tor and I had no idea where we would be going, and our new escort would tell us nothing. We waited for half an hour. I asked to phone grandfather but was again told politely that it could not be allowed.

A phone call informed us that our transport had arrived and we were led to the yard. There an NCO and two privates armed with machine-guns stood guarding a small truck. A tarpaulin hung across the metal frame of the open-back lorry. We climbed aboard and our luggage was lifted on, after which the entrance was covered with the tarpaulin. The NCO sat between myself and Tor, the soldiers opposite us, staring intently.

Then the lorry pulled away and I managed to catch a glimpse of a car that was now trailing us. I had seen it in the yard earlier, with its engine idling. They had clearly tightened security: armed soldiers and an extra guard. Did they really believe we might try to escape?

19

We had been given no clue as to where we were being taken and could see nothing of the journey. At first I tried to follow the route in my mind's eye, which streets we were driving along, and the junctions where we stopped. After all, I knew London quite well. I had to give in. It was impossible to tell if we were heading north or south.

One of the soldiers leaned forward to ask where we were from.

'Quiet!' yelled the corporal. He was a Cockney, but I somehow felt he might not appreciate my telling him that I, too, had been born in London.

Some minutes had passed when he pulled out some scraps of paper. He paused to leaf through them and held one of the scraps towards us. It was a dreadful caricature. A few simple pen strokes displayed Hitler's unmistakable hairstyle and short moustache. The cartoon was extremely obscene, but Tor and I burst out laughing. The corporal stared at us in amazement. He hadn't expected that.

'Do you have any more?' I asked.

He was now definitely confused but showed the rest of his collection all the same. There was Göering, his piece a field marshal's baton, and Göebbels with frogs hopping out of his mouth. We couldn't help but laugh. He really couldn't come to terms with our reaction.

It was a long journey and I realised that we had to be somewhere on the outskirts of the city. The lorry came to a sudden stop. The driver mumbled something and I heard heavy gates creak open. We drove on another hundred metres and stopped. The engine died. One of the soldiers loosened the tarpaulin cover and jumped to the ground. We had halted at a large building, perhaps a country estate of some kind.

A small man approached us from the house, a captain — I could tell that from his pips. He wore riding boots and clutched his stick firmly under his arm.

'Where are we?' I asked him.

He stopped dead in his tracks and stamped his foot. 'Get down, you bloody spies!' he screamed.

'Look, we're not spies,' I explained.

'Shut up, you bastards! Nazi pigs!'

'That will do,' I said, jumping from the truck.

The furious captain continued to stamp and rage. 'Take them inside!' he screamed to the two privates. 'We'll take care of the rest.' He pointed viciously towards the rucksacks and radio pack. There was no point in arguing, the man was hysterical. If I so much as uttered a single word, he would probably resort to physical violence.

We walked towards the house flanked by the two soldiers. Once inside we were shown into separate rooms. The door was locked behind me and I sat down on the narrow bed which stood alongside the wall. Besides the bed there was a chair and a small writing desk, and that was all. The single window was barred and impossible to see through. Where on earth were we?

I lay down. I hadn't slept much on the train and thought I had better try to sleep while I had the chance. But I couldn't, I was too much on edge. What was the meaning of it all? The horrid little officer, what had he meant? Were we simply foreign agents to him, people to despise?

A full hour passed by before the door was opened by an armed soldier. 'Come with me,' he spat.

His face told me not to ask our whereabouts or what was to become of us. I quietly followed him along the corridor. He took me into a large room where a doctor in a long white overall had been waiting for me. An eye-chart hung on the wall with a set of scales and an examination couch in the corner.

When the guard had left the room I asked the doctor the meaning of our ill-treatment. I explained that we were not what they thought we were, and I would demand an apology from that coarsely behaved captain we had met.

'Name?' asked the doctor. 'Date of birth?'

I gave him the date, adding that I had been born in London. He glanced at me and then continued with his questions. What illnesses had I had; had I been ill recently; were there any cases of TB, mental illness or heart disease in the family? He then asked me to unbutton my shirt to check my heart and lungs, and noted my appendix scar. After my eyesight and hearing had been checked, he called for the guard who had been waiting on the other side of the door.

I was escorted back to my room and the door was locked behind me. I was alone once again and none the wiser. None of my questions had been answered, and I still had no idea what would happen to us.

The guard returned after a short while and this time took me to a dentist. He meticulously examined my teeth, paying special attention to those teeth which Åge Berg had filled just a couple of weeks before we left Norway. 'Your teeth seem in very good condition,' he said at last and called for the guard.

I was returned to my cell and lay on the bed feeling totally helpless. I had been shaken by the hostility of our new prison. Both the doctor and the dentist had remained coldly distant; the guard said nothing more than 'Follow me!'; and then there was the brash rudeness of the captain. How long would this go on? Had Tor undergone the same treatment? Did he feel as confused as I now felt?

The guard returned a third time. We turned into a different corridor, with me following the heavily clumping boots of my escort. We climbed a staircase and swung down another corridor towards a large double door. I was shown into the room by the guard, who saluted. 'The prisoner!' he announced loudly. He left the room, closing the door behind me.

It looked like a huge dining-room. At the far end sat a group of men at a long table, between us a seemingly endless line of wooden floorboards. Light rectangular patches revealed the spots where mats had once decorated the floor. I recalled the same dark outlines of our own floor in Oslo when the mats had been sent for cleaning. French windows were on one side of the room and a large open fireplace lay empty on the other, but I recognised our radio on the mantelpiece. I felt I could see what they wanted. We were going to attempt to make radio contact with the Germans. It would be yet another test. I would show them the transmitter, how it worked, and then relay our first message. I walked across the wooden floor to the radio. The room was deathly silent apart from the hollow sound of my footsteps.

I examined the equipment to check that it was indeed ours. 'It's ours all right,' I announced to the table. 'Would you like me to set it up? My colleague really ought to be here — he's far better on the technical side than I am.'

There was a brief, horrid silence.

'Come here!' yelled a voice. 'And in future only speak when you're spoken to.'

I moved cautiously to the table which had been placed on a raised platform. I tipped my head back to try to make out their faces.

The table was covered by a green baize, upon which glasses, jugs of water, paper and pens had been neatly ordered. The two large windows behind them looked on to a garden. I was dazzled by the light and could scarcely see the faces of my interrogators. There had to be nine of them in total, only one of whom was dressed in civilian clothing, sitting at the far end of the table. A colonel sat in the very centre of the panel. He led the interrogation. He began with the usual questions — full name, date and place of birth. He spoke in a clipped monotone and his attitude was far from favourable. It slowly dawned on me that this was the military trial of which the men at Scotland Yard had spoken.

A verdict would be reached. If I were found guilty I could be sentenced to death. This was all too real. We had treated our double-crossing of the Germans as some sort of game. It had all felt like a well-acted theatre performance — our way of fighting the oppressive injustice of the occupation. Even the flight to Scotland and our landing by dinghy had the flavour of a boy scout adventure story, even if I had been very concerned about the films I was carrying. Had the Germans discovered them we could well have been arrested and imprisoned, but I was convinced that I could have talked our way out of it. Our visits to Banff and Aberdeen had even been quite pleasant. We had been treated with some respect as we proudly related our story to a curious audience. But this was different. I would have to work hard to gain their respect and trust, but I was determined to do so. I would not lie down now. I would convince them that I had a clear conscience and that my intentions were noble.

I looked at the chairman and realised the difficulty I would have to convince him. He looked to have a similar temperament to that of the captain. I would have to tread carefully. He was already annoyed by my unbecoming behaviour as I entered the room. I couldn't afford another mistake. All I had to do was tell the truth; I had nothing to hide. It was a good feeling and helped me stay calm despite the seriousness of the whole situation. I approached the colonel as I would a challenge. I had to persuade him.

'When were you last in England?' he asked.

'September 1939,' I replied.

'Sir!' he shouted.

'September 1939, sir.'

'Where?'

'I was working in London, on the film set of *The Thief of Baghdad*, sir.'

'As an actor?' asked a major sitting beside the chairman.

'I was a make-up artist, sir.'

'Did you go anywhere else?' asked the colonel.

'Manchester, sir.'

'What were you doing there?'

'Visiting my grandfather, sir.'

'What's his name?'

'Colonel Doctor Herbert Wade. His address is Rusholme Gardens, Manchester.'

'Is he a military doctor?'

'No, he's a colonel in the army.'

'Sir!' shouted the colonel once again. 'You will address me as sir.'

'I'm sorry, sir.'

'What regiment?'

'The Ninth Manchester Regiment, sir.'

The colonel turned to whisper to the major next to him. The major called to a lieutenant who was sitting at the far end of the table. The lieutenant disappeared quickly from the room.

The interrogation came to a temporary halt. I took a good look at the judges and jury. Three of them were majors, the remainder were captains, except for the colonel and the civilian. They all sat in silence, staring at me. I felt most uncomfortable and wanted to break the silence.

'I've asked to phone grandfather,' I said. 'But I've not been allowed to.'

The colonel glared angrily at me.

'Sir,' I added.

He gave no reply and the room was silent once again. The lieutenant returned with a thick binder beneath his arm. It had to be the army register. He placed it in front of the colonel who wet his finger and leafed through the pages of the register. One of the majors got to his feet and stood looking over the colonel's shoulder.

They eventually found grandfather's name. There was an exchange of whispers and nodding. My information was found to be correct.

'Yes,' said the colonel. 'There's a Colonel Wade in the Ninth Manchester Regiment.'

'Grandfather was at Gallipoli, sir,' I added.

The colonel looked up and turned to the major. His gaze returned to me. 'You said he was a doctor?'

'His Christian name is Doctor, sir,' I replied.

'He was christened "Doctor"?'

'His father was a chemist, sir,' I explained. 'He wanted to do something to honour his best customers, the doctors. They were the people who kept him in business. That's why he christened his first child "Doctor".'

I could see one of the captains smiling. The story was so incredible it just had to be true. No German spy could get hold of that sort of information. They were beginning to believe my story. After all, it was true.

The colonel sighed and turned to the lieutenant who leaped from his chair. 'Fetch a chair for Mr Moe,' he said.

He had called me 'Mr'. It was all over. I had done it, they believed me. Now it was just the formalities.

I thanked the lieutenant and sat down. The questioning continued but the atmosphere had changed. I still answered their questions with 'sir' but the colonel had softened his tone. His attitude towards me changed as he listened to my honest answers. I was no longer a spy on trial but an important witness informing them of the situation in Oslo, the organisation of Abwehr, and our training in the techniques of sabotage and telegraphy. I kept my answers precise and to the point. I now had their undivided attention. Notes were made now and then; a few details which they could follow up or a point of information they could pass on to the Intelligence Service.

'Did you want to try and make contact with the Germans? The equipment's all there. It would just take a couple of minutes to set everything up. My colleague could help.'

The colonel dismissed the suggestion with a wave of his hand. 'That can wait,' he said.

The interrogation had come to a close. I still had so much to tell them but I realised that the jury's only task had been to establish my trustworthiness; was I a spy or not?

'You can leave now, Mr Moe,' said the colonel.

'Thank you, sir,' I said. I got to my feet, bowed and turned to leave the room, treading lightly towards the door.

My guard was there, waiting. He escorted me back to my room. I smiled at him but he did not return the gesture. It didn't matter, it was all over now.

I was locked in, a prisoner once again. The verdict was not yet a public one, but that was a mere formality. I had to wait another hour. I impatiently paced up and down the room, or sat waiting, on the bed, trying occasionally to look out of the window. And then, at last, the door opened and the guard took me back to the interview room. He opened the door for me and I entered the familiar room. The trial was over. The nine men had left the table; two of them stood in the middle of the room talking to Tor.

20

I rushed over to Tor and slapped him on the back. 'How did it go?' I asked. 'What did you say?'

'Not much,' replied Tor. 'You had obviously told them most of it. They just asked me some personal questions, which they will probably double-check with their agents in Oslo.'

They would have to verify our stories. Our addresses, the employers at the Post Office and at Abwehr, and details of my work at the salon and with the film crew. Everything could be checked. It was not over yet. We would have to wait till they were satisfied with our stories before we could start work. I had no doubt that they would find everything I had said to be true, so I had nothing to fear.

I had told them about my mother, where she lived, and also given the letter addressed to Trygve Lie to the colonel, which had clearly impressed him. They could easily verify my mother's friendship with the exiled Norwegian Foreign Minister.

'The colonel leading the interrogation was infuriating,' Tor said. '"Have you been to England before?" "No," I replied. "You must have been concerned with how you might cope with the language," he tells me. I told him that I wasn't worried but he kept on insisting until I finally lost my temper. I pulled out my passport and slammed it down on the table in front of him. "There's my passport, look at it for yourself, I'm not used to being called a liar."'

'Then what happened?' I asked.

'He softened his approach after that,' replied Tor.

One of the jury members, a major, approached us and

asked us to demonstrate the use of our radio equipment. We walked over to the fireplace and Tor began to point out a few of the details.

'How is the aerial set up?' asked the major.

We explained that it could be set up indoors. We could transmit from anywhere as long as the building itself was set on high ground. The antenna had to be set up at right angles to the receiving station. It was as simple as that. We showed him the batteries, explaining the different dials and Morse keys.

'Colonel Stephens was extremely concerned,' said the major.

'I simply tried to explain things as they were,' I said. 'I had no idea what it was all about to start off with.'

'I think it's safe for me to tell you that we were prepared to sentence you to death.'

'Death,' replied Tor. 'Just like that?'

'There is a war going on. You were dropped by the Germans. Everything was against you, all the evidence was there. In any other country you would have been shot without question.'

So, we had come that close to death. He was right, of course. The evidence lay there on the mantelpiece. A wave of horror shivered through me. The verdict had already been reached before I walked into the room to find our equipment lying there before me. They had intended that the hearing be short and formal. It had been that clear cut.

What would have become of us had I not been given the opportunity to tell them about grandfather?

The major left us. A group of civilians came into the room. They were dressed in sports clothes: plus-fours, checked socks and tweed jackets with leather trim. They came towards us and introduced themselves. They were most informal, introducing themselves by their Christian names: Charles, Jock and Bill. I tried hard to remember their names but I soon forgot who was who. I presumed that they all worked for Military Intelligence, and from the way they spoke to us I gathered that they would be taking responsibility for Tor and myself; for the time being we were regarded as trustworthy.

A small, bearded man made his way towards us. He spoke to us in Danish and we answered in Norwegian. Keeping to our native tongues we exchanged some small-talk about the weather. He then excused himself and moved across the room to one of the civilians with whom he exchanged a few words.

I then understood the purpose of his chat. He had been sent over to hear what we were saying to one another. None of the others spoke our language, so they couldn't tell if we were genuinely from Oslo or not. They obviously had no Norwegians in the service so a Dane had had to suffice. After all, he understood our language well enough.

The Dane kept nearby. He watched us closely and as soon as we were alone he returned to us. He said little but listened intently, obviously more interested in what Tor and I might say to each other. We might give ourselves away, slip up and say something to imply that we may have been deceiving them during the hearing. He was rather obvious in his intentions. It was not difficult to see what he was after. If indeed we had something to hide he would never have got it out of us.

'We were thinking of going to London,' said one of the men in tweed jackets. 'Is there anything you want to do? Anywhere in particular you would like to go?'

There wasn't, so we let them decide.

I felt a lot happier. At least we were not returning to our rooms. Perhaps they had even booked us into a hotel for the night?

We climbed into the two cars. The outing was to a small restaurant called L'Ecu de France, not far from Piccadilly Circus. We sat at a round table, the Dane between Tor and myself. It was a wonderful, extravagant meal: drinks and starters, steak, well done, and a good red wine followed by dessert and port, coffee, brandy and enormous cigars.

Nobody showed any special interest in us; we were neither asked what we had been doing nor how we had come to Scotland. I understood why. We were in a public place. The people at the next table would easily overhear any talk of Norway and Abwehr. Anyone observing us would assume that we were out for a good night and nothing more.

I wanted to talk of the future. When would we start working? When would we make contact with the Germans? We wanted to be useful. No one showed any interest in any of this, but they kept a close eye on us. If we went to the toilet, the Dane and one of the other men came with us. I couldn't have contacted anyone, or phoned, or even exchanged words with a stranger if I had wanted to. As soon as I said something in Norwegian, the Dane's ears pricked up. On several occasions he asked me to repeat what I had said. I had spoken too quickly for him.

Tor and I eventually gave up and turned to using English, thus rendering the Dane's presence unnecessary. The group acted perfectly normally but I could see that they were keeping a close watch, constantly. They filled our glasses, laughed and joked with us, but it always seemed that they were looking for a weak spot.

Charles seemed to show the most interest in us. Like the others he spoke with an Oxford accent. I sounded like a Lancashire yokel in comparison with him. MI5 clearly recruited from the universities. As we were preparing to leave, a drunk staggered towards me in the hall. It was perfectly innocent, he simply wanted a match. Charles and another colleague rushed forward and pushed him away, gave him a light and told him to leave.

At that point it all became perfectly clear to me. We were still prisoners. We were no longer confined to a prison cell but we were still not free.

We walked down to Piccadilly Circus in a tight-knit group, with Tor and myself in the very centre. The neon signs had been switched off and the street lamps offered no light. London was like a ghost town. The men in tweeds took us down to the Underground which had been transformed into an enormous shelter. Rows of people lined the platform trying to sleep, bundled up in scarves, woollen hats, blankets and sleeping bags.

London had been transformed. We had heard on the BBC that Londoners had been taking refuge in the Underground, but I had never imagined there would be so many of them. The platform was packed with people sleeping, playing cards, smoking and eating, mothers with small children, OAPs, office girls — people of every description had come down to seek refuge from the constant air raids.

A train thundered into the station. The sleeping lay undisturbed, as did the card players, but a small girl began to cry. We climbed on to the train, sitting ourselves at the front end of the carriage, surrounded by the men in tweeds. At Earls Court we stepped off and we were taken to a high-rise estate.

'We've arranged your lodgings here in Argyll Mansions for tonight,' said Charles pointing to one of the buildings.

We were spending the night with one of their colleagues who owned a flat where the occasional guest could stay overnight. He spoke with a slight accent, possibly Dutch or even Flemish. He had been forewarned and had brought out the whisky. After a couple of drinks, we were left alone with our new host.

Tor was given a bedroom to himself and I was shown to a sofa in the living-room where I found sheets and blankets. I was given a book and our host then retired for the night. He didn't lock us in but I presumed that the outside door was bolted and impossible to open from the inside. I made my bed, lay down and flicked through the pages. It was a German pornographic book. This was the first night I had spent in London for one and a half years, and I was under guard; it was clearly not a prison, but we were under constant surveillance. My reading material was an obscure German book, probably another example of the English sense of humour. Or did they want to see if I could cope with the language, no matter the context? In the morning our host made us breakfast: toast, egg, bacon and orange juice. We said little over breakfast, and I later buried my head in the newspapers. The Germans were invading the Balkan Peninsula, Yugoslavia was about to fall into their hands, and Greece had all but fallen. The only glimmer of hope was that the British had seized Addis Ababa and driven out the Italians. We had nothing to fear from the Italians. Nazi Germany was the real enemy. Perhaps the attack on the Balkan Peninsula would ease the pressure on Britain.

I studied the advertisements: spring fashions were the same as they had been a year before, and the RAF were seeking volunteers. Colgate had released a new shaving foam which did away with the need for a shaving brush.

The doorbell rang and a uniformed major was shown in. He was attached to the Armoured Division and told us that he had come for information about the Norway occupation. He opened his briefcase and pulled out a pile of photographs and sketches.

This was not my department. I knew nothing about tanks. However, Tor knew a bit about them and recalled what he had seen in Oslo, pointing out those tanks which he knew to be in use.

We were later collected by one of the men we had dined with the night before. Jock was short, with a small moustache. We were taken in a large Citroën to a London office where two more of our friends were waiting, Charles, and the tall, thin man called Bill. The room had been set up for a film projection. I had given my rolls of film to Major Perfect in Banff. They had obviously been sent down to London for developing. We would be needed to describe the photographs.

The results were good. It was an 8mm film, and although the quality was not of the highest, the film had been given just the right exposure and the figures were clear and distinct. I pointed out our Abwehr colleagues, Müller, Andersen and Korsewitz. Charles made a note of their names. Bill showed some interest in a warship docked in the harbour and which appeared on several occasions. He wanted to know when I had taken the film and how long the ship had remained in Oslo. We couldn't help him. I couldn't remember, but we had at least done something useful. The men of the German Intelligence Service in Oslo would now be easily identified.

We returned to Argyll Mansions where the 'interrogation' continued. A stream of uniformed and civilian men came to visit us, posing all sorts of different questions which we duly answered. They were most inquisitive, each one a specialist. They requested details of the equipment used by the Germans, the system of rationing, the electricity supply, and so on. The questions went on, day after day, from early morning till late at night. We grew exhausted with the routine, and I could see that Tor was becoming more and more irritable. We had not come all the way to London simply to answer these endless questions. We wanted to do something. We were skilled and wanted to be used. We were opening up new horizons for them and they really ought to take advantage of it.

I had difficulty sleeping. I lay awake every night, waiting for the sirens, listening for the drone of the bombers, the explosions, anti-aircraft fire and the inevitable fire-engines. I felt helpless and claustrophobic, in fear of my life. Each night I was gripped by sheer terror, until I eventually fell asleep out of sheer exhaustion. In the morning I would stagger out of bed, covered in sweat, with dark rings circling my eyes, and struggle to the breakfast table. I had no inclination to join in the early morning conversation.

Charles tried hard to keep up my spirits, without success, and it was perhaps partly due to my fear of the raids that we moved after just one week.

One morning we loaded our luggage into Jock's Citroën and drove to Hendon in the north-west, far from the city centre. Jock turned the car into a small street, Crespigny Road, and we drew up outside a house of dark red brick. Two people came out to take care of our luggage. One of them, Andrew Corcoran, was a Scot, the other introduced himself as Philip Rea. Both were sergeants in the Intelligence Corps, although you couldn't tell from their dress.

'You'll be staying here from now on,' said Charles. 'I hope you find everything is OK.'

Our new home was built on two floors: three rooms on the ground floor and three upstairs; a kitchen, bathroom and a small garden round the back of the house. The furniture was plain, probably supplied by the army. There was a very military-like iron bed in my room, and even the pillowcases and blankets bore the army stamp.

Charles gave us our instructions. In all, four men had been given orders to keep an eye on us and accompany us should we wish to take a walk to get a newspaper or go for a drink at the local pub. Our arrival in Britain had been somewhat unorthodox and these were just a few necessary precautions which had to be followed for the time being.

We were also informed that we would have to obey the night curfew. We had Norwegian passports and would therefore have to act as other foreigners were having to. This meant leaving the pub no later than 10 p.m. This was all related to us in a very cheerful and polite manner, and it was not until Charles and Jock had left that the full implications really struck us. We were not to be left alone. Someone would always be with us, to escort us or keep watch. We couldn't even take a walk along the quiet suburban streets of our new home without somebody breathing down our necks.

21

At least in Hendon there was less risk of bombing. There were no heavy industries or docks or other strategic landmarks to interest the German Luftwaffe. The air-raid sirens did sound from time to time, but we rarely heard the hum of German planes. Hendon was certainly a lot safer than Earls Court.

At Argyll Mansions we had told our hosts all we knew about the German occupation forces in Oslo. Now it was the turn of the Intelligence Service, who concentrated on our relationship with the men from Abwehr and were extremely interested in hearing precisely what the Germans had planned for us. Someone from Intelligence came to visit every day and we would usually have lunch together in the pub. However, we were taken by Jock on two occasions to a central London office for questioning.

But prisoners we remained. We couldn't even step outside without being accompanied by Andrew, Philip, or one of the other pair who had been drafted in as reserves. They were there, whether we were shopping or simply taking a walk.

On Sunday morning, Andrew and I would walk down to Mrs Cohen's shop, a few streets away, to buy the newspapers. We spent the evenings down at the local pub, and apart from our visits here, and the occasional short walk, we had nothing else to do. I spent most of my time reading. Most mornings I would plough through a couple of papers, and on Sundays I would manage at least half a dozen. Our idleness made us nervous. Tor was the more visibly frustrated and often lost his temper with our 'hosts', accusing them of frustrating our willingness to do something constructive. 'I came to England to join the fight,' he screamed. 'Haven't you got anything for us to do? I have to join the Norwegian troops. I've got to do something.'

We tried our best to calm him. Deep down I felt as angry as he did, but all I could do was conceal my feelings. Perhaps I was a better actor than Tor?

The headquarters of MI5 were situated in a complex near Regent Street. We were usually taken there by either Jock or Charles, whose surnames were Horsefall and Cholmondely respectively, as we were to discover later. The entrance to the building was quite ordinary, with a small nameplate revealing the occupiers to be an export company.

We were met by a doorman who was clearly responsible for allowing entry only to those with the correct passes. A secretary sat in the entrance room, a tall, authoritative lady with long blonde hair. Her name was Mrs Brander but everyone called her Mrs B. She knew everyone and everything, and we turned to her if we ever needed to leave a message or ask about anything. It didn't take long for us to learn her number off by heart, Regent 6050.

We were always taken to an inner office for the clandestine meetings. Every day it was a different subject, but we soon noticed that the same old questions about our work kept recurring. Sometimes they phrased their questions as they had the previous day, at other times they tried from a different angle. We were still being tested. They continued to investigate our background, our training, Abwehr, everything. 'Try to remember' was a standing phrase of theirs.

After a couple of days we discovered that we were with MI5 and were now considered as part of their B division. The wheels were beginning to turn. A case officer was assigned to us. He would guide and advise us. We could only act with his permission. No specific messages were to be relayed to the Germans, nor could we answer any of

Abwehr's questions once we had established radio contact. The heads of MI5 had clearly decided to make use of us, but they didn't know precisely how.

If we were to succeed, everything would have to be meticulously planned. That much we did understand. If the Germans realised what we were really doing, all would be lost.

We sometimes felt as if we had already played our part. We had achieved the goal we set ourselves in Oslo. No longer free, we could not act on our own initiative, but were MI5's puppets. They pulled the strings and we danced. It was perhaps easier for me to accept — after all, I belonged in England. If anything went wrong, I could always retreat to my grandparents. Tor, on the other hand, had left both Norway and Gerd behind him in order to continue his fight. Neither of us could return. We had taken a positive step forward, there was no looking back, but for Tor England was still a foreign country.

Our case officer was introduced to us at Regent Street; he was about thirty years old, and clearly felt we would be working closely together in the future. Christopher Harmer was a lawyer and came from the same university circles as the other men who now worked for MI5. He was present for the remainder of our meetings and gradually got to know the details of our background.

Apart from that, little else happened during those first weeks at Crespigny Road. We remained under guard. Andrew and Philip escorted us everywhere, and Christopher occasionally joined us for lunch. The days passed. Our evenings were spent in the pub. An old pianist played music hall songs at an off-key piano as people sang along, laughing and swinging their pint glasses in time to the music. Blankets of smoke lay thick in the bar, and the waitresses weaved between the tables and chairs with their trays stacked with glasses. Andrew and Philip sat beside us and joined in with the happy atmosphere. They must have missed their families, even during the friendly evenings we spent in the pub. They did their best to relax and enjoy themselves, even though they were still on duty.

Things were not always easy. We were to speak to no one in the pub and the most innocent of contact was simply not permitted. Despite this we were expected to act naturally and reply to those who passed the occasional remarks to us. We didn't want to draw too much attention to ourselves. It was extremely difficult to create the right balance. We occasionally chatted to some of the girls who obviously missed male company with so many of them being called up for military service. But we weren't allowed to walk them home. We were told politely to decline any invitations to do so, but to arouse no suspicion.

On the second Sunday of our new imprisonment we went to Hampstead Heath and visited the famous pub the Bull and Bush. Here a new man appeared on the scene. He called himself Dick Townsend, but I was sure that was not his real name. He appeared very sure of himself, more domineering and less sympathetic than the others. We never discovered his actual role in the whole affair. Perhaps he was a doctor or psychologist. He certainly seemed to spend a lot of time probing and testing us.

The pub was packed with drinkers and I found myself face to face with a situation which would continue to haunt me. While we were standing at the bar, a hand clapped me solidly on the shoulder. I turned round to see an elderly gentleman with a large red nose and droopy moustache. 'On leave, I suppose, eh?' he asked.

I was lost for words. If I replied that I was, he would probably ask which regiment; if I said 'no', why wasn't I in uniform? Dick Townsend came to the rescue. 'We're with the Ministry of Information,' he said as he took me firmly by the arm.

Even civilian clothes drew people's attention. The country was at war, and any male civilian naturally provoked curiosity. The question might have been a perfectly innocent one but what he really wanted to know was why I was not in uniform. Dick suggested that, if asked, we reply that we worked for the Ministry of Information, reading foreign newspapers, preparing news reports. We spoke several languages and had been especially chosen for this highly specialised work for the war effort. It would satisfy most curiosities.

Dick Townsend spent several days with us, letting us do all the talking, with just the odd question. He seemed to be testing our potential — whether we were capable of playing the game. It was obviously important to assess our powers of observation. He might ask, 'Did you see that building back there?' Personally, I had seen nothing. I realised I was not particularly observant, and he obviously didn't hold out much hope for my level of intelligence — at least not in this respect. Tor, on the other hand, never missed a thing. He was accustomed to keeping his eyes peeled, perhaps because of his military background.

We had no suitable clothing with us for our stay in London. Our Norwegian military ski-suits were far from practical in London's spring weather, and my double-breasted suit was a bit exclusive. Dick Townsend took us to an Army and Navy store where we kitted ourselves out with some casual clothes: shirts, trousers, jackets, shoes. MI5 saw to the bill. Dick was quite generous. We chose what we wanted and he paid without hesitation.

On one occasion Dick and Tor went off by themselves. When he returned Tor was clearly agitated. 'He's mad. He still doesn't trust us,' exclaimed Tor.

They had gone for a walk on Hampstead Heath and decided to take a rest. The place was deserted. Townsend made sure that nobody was around and drew a revolver from his pocket.

'He just handed it to me,' said Tor.

'Why?' I asked.

'Just to see how I'd react. I could easily have shot him and escaped. He obviously thought it would be a good test for me.'

'What did you do?'

'I lost my temper,' replied Tor. 'I threw the revolver back at him and walked off. What a bastard!'

We told Christopher. Tor wondered how much longer this mistrust would continue, and how many more idiots he would have to deal with. If there were more, couldn't they be given something better to do? He hadn't come this far to be humiliated.

Dick Townsend was assigned to a different task. We never saw him again.

Our next door neighbour at Crespigny Road was Edward Poulton. Christopher introduced us to him, his wife Muriel and their son Jimmy. Edward, or Ted as we called him, was a radio expert with MI5. I realised why we had been moved there. Ted would be supervising all radio contact with the Germans. It was sensible to keep us nearby. However, it had not yet been decided when we would transmit for the first time. They still did not trust us entirely. I had perhaps managed to convince them more than Tor. With a British background, and being several years younger, I was perhaps a bit more innocent.

One evening Philip Rea took Tor on a pub crawl. They visited about half a dozen pubs, Tor told me the following day. From the very start he knew that it was no ordinary night out, not simply a friendly gesture on Philip's part. Philip had clearly intended to get Tor drunk, to see if he might crack. He needed to find out for himself. Yet another test. To see if Tor would betray himself under the influence of alcohol. In the end it was Tor who had to take charge of Philip. It was Philip who had got hopelessly drunk and even began talking of his past exploits with MI5. Tor managed to get him into a taxi and bring him home before the curfew. Philip looked extremely pale the following morning. He would be even paler when giving his report to Christopher.

Towards the end of the week Jock drove us back to Regent Street. We climbed the steps to be welcomed by Mrs B and Christopher. He never made mention of the episode with Philip, it had all been forgotten and hadn't damaged Tor's reputation anyway. 'You've been making life very difficult for the poor coastguard up in Scotland,' he said smiling.

We looked at him, puzzled.

'We followed up your story about the dinghy and your landing,' he continued. 'You had mentioned that Tor was signalling while you were coming in to land. The coastguard in command said that he was fully manned that night and they hadn't spotted a thing. So we naturally had our doubts.'

'I was signalling the whole time,' said Tor.

'I know,' said Christopher. 'It's been confirmed. Two bakers on their way to work spotted your signals. They thought the coastguard was probably on manoeuvres, and didn't report it. The coastguard in charge was sacked for the incompetence of his men.'

So, they had checked every detail. MI5 had to be one hundred per cent certain of us. Thank God for those two bakers.

Then Christopher grew more serious. 'There's something else,' he continued. 'You won't be too pleased. It may mean nothing, but the powers that be have decided that under no circumstances are you to make contact with the Germans.'

22

So it had all been in vain. All our hard work in Oslo, the training with Abwehr and all the risks we had taken. They had no use for us.

We were driven back to Hendon, silent in the rear of the car. I felt totally powerless. There was nothing we could do, not by ourselves. We had lost everything, our whole sense of purpose. I had tried to accept everything up until now. I felt sure that they would arrange something eventually. Christopher and the others must have known how we would react. That was probably why they allowed me to phone grandfather. I still hadn't made contact with my relatives in Manchester. At least I had done as I was told, in that respect, even though I had had every opportunity to phone. Now that they had given their permission it no longer seemed so urgent. On our arrival I had been desperate to contact him, as I was so uncertain about being accepted.

I phoned anyway. He was clearly pleased to hear from me. I told him that I had escaped from Norway in a fishing boat and was now working for the Ministry of Information. Dick had given us this cover story. Christopher had suggested that I use it to explain things to grandfather and my other relatives. It was best to stick to the one story. Despite being allowed to speak to grandfather, I felt bitterly disappointed. The reason for their decision was not for us to know. Christopher simply told us that the decision had been made. He either could not, or would not, say any more.

A few more boring days passed by, and Christopher paid us a visit. He said very little, especially when we asked what would happen.

'I want to join the Norwegian troops,' said Tor. 'Sitting here is a total waste of time.'

'I'm afraid that's not possible,' replied Christopher.

'Of course I can. I've already done my training. I was a sergeant. I want to fight for my country. I'm needed, damn it!'

'You've already seen too much,' Christopher explained.

'I didn't ask to see anything.'

'In the troops you could end up almost anywhere,' Christopher replied quietly. 'You might be taken as a prisoner-of-war and questioned.'

'I wouldn't say anything,' pleaded Tor.

Christopher shook his head. It slowly dawned that Tor would never be allowed to join the army during the war. That path was now firmly closed to him. He knew too much about MI5. They couldn't risk it. Even so, neither of us really knew very much in detail. No more than a few names and the address of their office in Regent Street. We had been told no more than was necessary to answer their questions. Now even that was more than enough.

I was not interested in joining the military. I hadn't done my military service. I couldn't even hold a pistol correctly, though the Germans had supplied me with one. There had to be something I could do. Perhaps I should try to get in touch with Trygve Lie. He must have received the letter from mother; that is if MI5 had actually sent it on.

I asked Christopher. He confirmed that the letter had indeed been delivered and that the exiled Minister remembered me, and knew why I was here. 'I talked to Mr Lie about you,' he said. 'If we can't find you something he'll see to it that you get a job at a consulate or in the Ministry. He'll take care of you, if necessary.'

I felt slightly better, certainly, but I was not especially happy with the solution. I hadn't come all this way to be packed off to a Norwegian Consulate. They ought at least to give me a chance to do something more constructive. However, MI5 were still undecided and Trygve Lie was not mentioned again.

One Saturday evening Christopher arrived at Crespigny Road. By this time we had spent several weeks with MI5. He asked to speak to me alone. 'Could I have your Norwegian passport?' he asked. I duly fetched it and gave it to him. 'You won't be needing it any longer. You're now a British citizen.'

He handed me an identity card in the name of Helge John Neal Moe. We had discussed the possibility before. By law, I was entitled to British citizenship as I had been born in London. That right had remained until I reached the age of twenty-one. I was twenty-two now and hadn't even requested British citizenship, but MI5 had considerable contacts and the authorities had turned a blind eye to my age.

'This is your other identity card,' Christopher told me.

The second card was written in the name of John Mooney. 'Why two?' I asked.

'Just a precaution,' came the reply.

'Which do I use?'

'That's up to you. If you know the person, then you obviously use the proper name, otherwise you show the second one. It might be best if your real name is not made too public.'

I could see the sense in that. At least he trusted my own judgement.

'You won't be restricted by the curfew any longer. And you won't be needing an escort either.'

At last, the gates had opened. I was so relieved and delighted. Although I hadn't exactly been treated as a prisoner-of-war, the psychological stress I had experienced over the past weeks had been extremely arduous. I was free at last of my minders.

'What about Tor?' I asked.

'I'm sorry, but he's a Norwegian citizen. I'm afraid my hands are tied. He'll have to stick to the usual routine.'

Tor seemed to understand the logic and accepted that I had the right to British citizenship and that he, quite simply, didn't. However, our positions had changed. Tor knew that and he was naturally upset. It was for his sake that I didn't immediately take advantage of my newly found freedom. I waited until Sunday morning.

'I'm just going to fetch the papers,' I said to Andrew.

'OK,' he replied. 'But don't expect me to come along.'

I walked out on to the doorstep and stood a while to take advantage of the warm spring air. I spotted some kids playing football against a brick wall. Striding across the road towards them, I took the ball at my feet, a skilful dribble, and then, a goal. It was a good shot too. Then I continued towards the shop, running, enjoying my freedom. I could do what I liked now. I fetched the papers from Mrs Cohen's.

'Is anything the matter?' she asked.

'It's spring,' I explained, tucking the bundle under my arm.

'It's taken a while for you to notice.'

'As far as I'm concerned, spring started just today.'

'I see,' said Mrs Cohen, and she gave me a knowing smile.

'What's that?' I asked.

'It's a girl, isn't it? I can see you're in love.'

'Maybe,' I said and skipped out of the shop. I walked back very slowly, smiling happily at the passers-by. Everybody looked so different, changed. I wanted to stop them all and tell them what had happened to me. Shout my freedom out loud; I could go anywhere, any time, wherever I chose, and alone. I felt so elated.

I tempered my enthusiasm upon my return to Crespigny Road. Tor looked sullen and impatient. I handed some of the papers to him and we read in silence.

Christopher had recognised the injustice of Tor's predicament. So, by Monday, Tor was allowed his freedom too, even if he still had to abide by the curfew. We decided to celebrate together and that evening we went to the Brent Bridge Hotel for a night out. It was not far from the Underground station at Brent Bridge. By the time we arrived the pavilion-like building was packed with people.

We were fortunate to find a table at the farthest corner from the orchestra. We asked some girls for a dance and they later joined us at our table.

Claire and Joan didn't spend all that much time with us. Tor had to return before the curfew and I went with him. The girls looked puzzled, so I explained that we were on a night-shift. They obviously didn't believe us, but Tor said that he was a foreigner and was working with me at the Ministry of Information. He had to return before the curfew. They could accept that story, so we agreed to meet again. We took the Underground back to Hendon and arrived at Crespigny Road with just a few minutes to spare.

Despite our more trusted positions, the questioning continued and Christopher visited us every day. It was a few days later that he informed us that it was still in the balance whether to allow our proposed 'scheme' to go ahead or not. Tor and I had already been cleared and the military had also shown some interest, but would the Germans fall for it? That was the million dollar question. It was a move in the right direction and a long-awaited morale boost.

Occasionally we visited the Poultons next door. Ted's wife Muriel was a journalist, and we seemed to get on very well. Ted himself was more difficult to get to know. He was a small, stocky man, quite quiet, but with a biting, sarcastic humour. I didn't get along with him too well and he positively irritated Tor. But we were in no position to show our feelings of discomfort. Poulton was the communications expert and we could be working with him a great deal. That is if everything went ahead.

'The real problem is establishing exactly how much information you could lay your hands on, if you were genuine German agents,' Christopher continued. 'We'll need some sort of cover story to explain where you've been, how you've kept a low profile, and so on. We have to wait for the go-ahead of course.'

We discussed it all in detail. I felt sure that MI5 had already thought of this, but we discussed it all the same. It made us feel as though we were getting somewhere. We brought up a few intelligent points which they noted down.

Christopher, in fact, filled in the gaps for us. We had managed to land safely, without arousing suspicion, sunk the dinghy and then hid the radio in a safe place. We then made our way to Aberdeen on the bikes. It went without saying that we had met crowds of refugees along the road, which had provided us with good cover. Abwehr were bound to fall for that as German propaganda made a point of emphasising it. After that I had travelled to Manchester and stayed with my grandparents for a week. I then returned to Scotland for the radio, which I found intact and fully functional. We were now in London, had rented a room and were looking for work. There had been no problem so far with the papers they had supplied.

To help pass the time, we pieced the sections of our cover story into imaginary reports that we put into code and sent to each other in Morse. It kept us busy for a few days and, besides, it helped us prepare for the real thing.

During this time Ted Poulton popped round to see us. Usually we only met at a meal time; lunch or dinner. But we were pleased to see him all the same. 'We'll give it a try tonight,' he said. 'The first report. Christopher telephoned and told me to ask you if you could put together a suitable report and then translate it into German.'

'At last,' laughed Tor. It was he who would send this, our first message, but we formulated and coded the report together. We prepared it all thoroughly and knew the routine off by heart. We worked and soon arrived at the finished report, translated into German.

Christopher did not arrive until late afternoon and we all moved into the Poultons' back garden to check the antenna which had been set up between two trees. The garden was already heavy in its summer foliage, which helped conceal the equipment. It was a perfect transmitting point.

Christopher checked over our text and decided to change a couple of details to help compact the information. Then we coded it. We ate dinner with the Poultons and then sat waiting impatiently for midnight.

Would we get through? Would they reply? Then, of course, would they believe us? It would be a crucial turning point of our mission. Everything hung on this one transmission.

A newspaper which Christopher had brought with him lay in front of me, so I picked it up and started leafing through it. I hadn't had a chance to up until now. A map of Europe covered half of the front page, from Hammerfest in the north to the Mediterranean. On top of the map stalked a terrifying messenger of death, scattering seeds that sprouted up like Nazi swastikas across the land. The dark symbols lay thick like a blanket of choking weeds. That was the current position on 16 June 1941. I recalled Abwehr and their talk of the low British morale and the panic caused by the mighty Luftwaffe. Here I was with just one of a million copies of this horrific statement of truth — the German war machine steamrolling its way through Europe.

Photographs inside the paper depicted the bomb craters and the aftermath of derelict, gutted buildings which followed the night's downpour of explosives and incendiary bombs. But there was no sign of panic. We had passed by scenes of devastation in London and had seen with our own eyes the boarded windows, and the shop signs 'Open For Business' and 'Still Going Strong'. The familiar V-sign covered the streets, 'V for Victory' — it had now gained the same symbolic meaning as the cross once had for the persecuted Christians.

The British were well aware of their position but it seemed simply to strengthen their resolve and their resistance. German bomber raids were not having the desired effect, and merely proved to show that the civilians on the Home Front were equally as brave and tenacious as the soldiers in the field. I was convinced that the Germans would never win the war. The question was, how would we defeat them?

23

Ted had set up the radio itself in the living-room, on a roll-top desk by the window overlooking the garden. In case of unexpected callers the top could be pulled down to conceal the set and our ciphering paraphernalia from inquisitive eyes. The cable to the antenna had been passed beneath a heavy curtain at the window. The curtains at the other side of the room had been drawn and would also help muffle the sound of the Morse keys. We repeated the message to Christopher in a test run and Tor practised his Morse. His first job would be to pass a brief message of our safe arrival and the hiding of our equipment. It would be important to mention the thousands of refugees who had delayed our collecting the equipment by a couple of weeks. We had first reported ourselves as refugees and were now in London in search of work.

The allotted hour arrived and Ted switched on the equipment. Tor, meanwhile, checked the batteries, giving Ted the time to put on his earphones so that he might follow the transmission. He gave Tor the signal to begin transmitting and the keys tapped nervously. After the call sign had been sent a few times, he paused and we waited in absolute silence.

Ted turned the receiver dial to the stipulated frequency which we had committed to memory. In the meantime Tor repeated the call again and again. Would they pick it up? The loudspeakers remained silent. If the Germans had received it they would have replied immediately. But there was no sign of their acknowledgement, code lettered SOW. There was nothing; nothing but the persistent crackle of the speakers.

'Perhaps they're not on the same frequency?' Tor whispered as he continued calling. 'They're probably not expecting us.'

While Tor kept tapping the keys, Ted fingered the dial delicately. And then, out of the blue, the receiver crackled into life and the acknowledgement came loudly over the speakers, so loud that Ted lowered the volume control. Klingenbergsgaten had received us at last. We listened carefully and jotted down the message — QSA4 — reception was loud and clear — GA! — Go ahead!

Tor began our initial report with CT139, the number representing the number of signals within the report. Somehow Tor was to try to relay a sense of nervousness. After all it was our first attempt. The message had to incorporate the fear of discovery, as if pausing for breath and then continuing at a fast, more panic-stricken rate. However, Tor had no need to play-act — he was nervous as it was. He fumbled through to the end of the report, finishing it with 'SK' and a final 'K' for 'Come'. We waited, but the reply was slow in coming.

'They probably have a pre-coded message waiting for us,' Ted suggested, 'but they will want to decipher ours before sending theirs.'

He was right. It didn't take long before their response could be heard.

We replied with our own code and then received the message CT176, the number of signals they were to transmit. Next came the code to tell us which of the crosswords to use in decoding, and at which point to begin. And then came the message. All three of us followed the short bursts, scribbling frantically. I was conscious of the beads of sweat forming on my forehead as I jotted down letter after letter. I caught Christopher's eye briefly and saw the happiness which, indeed, we all felt at this moment, even before we had decoded the message. It was soon all over. The room fell silent and we leaped into the air. The tense atmosphere was broken by an overwhelming sense of relief and joy.

Christopher was the first to settle. 'Let's take a look at the key,' he said. 'Let's hope we really do have something to shout about.'

Tor found the reference and together we started to decode our first message. It was very general and, as Ted had suggested, they had obviously prepared it well in advance. They were pleased that all had gone well and asked where we were living, what we were doing, and when might we be ready to start work. They also said that they would reply to our message the following evening.

I felt slightly disappointed, but it was all we could expect under the circumstances. They were hardly ready to send us on a mission on our initial contact. It was necessarily an ordinary, general reply. They understood that we would need to settle and find a convenient base for operations. It could take us some time and there was no particular hurry. But we were impatient. I suggested that we respond immediately to say that we were well prepared and awaiting orders.

Christopher smiled at my enthusiasm. 'I think that's enough for today,' he replied. 'We'll have to sit down and analyse our position carefully before we go any further. We have to be sure that Abwehr are convinced, first and foremost. I expect that they will want to be sure that you have arrived in London without any problems. You are probably the first to do so.'

'First?' I was surprised.

'Yes, the first from Norway. I'm afraid your predecessors did not fare as well. I can tell you no more than that. You told us yourselves that your mission was codenamed "Hummer Nord III".'

Christopher did not elaborate, but it was food for thought. Tor and I realised that we were by no means unique. We were the third in line, and the former two had clearly failed to meet their objectives. But what exactly had he meant? Had they been genuine spies? Were we the first to offer our services as double agents? The first to betray Abwehr?

My question remained unanswered. I was a small cog in a very large wheel, and whatever happened we would not be trusted with the information. Once again I felt like a small puppet in the hands of a giant organisation. We had played our part. Abwehr trusted us; we had convinced the British of our loyalty to the Allies. We were accepted. However, we were not our own masters. MI5 were pulling the strings — our hands were tied. We were forced to dance to their tune — and only occasionally allowed to make our own decisions; where it didn't really matter. That was how it was to be. I realised that we would never fully understand the rules of the game, we were simply pawns on a giant chessboard. It was the only feasible way. As long as Abwehr had confidence in us, we could work for the Allies; they were calling all the shots.

It was perhaps for that reason that I felt less happy than I might have been, having successfully made contact. Perhaps I'd feel better once we really started work. What did it matter? There was a war and we had a job to do.

Christopher left and Tor and I went next door to our new home. We had little to say to each other, but I felt sure that Tor felt the same way. At last we had something to feel pleased about, our first aim had been achieved. There was no alternative but to carry on. MI5 decided against sending another message the following evening as it might arouse suspicion. It would be most unlikely as far as the Germans were concerned. Instead we would await further information from Abwehr. Christopher was certain they would reply to our report. He was right. It didn't take long before the loudspeaker sparked into life once again. We duly recorded the message but did acknowledge receipt.

It was not what we had expected. They were interested in the quality of our transmission. Our report had been received QSA4, which indicated that reception had been almost perfect, the peak of the scale being QSA5. We had a problem. Ted had done too good a job, not the sort of quality you might expect from a couple of inexperienced amateurs. The Germans were curious as to which antenna we had used, how we had set it up and where. Although they congratulated us on the quality we realised that they had been somewhat surprised and even, perhaps, slightly suspicious.

A few days later Christopher returned to tell us we were to contact Oslo. In response to their last message we had used our own antenna, transmitting from a wooden-built house perched on a hill. We had rented a flat and the landlady was hard of hearing. It was an attic flat, cut off from the rest of the house. She had few friends, so there was no risk of unwelcome guests. The spot was ideal and the transmission was therefore excellent. We tightened up the content, leaving the bare essentials; flat with deaf widow, wooden house on hill, no visitors, etc.

Christopher seemed happy and left it to us to formulate the coded translation. It had to sound genuine, so we tried hard to put ourselves in that particular, albeit hypothetical, situation and then go on from there.

'We'd better ask for money,' I said.

'Why?' asked Christopher.

'Our initial supply would have run out by now. We need it for a few essentials — curtains, and we've been asked for double rent as there are two of us.'

'Curtains?'

'Well, to seal the windows and avoid being spotted at the transmitter. And we need a radio to muffle the sound of the transmitter.'

Christopher paused, then nodded his agreement. So we would tell them that we were desperate for money and that unless we got it we would soon be unable to continue with our work. This time the Germans responded immediately. Tor tapped out our message and we awaited their reply. They congratulated us on our work with the antenna once again and sent their best wishes. We were to take no risks and to avoid long messages in order to evade detection. They also requested information about morale in the capital, the success of the night raids, and how the overall spirit of resistance was. They requested a short *Stimmungsbericht*.

A week later we sent back a report which Christopher delivered to us. Resistance was still strong but not unscathed. Raids were of some effect, but the British people were a tough race. That evening we commenced the transmission to Klingenbergsgaten, it being my turn to operate the key. The same routine continued for some weeks, perhaps once or twice in any one week. For the most part I left Tor to the job of communicating our messages. Everything that was ever sent had been carefully prepared by MI5. Christopher delivered the text and we dealt with the rest — translation, coding and transmitting. To begin with, Christopher would ask us to decipher our messages before transmitting just to check that no mistakes had been made.

Abwehr had instructed us to include the codename 'Henry' in all our messages, if all was well. If something was wrong we were to leave it out and they would know that we had been captured and were relaying messages by order of the Secret Service. It was simply a safety precaution and it was up to us to ensure that we never forgot. Our objective during this period was to gain the trust of our contacts and simply establish mutual confidence. Their response was a favourable one.

Our first tasks were basically simple. We were to report the effect of certain air raids, possibly as a test. As they could obtain the information from aerial photographs we always had to keep close to the truth. Perhaps several rows of terraced houses had been destroyed, with many killed, and the remains still smouldering.

Slowly we tried to build up a rapport with our contacts. They were no fools. We had to do precisely as they asked. Occasionally we would halt transmission, as if we had been cut off suddenly. Tor would simply stop relaying our message and only after a few days would we continue, saying that we had been disturbed and had not dared go on.

One thing was certain: we couldn't carry on using the Poultons' house as a base for too long. They would certainly grow suspicious. We presumed that the Germans had long since located our position and knew we were somewhere in North London. And if the Germans had done so, then the British were bound to have done the same. The Germans would know that any unusual transmissions would be picked up by keen radio amateurs and relayed to the authorities. The question that would be on their minds was why the English had not managed to locate us. For this reason MI5 constructed another cover story. We had now been allowed to register as Norwegian refugees and, after a thorough investigation, I had enrolled with the Norwegian troops. Following two weeks basic training, I had been transferred to the Intelligence Corps and been sent north to Scotland. Tor, meanwhile, had been made a translator to help with the registering of Norwegian refugees.

Abwehr's reaction was extremely positive. They were delighted with the progress we had made in infiltrating sensitive areas. They had swallowed the bait. There would be no problem now in making our transmissions less frequent; we could move our location and therefore also see plenty of the country with whom they were at war.

Tor and I were proud of our success with both the Germans and with MI5. They had complete faith in us and, even if Tor still had to respect the curfew, at least we were no longer under constant observation. But there didn't seem to be enough to do. We were solely occupied with the messages which Christopher passed on to us, perhaps once or twice a week. In all, it could only be a couple of hours' work. We had so much spare time on our hands that frustration began to set in again.

The days were long. We slept late, eventually dragging ourselves out of bed for a late breakfast before reading the papers. Lunch was spent in the pub with either Andrew or Charles and on the odd occasion we would be visited by a general staff officer, perhaps curious to get to know us better. Was the War Office going to accept our offer to help deceive Adolf Hitler? In the afternoons I would try to read. Muriel took me to Hendon Central Library and introduced me to contemporary English and American literature. I ploughed my way through some of the better-known works and we had the occasional evening chat together to discuss the finer points.

At times our existence felt all too insignificant. With the war at its height and Norway still under occupation, we felt we weren't doing enough. MI5 were practically in a position to take over the operation. Tege and Ja had been well established and we were no longer necessary.

The frustration and boredom grew worse. When would it all end? Trying to fill the days was becoming increasingly difficult. MI5 supplied us with everything — roof over our heads, clothing, food and money; not a great deal of money but we were never left wanting. Tor suffered most during this period of inactivity. He desperately wanted to enlist but knew that any attempt would be frustrated. His temper often got the better of him and he snapped bitterly at our colleagues. He told them that he had had enough. If all he could do was operate a radio once a week, he wanted out. The more the monotony of the routine settled into our work, the worse the atmosphere became. Christopher did all he could to help, testing our reflexes, going through our messages with a fine tooth comb. He would describe hypothetical situations and ask us to go over them with him. What would we do in such and such an event, how would we react, what might we request from the Germans? We had the occasional lengthy discussion, during which points were noted and ideas swapped, but it wasn't really up to us to decide anything. The decisions were made higher up the ladder.

So it was good news for all of us when we were told that Tor would be spending a couple of weeks with Andrew at his home in Carlisle. In the meantime I would take charge of the transmissions, perhaps from another location this time.

24

Tor and Andrew travelled north, leaving me to occupy myself as best I could. I paid a visit to Mrs Cohen's every day and chatted to the young girl who worked for her. She was constantly moaning about her poor wages, so I would collect the papers and return home, leaving her to get on with it. Lunchtimes were spent in the pub; a quick drink, some soup and a couple of fresh rolls would keep me going till dinner time. Occasionally I was invited to join in a game of darts with some of the other locals but I'm afraid I was never particularly good.

By this time Crespigny Road was beginning to feel like home. Every day I would listen to the BBC news broadcasts, following them in every language; first, English, followed by German, French, Norwegian, Danish, Czech and Polish. I thought it might keep my mind occupied to take the opportunity of learning Czech and Polish, so I continued listening to the broadcasts for several months. I managed to pick up quite a lot and although I could never say that I had mastered the two languages, I enjoyed the mental stimulus, and besides, it helped pass the hours.

It was around this time that the builders arrived at the Poultons' house. They tore out some cupboards downstairs, knocked through a wall and began to construct a shelter of thick metal plate. A heavy steel door was set into the metalwork and the room fitted with air ducts, bunk beds and a small table. Ted showed me round once it had been completed. It was intended for our protection during air raids and for safe-keeping of the radio in case of a near hit. We were clearly worth the trouble. They were taking no chances, ensuring that we were well taken care of in every way.

Tor's trip had been for the same reason. Over the past few weeks he had grown ever more sullen and irritable. He desperately needed a change of scenery. If he was to be of any use to MI5 they would have to ensure that he remained healthy and mentally alert.

During Tor's absence I was given the chance to send a couple of reports. The Germans had asked about the official procedure which Norwegian refugees had to pass through before registration and it had been decided to tell it as it was, for it wasn't impossible that the Germans already knew the answer and were testing us or that they would be able to find out from elsewhere by making a double-check. We had had no experience of the procedure but I learned that usually Norwegian citizens were required to spend three weeks in a refugee camp, where they would be interrogated thoroughly. If all was well, official identity papers and ration cards would be provided and the refugee was then free to join the Norwegian troops. This wasn't secret information, but passing it on could do no harm to our standing in the Germans' eyes. It also gave me the chance to remind them of our hardship and that we needed immediate help.

In their reply Abwehr declared that they were pleased with our progress and promised us more money. But in return we would have to prove our real worth. *Stimmungs-bericht* and damage reports were all well and good but the main objective of our mission had been to create disorder, commit sabotage and help undermine the British fighting spirit from within. Our new orders were to get to work as soon as possible. I replied that as soon as the opportunity arose we would gladly comply but that the necessary preparations would cost money. With a further supply of a few hundred pounds we could start right away.

Christopher returned next door with me. The transmission had gone well once again and the quality of reception had been first class. I asked Christopher if he would like a drop of sherry.

'Where did you manage to get hold of it?' he asked. 'I can't find any anywhere.'

'Grandfather,' I replied, filling his glass. I had a relative who worked in the industry and we frequently received our drinks through him. When the war actually broke out there had been plentiful supplies of wine and spirits and I had been given a whole case of sherry. You had to have the right connections.

Christopher savoured every drop.

'Have you been working in the Intelligence Service very long?' I asked.

'No, not very long, actually. The two of you are my first case.'

'The first?'

'That's why I'm so anxious that it all goes well. I was originally gunnery officer on an anti-aircraft site in London, but was forced to leave because of poor eyesight and here I am.'

He had never been so open about himself before now. The only information we had been given was that he was a qualified lawyer and that before the war he had spent a short time at the Bar. So we were the first double agents in his charge. It explained why he had not yet been free to take independent decisions and was constantly referring upwards to his superiors. With Tor he had shown unlimited patience and was always keen to oblige, always polite. He never seemed to lose his temper, regardless of Tor's abuse and frustration. He never spoke of his private life. He was here to do a job and remained ever formal, never stepping from behind his role as MI5 officer. We respected him for that; his job was not an easy one. He was given his orders and expected to follow them to the letter. Ultimately he would be held responsible for the success or failure of our operations.

Christopher didn't stay long. He thanked me for the sherry, perhaps slightly put out that I had managed to lay my hands on an entire case. But before he left he told me the date which had been set for my mission. Ted would travel with me to a place called Winchester and we would attempt to transmit from there.

I eventually found it on the map, a small town in the south of England, a few miles north of Southampton. My cover story had allowed for the fact that some travelling would be involved in my job. It seemed a perfect location. Ted would not have been my first choice as travelling companion. Although I had learned to reply to his sense of humour with the appropriate sarcasm, I still hadn't really taken to him. At times he could be extremely unpleasant, seldom answering my questions, and he seemed ever suspicious. His eyes seemed to be following me constantly, waiting for the slip that would betray me as a German agent. However, there was little I could do. It had all been decided. We packed and double-checked our equipment, the transmitter, antenna and other supplies.

We travelled to Winchester by train and then caught a taxi as far as the police station. Once Ted had shown the sergeant his identity card we had no problems getting what we wanted and the sergeant's attitude was clearly one of respect. He duly introduced us to Inspector Walters, his superior, who asked us into his office.

Ted explained that we were testing some radio equipment and would need somewhere near Winchester to use as a radio station. Our work was of some secrecy and we didn't want to arouse any curiosity but we did need a site on reasonably high ground for the antenna. The inspector suggested that we use his own home, which fitted the bill perfectly. It was a secluded spot and we could have use of an attic room where we wouldn't be disturbed.

Perfectly happy with this arrangement we left the station and booked into a hotel before being taken to Walters' house. Both his wife and daughter were at home. The girl was, as yet, too young for school. The site was ideal as the house lay on the very outskirts of town in an enormous garden surrounded by heavily laden fruit trees. It would be a good harvest this year.

When we arrived Walters' wife was busy amongst the flower beds. She apologised for her appearance and ran inside to prepare tea. In the meantime Ted and I carried the transmitter up to the attic. We placed it on a table by the window, connected it up, leaving the antenna until we were ready to transmit. Over tea we chatted about the war, the rationing and the possible invasion of Britain. Southampton had to be a prime target for the Germans. It was a bit too close for comfort as far as they were concerned. But they assured us of their readiness. No German would ever set foot in Winchester, of that we could be sure.

Much later in the evening we climbed up to the attic to prepare the antenna for transmission to Oslo. Inspector Walters would clearly have liked to join us but he remained with his family.

On this occasion the message was not a particularly desperate one. I was working in the south of England, temporarily, and had set up base on a wooded hillside. Tege was currently in Scotland and, as usual, we needed more money. Tor always wrote his report in Norwegian before the German translation, but I began with English; it was more natural. It meant, however, that the style and tone of my messages might be slightly different. If anything that was an advantage. It would help our contacts recognise the identity of their operator. It was a nice touch. Once I was satisfied with the content of my reports, I practised the Morse, simply by tapping my fingers on the table. We were then ready to start. Ted switched on the equipment and tuned in to the appropriate frequency.

When I had finished my call we sat back waiting for the reply. I tried again and again but we heard nothing. After half an hour we gave up. There was little else we could do. Perhaps atmospheric disturbances had checked our transmission. It was a possibility we hadn't foreseen. We had wanted to vary our location and that was the whole point of the trip to Winchester. Apparently MI5 wanted us to keep on the move. It would open doors, widen the scope of our operations. We would be able to relay different information from the various locations. I had no idea precisely what MI5 had in mind but I could draw my own conclusions. Nobody could stop me doing that.

Disappointed, we packed up our equipment and returned to the hotel. The following morning Inspector Walters arrived to collect us. Our train wasn't due to leave until the afternoon so he invited us back to his home. We discovered that the inspector was a keen amateur photographer and he showed us part of his collection. He then invited us into the garden, where Ted and I sat on a low wall with the daughter between us while Walters took a few snaps.

I was slightly surprised that Ted allowed him to take our picture. The Germans would have loved to have seen their agent Ja happily smiling alongside MI5's communications expert. Ted obviously hadn't given it a second thought. Perhaps he enjoyed having his photograph taken and was too vain to decline the request. So I put on a brave face. It wasn't that I mistrusted the inspector; he was a devoted amateur and nothing more. All the same, the prints might get into the wrong hands.

Christopher met us at Hendon and handed me a large envelope. It had grandfather's address on it, but was in my name. I opened it up to find a wad of used five-pound notes. I counted £400 in all. It was the Germans' response to our earlier pleas.

'What did grandfather say?' I asked.

Christopher laughed. 'Nothing. He didn't even see the letter. We don't take risks like that. He might have opened it by mistake.'

We had agreed that any correspondence should be sent to my grandfather, who was well above suspicion. I had let this be known to MI5 who had obviously been keeping a watch and intercepted the letter. The envelope was perfectly ordinary: you could have found it at any stationer. The George VI profile had been stamped 'Piccadilly

Circus'. So, Abwehr had connections in the very heart of London.

I counted the notes once again. It was a lot of money to me. I would have no problems spending it. MI5's contributions did not allow for extravagance and I was quite happy to accept it and to convey my thanks.

Just as I was about to put the bundle of notes in my wallet, Christopher held out his hand. 'Sorry, John,' he said, 'I'm afraid you can't keep it. We'll need the envelope too, to try and trace the source.'

I should have known. They would want to track down whoever had sent the money; it was a perfect opportunity.

'I felt that you ought to know, just in case Abwehr asked if the money had arrived.'

25

The Germans weren't given the chance to ask. We told them ourselves, adding that we would make sure that we earned it. In reply, they told us that they had high expectations of us. We were to start work immediately. Warehouses, ammunition depots, power stations — it didn't matter which target we chose, as long as it achieved the right ends. But we were to take no risks. It might take longer to plan but we were too important to take unnecessary risks.

Tor and Andrew returned from Carlisle. Tor seemed to have benefited from the break and looked a lot healthier. I was pleased to see him so calm and relaxed. His attitude had changed too.

However, it didn't last for long — barely a week in fact. The wasting idleness of our existence took its toll. The same old routine: the newspapers, the pub, the endless afternoons and the same evening haunts. Tor gradually lost his patience, just as he had done before. The slightest thing seemed to aggravate him. Christopher was greeted with the same questions every day; Tor desperately wanted more to do. He hadn't risked his life to rot away in a London suburb. He wanted to fight, be in the front line. Ted could manage by himself, and besides, MI5 were calling all the shots now. We had paved the way for them and they could now take over control. Anything to escape.

Christopher, as usual, listened quietly and patiently. I would try to calm Tor, occasionally with success, but the atmosphere in the house grew as tense as it had been before.

Tor was only ever happy when we arranged to meet Claire and Joan, the girls we had met at the Brent Bridge Hotel. However, our evenings out still posed problems. There was the curfew to remember. Come ten o'clock we were expected back at Crespigny Road without fail. I occasionally stayed out with Claire. I didn't feel guilty — it was simply something that Tor would have to come to terms with. It certainly didn't affect our friendship, for he could see I wasn't to blame.

One particular evening Claire and I were left at the Brent Bridge to dance as long as the music lasted. As the evening was drawing to a close, we decided to walk home in the warm, late-summer night. I stayed with Claire at her house, not returning until early the following morning. Andrew met me in the hall, fully dressed and looking rather worried.

'Where's Tor?' he asked.

I told him that he had left well before ten. I had simply assumed that he had gone straight home. He clearly hadn't.

Andrew was furious, and he cursed Tor with a flood of abuse. He telephoned Christopher to tell him that Tor had disappeared. He had to be found; should we would call the police? Andrew slammed down the receiver. 'Christopher's on his way,' he blurted out. 'Do you have any idea where he could be?'

I did have a rough idea, but before I could say anything the door opened and Tor stepped into the hall. He smiled and hung up his jacket.

'Where the hell have you been?' demanded Andrew.

'Out,' replied Tor. 'At a party.'

'What on earth are you playing at?'

'Well, I was about to leave when I realised I was too late. I couldn't risk being stopped on the way back, so I stayed the night.'

Tor obviously didn't realise how serious it was. As far as he could see he had done the right thing. So what was the fuss about? Surely it didn't matter where he stayed as long as he was indoors before curfew?

'You should have phoned,' I said. 'Andrew could have collected you in the car.'

'They didn't have a phone.'

Christopher arrived and took Tor aside to have a word with him. I didn't overhear what was said from the next room. I felt they were making a fuss about nothing. Andrew and Christopher should have seen the funny side of it and just forgotten about it. But they were far from amused. They were treating it as a grave breach of discipline; they were extremely serious. MI5 had to feel they could trust us no matter the circumstances. This trust was the basis of our continued operations. We simply couldn't afford to make mistakes.

'Don't ever let it happen again,' warned Christopher.

Tor promised but still looked puzzled by all the fuss he had caused. He had only spent the night with a girlfriend.

'It's not a question of morals,' Christopher explained.

The episode was soon forgotten. Christopher never mentioned it again, and Tor did as he had promised. Our radio transmissions continued as usual, but it was clear that the batteries were dying out. We had already told the Germans we would soon need to replace them and Andersen had said that we would easily find a new set. His assumption proved to be correct. The same type of battery was used to power large portable receivers we had seen in several of the shops. We told the Germans that we had had no problems finding a replacement battery, but to avoid suspicion we would get an extra portable radio receiver that ran on the same battery and for which we could pretend we were getting a replacement. Tor and I thought this was a bright idea — in fact, something that real spies would do. However, our action didn't go unnoticed, because a week later Christopher arrived to warn us that shop owners had been asked to watch out for anyone buying the very same make of battery. At least this meant that any other German spies' supplies were in danger of being traced.

Christopher surprised us again soon after this episode. 'We've decided that it's time we see what you can really do,' he said. 'For the purposes of the exercise, you will be actively spying for the Germans. We want to see just how much information you can compile by yourselves. After all, we don't want to give you any more information than you could compile in the field.'

He turned to Tor. 'You'll be first. Let's assume that the Germans want to know which Norwegian ships have docked at Glasgow over the past few days. You'll be on your own. It's up to you to find out as much as you can, speaking to the crews and so on.'

'I'm not playing any more games,' replied Tor. 'I need something more than that.'

Christopher pretended not to hear him.

'Andrew will travel with you, tomorrow.'

Tor sighed. It would be a break from the boredom and frustration, but the task was not especially exciting.

'If we are to be successful in the future the information you relay to the Germans must be as authentic as possible. The Germans know what you are capable of and we don't want to arouse their suspicions now.'

Tor couldn't see the point of it all. It would prove nothing.

'There's one other thing,' continued Christopher. 'The curfew no longer applies to citizens of Allied countries, and as Norway comes under that heading . . .'

Tor looked pleased, at last. I felt happy for him. We were on a par once again. It helped him to accept the trip to Glasgow.

I spent most of my time with the Poultons while Tor was away. Muriel and I would talk for hours about music, literature and the news that the Americans might soon join the war. She was a witty, clear-headed lady and I feel I learned a lot from her. It was certainly thanks to her that my English improved. Of course I spoke the language as I had grown up with it as a child and spent my summer holidays in Manchester. But there was still plenty I had yet to learn. Muriel proved to be a first-class teacher. I gradually developed a much better feel for the language.

Then Tor and Andrew arrived back from Glasgow. From the minute they set foot in the hall I could tell that something had gone wrong.

'How did it go?' I asked.

'Terrible,' Andrew replied. He looked rather disgruntled.

'I told you from the start that it was a crazy idea. I'm just not a spy,' said Tor.

Tor and Andrew had arrived in Glasgow in the evening and checked into a hotel. The following day they travelled to the docks and eventually found a public bar which was a haunt for Norwegian sailors. They had seen several Norwegian ships in the harbour and knew that the pub would be busy. Andrew sat himself down in a corner and let Tor get on with his work. He ordered a beer and began to chat to some of the men around the bar, asking them the usual things. Where were they from? When had they arrived? and so on. There was nothing particularly unusual about his questions, and besides, he was a Norwegian.

Once he had gathered a few details, he pulled out a notebook to record the information. He walked over to another group, ordered another beer and began to ask the same questions. There were plenty of Norwegians in the pub and he soon had a few pages of notes.

Tor continued for an hour. That was when the police arrived, probably alerted by the publican or a plain-clothes policeman. He was arrested along with Andrew, who had been pointed out as a friend.

Tor found it all very amusing. 'At least it proves that no German spy would last much more than an hour over here.'

After an hour or so they were released. The Glasgow police were delighted with their catch. There was a good deal of rivalry between themselves and MI5, and it wasn't often they were given the opportunity to get their own back. Two of them caught red-handed. It was a sweet triumph.

'I've never been so embarrassed in my whole life,' groaned Andrew.

I couldn't help but feel sorry for him. He had been good to us and had done all he could to help keep our spirits up.

Christopher was equally ashamed. It was a blow for him too. No doubt his superiors at MI5 had told him what they thought of the whole idea.

It was 16 August 1941. We had been in England for over four months. The dozen or so transmissions we had made had helped us establish ourselves in the eyes of our German colleagues, despite the fact that we had neither handled sensitive information nor committed any acts of sabotage. It was a good start and we had found our feet. The four hundred pounds we had received testified to that.

As usual, the mornings were spent with the newspapers. The Nazis were flooding into the Soviet Union, spearheading attacks on Crimea, Moscow and Leningrad. Marshal Pétain was establishing dictatorial power at Vichy. It was not looking good. Hitler would soon have the whole of Europe bar Britain. Once Moscow fell, they would concentrate on the British Isles and intensify their operations. We would soon be in the front line. The BBC news broadcast that we had just been listening to wasn't exactly encouraging.

'Won't we ever get something real to do?' grumbled Tor. 'This is pointless. MI5 might as well take over the lot!'

Tor was probably quite right. We were superfluous. Even if it all grew into something more far-reaching, we were not needed.

Andrew came into the room and said he had something to discuss with Tor. As it was lunchtime, they went out to the pub. I was curious but decided not to ask why. They were gone all afternoon. I tried hard to concentrate on the book which Muriel had recommended but my mind kept wandering. There had been something in Andrew's face which had worried me. Something was wrong.

A car drew up outside the house. I rushed to the window and saw Jock's Citroën. Tor and Andrew climbed out, followed by Christopher. Tor stood motionless on the pavement, staring along the row of houses. He was startled when Andrew disturbed his daydreaming, and all three of them marched towards the house, Tor between the two men like a prisoner under escort.

I ran down the hall. Tor didn't even look up at me, but carried on upstairs to his room. I ran after him. 'What's happened?' I asked when I caught up with him. 'Where have you been?'

'We went out for lunch, then Jock appeared and drove us to Regent Street.'

'What did they want there?'

'I just met Christopher,' Tor replied.

'Why?'

'He told me to be calm and then said that I was being placed in a detention camp. I'm going tonight. They've dismissed me.'

'They can't do that!'

It simply couldn't be true. There had to be some mistake. Tor had misunderstood him. But Christopher confirmed Tor's story after I had rushed downstairs. 'I'm sorry,' he said. 'I can do nothing about it.'

'But why? You can't still have any doubts about him?'

'There was no way we could make enquiries in Oslo, naturally. We couldn't risk the Germans finding out.'

'But we've told you the truth,' I exclaimed, 'and we've given you a unique chance to deceive the enemy.'

'Tor is too unreliable. He's made one mistake too many.'

'But little things — they were not important.'

'True, but that's not the point. We have to be one hundred per cent certain of our choice.'

'Give him another chance,' I pleaded. 'He can do it.'

'In war there are no second chances,' replied Christopher. 'You'd better go and say goodbye to him.'

There was no way I could persuade Christopher. It was hopeless. I climbed the stairs to find Tor staring out of the window. At the back of the house lay a small garden. We had often fixed the antenna to the trees out there, under cover of night. I watched the trees sway gently in the breeze. Tor stood motionless, looking out at the late summer greenery.

26

My first thought was that Tor would go berserk and vent his anger on anything he could lay his hands on. I prepared myself for the worst. Instead he simply turned round and looked at me. He was pale and spoke deliberately. 'I'll have to pack. I'd like to be alone.'

I left him upstairs to prepare himself. The whole thing had to be some sort of sick joke. They couldn't do this to him for a few silly mistakes. We had all made mistakes at some stage. Even Philip, when he had tried to ply Tor with drink. He hadn't suffered for his foolishness. And Andrew had allowed Tor to make a fool of himself in Glasgow.

'Can't you give him something else to do?' I asked Christopher. 'He can still make himself useful.'

'Perhaps later,' came the reply. 'For the time being he's going to the Isle of Man.'

'But you can't put him in prison. He simply hasn't deserved it.'

'It's not a prison. He'll be well looked after. He won't have the same freedom he's had in London but he's not going to be locked away.'

It was so unfair. It was all thanks to Tor that I was here now. If it hadn't been for him we never would have been able to get this far. And this was his reward! Did they not realise that if it hadn't been for the interminable boredom, Tor would not have been so frustrated and clumsy?

'I realise that there have been times when he's been right to complain,' said Christopher. 'But we can't afford to take the risk. One silly move and we could blow our cover.'

'You could be a little more understanding,' I pleaded.

'There's a war going on and a limit to how much understanding we can allow.'

There was no point in carrying on, the decision had been made by others higher up the ladder. It was Christopher's job to carry out orders.

Tor had closed the door to his room and I didn't want to disturb him, so I simply waited outside. He eventually appeared at the door with his suitcase. He put it down and held out his hand. 'I'll be seeing you, John.'

'It'll be all right,' I explained. 'You'll be back soon. I'll try to keep things going until then.'

'Back?' he said, trying to smile.

Christopher put his hand on Tor's shoulder. 'Are you ready?' he asked. 'Have you got everything?'

'John can take care of what's left,' replied Tor.

'Well, we'd better go then.'

Andrew took Tor's case and put it in the boot of the car. Tor and Christopher climbed into the back of the Citroën. I could see that Andrew had tears in his eyes too. I asked him if he wasn't going with them.

'I'll stay here with you, if you don't mind.'

In other words, he was left to keep an eye on me. Or perhaps it was simply a thoughtful gesture.

Jock started the engine. Andrew and I stayed to wave goodbye to the car as it turned the corner and was gone.

'And that's the thanks he gets,' I whispered.

'What do you mean?' Andrew asked.

'It was Tor who made it all possible.'

'Come on. Let's go inside.'

Andrew was a good choice. You could never lose your temper with him. He was like a huge, lovable bear. I wouldn't pick on Andrew, and Christopher knew it.

I tried to read but nothing sank in. I even turned on the radio, but I was no longer interested. Andrew suggested we take the Underground to the city centre. We could go to the cinema and have a meal out.

As we left the cinema I was as oblivious of what the film had been about as when I walked in. My mind was too preoccupied with Tor. What had they said to him at Regent Street? What had decided them on this course of action? Was Tor already on his way to the Isle of Man? Had he been handed over to the prison authorities? Or was it a special division that took care of suspect foreigners? Would Tor stand trial? Or could they simply place him in detention without going through the red tape? How long would he be forced to stay there? Would I be able to get in touch with him?

We had dinner somewhere, I don't know where, and somehow Andrew got me back home.

Christopher came round the next day. 'How are you feeling?' he asked.

'Empty,' I said. 'And lonely. How long does he have to stay there?'

'I don't know. I'm afraid that I have no influence over the decision.'

'What if I was to go to Trygve Lie?' I said. 'He could talk to the authorities.'

'I don't think so,' Christopher replied. 'This is a purely British matter. We were forced to intern several thousand people at the outbreak of war, mostly foreigners whom we did not want running free, but there are also a lot of British people who were found to be security risks.'

Was this a reminder that I, despite my British citizenship, could not feel totally secure?

'You can trust Tor,' I said.

'I know,' said Christopher, 'but it doesn't change anything. As far as we're concerned the case is closed.'

'What about Tege?' I asked. 'What's going to happen to him? Or is the idea to let Ja disappear too?'

'Ja will continue as usual,' said Christopher. 'So will Tege.'

I looked at him. He was serious. 'From the detention camp?'

'We'll have to pull in a reserve.'

'A reserve?'

'Tege's role will be taken over by Ted Poulton,' said Christopher.

I laughed. 'Impossible,' I said. 'He can't transmit the same way Tor does. The Germans will know that someone else has taken over.'

'Ted's been practising,' Christopher said. 'He can imitate Tor perfectly. Our experts can't tell the difference.'

'He'll never do it,' I stated.

Naturally Ted had sat with headphones on during both Tor's and my transmissions. However, we had not managed to transmit enough for Ted to have had time to learn Tor's unique style with the Morse key.

'We recorded Tege's messages,' Christopher explained. 'Ted's been practising very hard.'

I started to be suspicious. Had they decided long ago to remove Tor from the operation? Was that why they had recorded his messages? Were mine on tape too? I asked Christopher.

'Of course,' he replied.

During the next few days I really felt that the whole situation had changed. It was desolate without Tor and I was not particularly pleased to have been given a new Tege. Perhaps, in purely technical terms, he could replace Tor but as a person he was no substitute. It slowly sank in that there was nothing I could say or do to help Tor. I simply had no choice other than to continue work with Ted. Ja and Tege would have to carry on as they had done, as a team, or the whole operation would be jeopardised.

Once Tor had left I grew more sullen and withdrawn. And then another mission was organised for me, this time to Aberdeen, perhaps to help me forget about Tor. After the failure of Winchester we would be sent north to try again. The decision was a welcome one; not that I was desperate for Ted's company, but it would be a good break from the present routine.

We had reserved bunks on the night sleeper and made sure that the radio was well hidden beneath the blankets on the spare bed. When we arrived we immediately looked up Chief Constable McConnought who had taken charge of us before we left Aberdeen for London some months ago.

He recognised me straight away. I could see he was surprised. The last time we had met, Tor and I were prisoners awaiting interrogation and possibly execution. And here I was, alive and kicking, working with MI5!

Ted revealed no more than was necessary. We were simply testing radio equipment. He said no more than he had had to say at Winchester.

McConnought lit his pipe amidst the familiar cloud of smoke and cleared his throat. 'Superintendent Westland will take care of everything.'

I thought I could detect a hint of disappointment in his tone. Perhaps he had expected more. It was not a routine request and he had to be mildly curious as to why I was now testing radio equipment with MI5. However, he asked no questions and simply introduced us to Westland. Ted explained what he needed and Westland offered the security of his home, as had Inspector Walters. He, too, had a spare room upstairs where we could work undisturbed. So we were driven to his home and introduced to his wife and two teenage daughters. He had arranged for us to use one of their rooms.

Ted and I spent the afternoon setting up the aerial and getting the 'piano' ready for use, and I then prepared the report itself. It was a short message stating that I was working in Scotland and had seen large numbers of troops at a railway station, equipped with skis and winter supplies, on their way north. I was transmitting from the outskirts of the city but was concerned as to my safety.

I had no idea of the significance of my mentioning the ski troops. It was obviously falsified information to lead the Germans into thinking that a large-scale operation was in preparation north of the border. Why, exactly, I had no idea. I could think of no logical explanation for it. Ted and I remained silent about our activities and Westland knew nothing anyway. Absolute secrecy had to be maintained.

That evening we were invited down for tea. I sat playing their piano for some time encouraging the girls to sing along. They were obviously having fun. Our visit had to be quite exciting for them. Two strangers locking themselves away in a room with a host of packages and cases.

The girls were sent to bed later in the evening and Ted and I moved upstairs. We locked the door behind us, sealing the entrance with some blankets to help muffle the sound of the keys. But once again our efforts were unsuccessful. I persevered at the keys for almost an hour while Ted tried his best to keep tuned to the right frequency.

The following evening we tried again, but we were still receiving no reply. Dinner with the Westlands was the only thing that seemed to go right. We knew that the Aberdeen police had their own radio station, which they had established on the top floor of their headquarters, and we decided to try from there. The chief radio technician, Ted Ingram, took us upstairs and helped us set up the equipment.

We got our reply at last. The response was immediate: reception was QSA3, slightly poorer than our transmissions from the Poultons. Their message came back, loud and clear: 'Sabotage — top priority'.

MI5 were told discreetly by phone of the news. The following day we returned to London, mission accomplished. It had been a step in the right direction and Christopher was clearly delighted that we had been able to establish radio contact with Abwehr.

He was even happier when the Germans contacted us a few days later. They made no mention of sabotage but, instead, requested that we move to the south coast to establish if there were any pipeline workings on the beaches. I was somewhat confused by their request, as was Christopher. However, the following day all was revealed. After consultation with an MI5 expert, Christopher could tell us that the Germans had been referring to coastal defences. Pipelines could be built extending from the land out to sea and be used to pump oil and petrol out into the sea in case of attack. The invading forces would be met with a wall of fire before they had even had a chance to set foot on land.

MI5 examined the possible consequences of my reply. Could we tell them there was no sign of such defences? Should we reply that the beaches were strewn with them? The question was, could I possibly have gained access to such information? The coastline was strictly guarded: access was only for those with special permission. We would also have to think of something else — what did Abwehr already know?

Christopher and I agreed to make up an imaginary itinerary. I had been sent to the south of England and on my travels I had caught sight of a crashed vehicle by a railway crossing; a truck loaded with heavy piping had been hit by a train. I had seen the damaged pipes lying buckled and unusable beside the track, but had noticed that they were fitted with heavy duty couplings, which suggested they would be used for liquid transportation. I had grown curious and gone into the nearby pub to speak to some of the locals.

'I see there's been a nasty accident,' I said.

'A shunter hit a truck,' replied one man.

'Was anyone hurt?'

'No, not seriously.'

I had been told that a similar accident had taken place a few miles away. There were always lorry-loads of pipes passing through the area. We decided that I had seen the pipe-carriers myself and that the loads were moved under cover of darkness.

Christopher cleared the story with MI5 before I was allowed to send it. We would relay the message to the Germans in a couple of weeks — a sufficient time lapse. Then the Germans could draw their own conclusions from the information I had given.

The Germans were impressed, but Christopher was slightly on edge. 'We don't want it to look too easy,' he said.

Perhaps that was why MI5 decided that I should lie low for a while. During the following weeks I made contact only once. My German contacts didn't appear too disgruntled but, then again, there was little they could do anyway.

One morning Christopher and Jock appeared to tell me that Trygve Lie had asked to see me.

'Is it about Tor?' I asked.

'As far as I know he simply wants to meet you,' replied Christopher.

I hoped that Trygve would be able to do something for Tor. I had written to him several times but had received no reply. Christopher thought that his replies had probably been delayed by the censor. Their system clearly wasn't as efficient as the Norwegians'.

Jock parked the car some distance from the office and Christopher got out to check that we were expected. He returned shortly after to say that everything had been arranged. I was expecting some progress from the visit; the walk into the embassy made me feel especially important — the invitation was not one everybody could expect.

I was surprised to find there was nobody to meet me in the entrance hall, not even a doorman. The corridors were deserted and the lift doors stood wide open, waiting for us. It all seemed slightly odd. When we walked out of the lift I realised why the place had been so empty. It was a security precaution. I might be recognised. It was not impossible that I had been seen working at the Regnbuen or at the salon. The visit was not one which would be commonly known, it would be too risky.

Christopher knocked at the door of Trygve Lie's office and showed me into the room. He stayed outside. Uncle Trygve was the same as I had remembered him from our parties at home. His face perhaps a little thinner and his suit hung more loosely than before, but otherwise he hadn't changed at all.

'John, it's so good to see you again. I hope you weren't seen. I thought most people would be out to lunch at this hour. You seem to be doing very well for yourself.'

I couldn't complain. We had done what we had intended to do and hopefully been of some use.

'I know what drove you over here,' he said. 'Oslo

informed me. But what you've done since then is none of my business.'

'You know that Tor has been interned?' I asked. I had been prepared to speak out in Tor's defence but I was interrupted.

'Yes,' I was told, 'but there's nothing we can do. The Norwegian authorities have no influence over the decision. I've already looked into it.'

'But I thought that was why you had called for me.'

'No.'

He showed me to an armchair in the corner of the room and we sat down. 'There's something else.'

He poured out two sherries, offered me a glass, nodded and lifted the glass to his lips. I waited for him to speak. 'There have been a lot of changes in Oslo,' he said. 'I don't know how much you've heard.'

'No more than what I've read in the newspapers. I've had no letters, obviously.'

'Your mother's fine, you don't need to worry about her. But I'm afraid your father has been arrested and is now in Grini prison.'

I stared at him in disbelief. I was going to ask if he had received any news of mother and father, but I never imagined father would be anywhere else but at his Tivolihallen salon.

'I realise it's a bit of a shock,' he went on. 'But it may not be as serious as it appears. He's keeping well and we've not lost hope yet.'

He moved to the heavily taped windows as a flock of pigeons flew by and settled on the opposite roof. But Trygve's thoughts were clearly in Oslo and with the woman he had once courted and whom he still thought so much of — my mother. He turned to me slowly. 'You can be proud of your father,' he said. 'Helge had been very busy.'

Uncle Trygve had been well informed through the various well-established channels from Oslo. Father had been arrested at the end of May, scarcely two months after Tor and I had arrived in Britain. He had been reported to the authorities by the wife of one of Quisling's supporters. Father had never been particularly discreet about his opinions. It had to happen sooner or later. I had warned him, but he never listened to me.

'They first took him to Möllergatan 19. He was put in a cell along with Harald Grieg, Arnulf Överland and several others you probably know. At the end of June he was transferred to Grini. He's been there ever since.'

'Is he being treated well?' I asked.

I was amazed by the detailed information Uncle Trygve was able to give me. Father had taken over as the prison hairdresser. As such he was given the opportunity to act as go-between, passing messages along the line. He would pass messages between married couples and when a new inmate arrived he would get as much outside information as possible and pass it on to the other prisoners. Every morning he would shave the prison commandant. While he was waiting for him to get out of his bed he would stand in the living-room and tune into the BBC or Swedish stations to pick up what information he could. The news would find its way round the prison.

'Helge does so much to help morale,' said Trygve. 'He's doing a marvellous job.'

He fell silent. Perhaps he was thinking along the same lines as myself. When would it all be over? How long would we have to wait for our freedom? Would father survive till then, or would he get into deeper trouble? Uncle Trygve looked at his watch. It was time for me to leave. I got up to shake his hand.

'Thank you,' I said to him. 'If anything happens . . .'

'I promise to keep you informed. Take good care of yourself. You're doing a fine job.' He took me by the arm and walked me to the door. 'I'll try to let your mother know that you're well.'

I nodded and walked out into the hallway. Christopher followed me into the elevator. The building was as deserted as it had been when we arrived. Jock was waiting for us outside. The journey back to Hendon was heavy with silence.

27

Autumn arrived with its mist and rain. Father was in Grini and Tor in detention on the Isle of Man. The leaves turned to a golden yellow, faded to brown and were plucked away by the blustering winds. The days were dismal. I felt helpless. I could do nothing to escape the dull monotony. I had completely lost touch with Tor and had no idea how he was or if he was being treated well. And father was even further away, if he was still alive.

Some nights I would fantasise that I had sent an ultimatum to Abwehr. Release my father or I defect. But I knew that I could never do it. We had achieved little this far and within MI5 there were still those who were hesitant about the whole operation.

'We can't be sure that the Germans are entirely convinced,' Christopher told me one November day.

'Well, why don't we organise some sabotage?' I asked. 'That should allay any doubts they might have!'

'That's not a bad idea. I'll look into it,' Christopher smiled. He was as friendly and as obliging as ever.

We still met solely on a professional level and never discussed personal matters outside the bounds of our duties. Perhaps he simply saw me as another cog in the wheel. I knew that he came from a family of doctors. His father had a practice in Harley Street. Perhaps he had learned from them to separate work from his social life. He was always very professional and clear thinking on the job, but at the end of the day he would retreat to his own friends, his own world.

I found him very easy to work with. He was open-minded

and always willing to discuss any work-related problems. He always tried to put me into the frame of mind of a loyal German spy and to make me imagine how and what — as such — I might be able to perform. It was critical that I be as natural as possible in both of the parts that I was playing, with two scripts to follow. I had to be consistent. It was not easy.

The thing I feared most was meeting someone I had known in Oslo. There was always the risk that it might follow the grapevine back to my contacts in Abwehr. It was clearly a problem which MI5 had also considered, as I discovered at lunch with Christopher and some other colleagues.

We had gone to a restaurant near Piccadilly Circus. I suddenly felt someone's hand clap me on the back. 'John, what the devil are you doing here? I thought you had gone back to Norway,' cried the man.

I turned to see his face, which I couldn't immediately place. A moment's reflection and I remembered that he, too, had been working on the set of *The Thief of Baghdad*. He had also been in the make-up department. I wasn't given a chance to reply.

'So, you two know each other?' said one of the MI5 officers.

I explained how the stranger and I had met.

'Take a seat,' said the officer. 'It must be good to meet old friends after such a time.'

He fetched a seat and my former colleague sat himself down, looking slightly bemused. The conversation took the line of a well-veiled questioning. How had we met? How much did my friend know about me? By the end of the evening it was clear that Christopher and the others were not too concerned about the security risk and we left my old friend in the restaurant. However, it was a frightening experience. Had he been Norwegian I would have been totally on my own.

Following this event I was given strict instructions should it occur again in the future. I would have to excuse myself politely and phone Regent 6050 immediately. There would always be someone available to take care of the situation. I was to carry change at all times. We couldn't be too careful.

The Germans continued a 24-hour radio surveillance. This meant that Ted and I took the initiative and not Abwehr. Unlike the Germans we did not keep the lines open round the clock. They would have to wait until we contacted them if they wished to relay any messages themselves. It was a distinct advantage to have the upper hand. We could also manipulate the situation at will. We might well be transmitting under poor cover and therefore only dared maintain contact for very short periods of time. We held the reins, tightly controlling the situation. Even if we had received them loud and clear, we could pretend conditions were too poor for us to comprehend. A few days later we would contact them again and ask them to repeat their question. This would give us sufficient breathing space to invent a suitable response.

It worked well, too! The Germans could do nothing but sit back and wait. They had to accept that we were operating under severely difficult conditions. What with moving locations and still trying to maintain good cover, we were not short of excuses. However, we wouldn't be able to carry on like that for ever. The Germans expected results. We had been trained as espionage agents and they expected us to create as much havoc as possible. It was now winter and we had still not been able to report any successful sabotage results.

Christopher arrived one particular morning, bubbling with excitement. 'This is it. We've been given the go-ahead for our first sabotage mission.'

'Great,' I replied. 'It'll be a welcome change.'

Christopher smiled apologetically. 'I'm afraid you won't be involved. We have our own people to take care of that. But you'll be given all the details for your friends.'

MI5 had chosen a warehouse depot in Wealdstone as the first target for Ja and Tege. The idea was that, naturally, with shorter supplies of food and provisions, the morale and resistance of the British would be considerably weakened. There was a blockade on all imports, so it was an ideal target. These depots were scattered all over the country and difficult for bombers to pinpoint precisely, and besides, the Luftwaffe had better things to do.

'What's kept in the warehouse?' I asked.

'It's full of spoiled sugar supplies. The whole stock was damaged in a leakage. The depot was to be destroyed anyway but we managed to delay things.'

Wealdstone was not far from Hendon. I had hoped that Christopher would take me to see it beforehand, but I was disappointed. There was always a chance that someone might recognise me and that was a risk we could not take. A group of explosives experts had been roped in to carry out the mission. It was much safer that way.

'I would have liked to have done it myself,' I said. 'I have had experience with explosives before, you know.'

It didn't help. I would have to be content where I was.

'When you contact the Germans you're to tell them you detonated the building and retreated immediately, without being seen.'

There was to be no mention of whether the mission had been successful or not. They would not know if it had been totally destroyed, details of numbers killed, or if the fire had been successfully extinguished. We would have left the scene immediately and not dared to return to view the results. The Germans would understand that.

The night of the mission was long and uneventful. I stayed up waiting to hear from Christopher if all had gone well. But there was no phone call and nobody came round. Christopher did not appear until the following morning.

'How did it go?' I asked before he had stepped into the hall.

'The operation was a success,' he replied.

But the mission had not been a straightforward one, I was told. There were several problems to consider. In order to attract the attention of the press they had to ensure that the whole building went up in a blaze of smoke. The

Germans would need to read about it if they were to believe us. At the same time they didn't want to do too good a job and endanger the lives of nearby residents. The fire brigade, too, would need to be on the scene quickly in order to sufficiently control the blaze without extinguishing the fire too efficiently. It had been a difficult operation.

'We had one or two problems with the watchmen on duty. They were asleep at the time and had to be woken up so they could get to safety.'

They also had to make sure that the explosives were of sufficient strength and additional incendiary devices were placed around the building as a precaution. And if that wasn't enough, the saboteurs had been arrested by a zealous young policeman on night duty.

'It was certainly a new experience, that's for sure,' Christopher explained. Indeed, it wasn't simply a question of taking in the Germans, but also our own countrymen. The newspapers had to react spontaneously to the situation and for that to happen we had needed to ensure that the fire was a good one. No journalist is going to be interested in a small bonfire when the entire city is subjected to perpetual air raids.

Our report to the Germans was a short one: last night, attacked warehouse, north-west London: great difficulties, almost discovered, escaped successfully: need more money. The Germans acknowledged our message but made no comment. They did request further information about conditions north of the border. Although they did not express the opinion directly, it was evident that they suspected a direct attack along Norway's coastline.

We broke contact following their request. It was now simply a question of whether or not they spotted the report of the fire. It didn't make front-page news but we hadn't expected it to. Current events on the Russian front were of much greater significance, and the *Barham*, a battleship, had been torpedoed in the Mediterranean. These were far more important than a north-west London warehouse. However, the fire was mentioned in all of the newspapers. Police and fire experts had not ruled out the possibility of sabotage. The public were urged to be more alert. The police would be grateful for any information, any sightings of suspicious characters in the area.

I suggested to Christopher that we mention our 'success' to the Germans. He did not like the idea at first but then realised that, in our delight, we would no doubt do just that; besides, it was a cry for recognition and praise. And it would smooth the way to obtaining additional funds. So we got in contact once again to let the Germans know when the newspaper articles had appeared and we demanded money to cover our expenses. Midway through the transmission I broke off. The Germans replied immediately, but we did not respond. Shortly after they began again and this time expressed concern as to what might be happening in Scotland once more. They clearly suspected a building-up of forces in preparation for an assault on Norway.

'Will we be sending more reports from Scotland?' I asked.

'Yes, military high command feels it's important,' replied Christopher.

'So it will mean another trip to Aberdeen?'

Christopher nodded. I was all in favour of a break from the usual routine, even if it meant being away from Claire for a few days. The greatest problem was that I had too little to do during the day. For all Claire knew, I was working for the Ministry of Information. It helped explain my occasional trips away from London but did nothing to account for my empty days of doing nothing. It was only every two or three days that I would meet Christopher to discuss the next report. Perhaps I should have thought myself lucky, but at twenty-two years of age I was too full of energy to enjoy so much inactivity. To keep myself busy I enrolled for an Italian language course at the Linguists' Club in Baker Street. Adopting the name John Mooney, I attended as many classes as I could.

It had been a considerable time since Tor had last keyed any Morse. Consequently, it was decided that it was time for a different cover story. So the Germans were informed that he had now joined a military unit and been sent across to Iceland. I had no idea how long for, the Germans would just have to be patient.

A date for the trip to Aberdeen was arranged. Ted and I caught the overnight train once again, arriving in the north-eastern city in early morning. We promptly set up the equipment in the police station, then went outside for a short walk before preparing for our evening's work. I was most curious to hear if the Germans had actually read the newspaper articles detailing our mission during the previous week.

Ted Ingram helped us in the final stages of setting up the transmitter. My cover story read that I was frequently sent to Scotland by the Intelligence Corps as Security Officer. It gave me the opportunity to report that many Norwegian troops were assembling in the north. There had also been rumours that a regiment of Austrian mountain troops were joining them for training. The report was to be kept to a minimum, as usual. I was constantly on the move and had no idea when exactly I would be able to contact them following this last transmission.

The Germans' reply was what I had hoped for. It was an unusually lengthy message of congratulations. They were delighted with Ja and Tege's excellently executed act of sabotage. The Abwehr high command expressed their admiration and fully understood the difficult conditions in which we were operating. We were advised to be cautious. The Germans had no desire to lose their two most successful agents and realised that the nature of our operations meant that regular contact was impossible. They were also sorry that Tege had been temporarily rendered less active in Iceland.

Once the transmission was over, I translated the code into English and read the message to Ted. For the first time I saw his expression change from the sullenness to which I had grown accustomed as he smiled broadly with the satisfaction of a job well done.

28

For the most part a double agent's life was nothing out of the ordinary. In fact it tended to be rather boring, always waiting for something to happen.

There were even fewer people residing in Crespigny Road now, and by the autumn of 1941 Andrew and I were the only ones left. It was proof that MI5 had finally made up their minds and had accepted me. Tor was stuck in a detention camp and I was allowed to run free, acting as a sort of messenger boy, trusted yet not enough to be a member of the élite circles.

Andrew and I tried to pass the time as best we could. Every morning we bought fresh bread from the baker at Hendon Central and made breakfast: tea, toast and marmalade or peanut butter and, occasionally, scrambled eggs made from egg powder. Then we read the papers, listened to the news on the radio and held shoe-polishing competitions, where Andrew was the undisputed winner.

I met Claire several times a week. We used to go to the cinema, visit a dance restaurant or spend a couple of hours in the pub. Andrew discovered a swimming pool in the area which was open once a week. We went there on a regular basis for a couple of hours at a time.

We also wrote to Tor and clubbed together for a carton of cigarettes which we sent via Christopher. Anything for Tor had to go through MI5, not the normal channels, and I assumed that all the messages were read by both the Intelligence Service and the post censor. It was strange to think that only a year ago Tor and I had been censoring the post in Oslo and now our letters were being censored by the English.

The weeks passed and not a word was heard from Tor.

Now and again Christopher appeared with work for us. It was formulated, coded and then transmitted late at night. There was not much to report during the autumn, except to relay the general feeling in Britain. We told the Germans that because of the sabotage I had to lie low and with Tor away in Iceland I could not accomplish much anyway. At first the Germans were quite content. The successful sabotage of the provisions depot had temporarily quelled their demands on us.

I had difficulty staying awake during the night passes, which ended only when the Germans' message had been deciphered. Luckily there was a small chemist shop a couple of streets away. The chemist himself was a tall, well-built man with enormous hands. He also had a Canadian accent. The good thing was that he was not very fussy about prescriptions, and under the counter he kept a small supply of fenedrin. With the aid of an occasional tablet I managed the night passes without any trouble. These tablets were easier to take and more effective than the pieces of bitter chocolate the Germans had given us.

The chemist had something else of value. After a late session in the pub we would crawl into his shop where he would look at us knowingly and sigh so heavily that the buttons would almost pop off his white coat. Then, behind the counter, he would mix a brown concoction. It tasted revolting, but that morning-after feeling disappeared instantly.

The whole situation seemed unreal. The war had been going on for more than two years now; Londoners were used to the air raids and had adapted themselves to the inevitable. Evidence of the war could be seen everywhere: sandbags on the pavements, the crowds of men in uniform, and the many women who had suddenly started working in unusual places like arms factories, warehouses and garages, and as bus drivers and railway staff.

One day the tobacconist's assistant told me that she was leaving to work in an aeroplane factory. Mrs Cohen was not pleased, but the girl was extremely happy. Not only would she be getting twice the money, she would also be doing something useful. Doing something useful, aiding the war effort, was an on-going theme in London during these years. In that respect I thought of myself as important, a necessary piece on the chessboard, on a par with a U-boat lieutenant or a tank driver in North Africa. Mind you, I was not exactly active!

Towards the end of November Christopher arrived holding a letter. This first sign of life from Tor had, via every thinkable authority, finally ended up in the right hands. It was written on special paper and the sender's address was Camp WX, c/o Chief Postal Censor, Liverpool. The tone of the letter was bitter. 'This is the most loathsome place you could possibly imagine,' he wrote. 'Surely they're not keeping me here for ever? They can't be that crazy? You can't believe how frustrating this place is. I get thinner with every passing day, even my hair's turning grey! Do you remember how excited we were about going to England?' He thanked us for our package and hoped we would not forget him. However, he realised that the postal system wasn't the fastest imaginable!

I gave the letter to Andrew. He read it. I could see him clenching his fists in anger over the treatment Tor was being subjected to.

Tor was living in a fantasy world too, being confined without a real reason. Surely the Department would realise their mistake soon. Or was that too much to ask for? Andrew and I never discussed Tor's letter but I could tell he felt just as powerless as I did and that he found it hard to control his anger.

The days drifted by. December arrived and the shops in the centre of London tried to simulate a Christmas feeling. Out of the stockroom and into the display windows came the old pre-war Father Christmases. Children's eyes lit up but there was no rush to buy Christmas presents. Everything was rationed and the rations were not generous. If someone wanted to give a jumper or a shirt, they either had to save up clothing coupons or get some from the receiver of the present. Still, there were a lot of people about despite the lack of goods and the bomb threat. One had to make one's way through sandbags and bus fumes in Oxford Street, as I found out when I caught the Underground there from time to time. I had to get out amongst real people, even if they wondered why I was not in uniform. Should the conversation turn to that, I had an answer ready.

One day the newspaper boys were shouting excitedly on the streets. Something startling had happened — the Japanese had attacked Pearl Harbor and the USA had entered the war. This had been long awaited. The USA had been expected to step into this fight against the Nazis, but no one expected that it would happen like this.

We had long discussions about what it could mean to us. Would the Germans' attitude towards their special agents change? We sent them a non-committal report relaying the feelings after the big news, and then waited for their reply. They did not touch on the subject but thought we ought to try to get back to work. They also wanted to know when Tor was expected back from Iceland.

We waited a week then I sent a reply. Tor was not due back in England for another couple of months yet. As for myself, I was going to celebrate Christmas in Manchester with my grandparents, but I would resume contact upon my return to my regiment. I did not dare take the radio to Manchester with me as it was far too risky.

One detail in the message was true. I was going to spend Christmas in Manchester, and a few days before Christmas Eve I was sitting in a north-bound train.

Mitchell, the family chauffeur, met me at the station with the Daimler. I suddenly felt I had landed in yet another fantasy world. Admittedly, the city was full of soldiers dressed in a multitude of different uniforms and, sooner or later, grandfather would start talking about the war. However, neither Mitchell nor my grandfather had changed their way of life. Grandfather had sold his big house though and had moved into a serviced flat in Rusholme Gardens. Mitchell was working at the family brewery in Manchester for the most part, but was at hand whenever his services were required. A maid came in every day to do the cleaning and cooking despite the fact that there was an excellent restaurant in the block.

My grandparents were pleased to see me, but not exactly overjoyed. Grandfather thought me a burden. I realised that the first night when we had gone to his local at Withington. The White Lion, a place I remembered well. All his friends were there, savouring their frothy pints and whiskies. I was introduced. Then someone asked what I did and why I wasn't in uniform. I replied in my usual way that I worked at the Ministry of Information. Nothing more was said about it, but on the way home grandfather asked me why the Ministry could not supply me with a uniform.

'You're a part of the war machine too,' he said.

'I'll ask about it.'

I knew that in grandfather's world every man had a duty to fulfil — duty being to dress in khaki and help save the nation. In order to play one's part it had to be this way. Wearing a uniform was proof to your neighbours and friends that you were doing your bit.

'If not, you ought to look elsewhere for a job,' said grandfather.

'I'm perfectly happy where I am,' I said, 'but perhaps I can arrange a uniform if you deem it important. I'll probably get a sergeant's grade.'

Grandfather stopped dead in his tracks and glared at me. 'Sergeant?' he said. 'An NCO?' That had not been a good thing to say either. Everyone in the family had been officers and it was my duty to uphold this tradition. 'There must be some way you can get a commission,' said grandfather.

'No,' I replied. 'The possibility doesn't exist and anyway I'm not that keen.'

Grandfather muttered to himself, marching off home with long strides. He had been acting brigadier-general at Gallipoli, but pensioned in his old rank of colonel.

Apparently it had been a question of a couple weeks more service for him to have called himself a retired general. It was something he never quite got over.

I thought about what would have happened if I had accepted grandfather's offer before the war of financing me through university. In 1940 hundreds of medical students were commissioned as officers and sent out to the Allied front line. His dream would have come true. I would have been able to visit him in an officer's uniform. However, I might also have been killed like thousands of others, and then perhaps grandfather's dream would have become a nightmare. My photograph would have been placed beside that of his son who died at Gallipoli. He would have two photographs and two mass-produced medals for valour. Not much of a memory, but at least we'd have done our bit.

Grandmother still lived in the good old days. When I had been younger and used to spend my summers with them, it had seemed natural for me to accept their way of thinking. They were as they were and I didn't react. Now that I was older and a war was going on, I assumed their attitude would change, but it hadn't.

One day, the maid, Ethel, a conscientious girl whose face was unfortunately scarred by pockmarks, asked if I wanted to go to listen to a military band with her. They were holding their Christmas concert in a nearby park. I said that I would like to go and dutifully informed my grandmother that I was thinking of going out for a couple of hours to listen to a band.

'Are you going by yourself?' she enquired.

'No, I'm going with Ethel.'

She looked at me as if I had sworn. 'But you can't go with a servant,' she said.

'Why ever not?'

'It's not proper. Besides, she just wants to show you off.'

'Well, let her!' I said.

Grandmother was obviously upset. It just wasn't the done thing, fraternising with the servants. It was then that I suddenly sensed the gap between us, a generation gap.

Long ago I had been moulded into their world in all innocence, but now I was independent of them. I no longer fitted in with their traditions, despite the fact that I respected them.

'We won't be long,' I said, leaving quickly. Grandmother turned round and went into the living-room. Ethel gave me a smile; it was almost a smile of victory.

We spent Christmas Day alone in the flat. There was plenty to eat and drink, but the atmosphere was not good. Their grandson was not in uniform, his heroism was not a topic for discussion in the pub. Their grandson went about with the servants and did not show the right respect for his social standing.

It had been decided that I would remain until the middle of January, which I did despite the fact it proved extremely trying. Grandfather was troubled by my presence and I was troubled because of it. That is why I felt some sort of relief in not accepting Mitchell's offer of a lift to the station. I caught the bus instead.

An hour later I was sitting on the train to London. During the journey I regretted not having told grandfather my reason for coming to England and what I was doing. I could have made him swear an oath of silence. Then he would have understood me better and even accepted me. However, that was not possible. I had to play the role in which I had been cast. If I did not, everything we had achieved so far would have been for nothing.

Back at Crespigny Road there was a letter from Tor waiting for me. It was full of the same bitterness. The only highlight in his existence was a package from me. I felt guilty that I had not sent more packages, with cigarettes, books or a gramophone to keep him amused. Tor also told me that his request to the exiled Norwegian Lord Chancellor for help to have his case tried had been rejected. Apparently there had been no new information which could change his situation. A very cynical reply indeed.

Andrew returned from Carlisle where he had spent

Christmas with his family. Christopher reappeared and informed us that the High Command had decided that MI5 should carry on planning the continuation of our operations, but as yet he could not disclose what it would be.

In the meantime, Andrew and I registered for a French course at the Berlitz School in London. This was just one of the things we tried to pass the time. February passed by aimlessly. Claire and I spent a lot of time together, but mostly I was with Andrew. We continued sending our weekly reports and once again I asked for money. I told the Germans that I had lots of ideas for new sabotage attempts and that I was looking into it. However, my work took up a lot of my time and I had to carry out my duties so as not to arouse suspicion.

Then, suddenly, the Germans issued an order. They wanted me to get information about the Bofors 4.5 gun which the British air defence used. The Germans wanted to know all about this anti-aircraft weapon. How many rounds did it fire? How long was the barrel? Did the gun have a mobile version? What instructions were there about the main instrument?

I did not understand any of it, but Christopher was overjoyed. 'It's getting really interesting now,' he said.

29

I was concerned. 'I don't know anything about anti-aircraft guns,' I said.

'That's not the main problem,' said Christopher. 'The question is how best you can find out what the Germans want to know.'

I understood that MI5 had received instructions from the military authorities to release certain bits of information about the gun the Germans were so interested in. If I could send them a report it would enhance my position as an effective agent and might, in the long run, be of use to mislead them. Now it was a matter of working it out in a practical fashion. The Germans were aware of my background, that I was no weapons expert and also that it would be difficult for me to get hold of intricate technical information, let alone understand it. Tor, who knew more about the subject, was still in Iceland.

'There was a short, somewhat insignificant article in one of the internal aviation magazines,' said Christopher. 'You can start with that.'

'Where am I meant to have got hold of the magazine?'

'In a camp when you were out on a job.'

So far it sounded believable. It was perfectly possible for me to have got hold of the magazine because, as we had often reminded the Germans, I frequently travelled around as part of my job.

'Then what? The Germans won't be happy. They might already have the magazine. We'll have to give them something else.'

'We'll let you visit a regiment that's been equipped with

the gun,' said Christopher.

We agreed on that and in my first reply to the Germans I analysed the magazine article in detail. In passing I mentioned that I'd be travelling to the south of England on work and that when I was there I would endeavour to glean more information. The Germans were pleased but asked me to hurry; it was important that I got hold of the required information as soon as possible.

Now it was a question of balance. There was no way I could get hold of all the technical details without problems. At the same time I had to show the Germans that I could work effectively when required. So we divided up the answer bit by bit. In a mess I managed to get an NCO to reveal the firing rate of the gun. On another occasion a transport officer had boasted of the excellence of the new weapon, a fact I noted gratefully. The Germans obviously thought I had done well, because they dropped the subject and suggested a new sabotage instead. I replied that I was preparing for one, but as usual I needed more money.

In one respect the whole thing was like a game to me. Out in the world there was a war going on but at Crespigny Road, Christopher, Andrew and I were sitting planning a fictitious game. I was the pawn to be moved around. Together we made up conversations in an imaginary mess and discussion in an imaginary canteen. If I had been sent out to inspect a security building somewhere, what could I possibly see? What might I overhear? What information could I gather? The contents of my reports to the Germans were decided by MI5 in advance. At the game table we just arranged the message into a believable package for the Germans. I often thought about my part in the whole thing. Was warfare affected by the reports I sent, assigned to me by MI5? Was any action taken, and was this what MI5 hoped for?

None of these questions were ever answered. I was just the little man in the set-up. I went along with my group, obeyed orders, although I rarely knew where we were going or what purpose it served. I had, however, noticed one thing. The Germans' questions had changed of late. In the beginning they had been most interested in the atmosphere, the will to fight and the effect of bombings. Of course, this was part of their preparations for the main invasion of Britain. However, after the attack on the Soviet Union my employers had been more interested in other things: the state of provisions in England, what goods were rationed, and whether there was enough food and clothes to be bought with ration cards.

Was this proof that Hitler had decided not to invade England? Were the people in Berlin more interested in knowing how long British supplies would last because of their intention to starve the British into surrender? Then came their questions about the anti-aircraft guns. Did this mean that the Germans were no longer convinced of the victory they had talked about in Oslo? Were they afraid that the British possessed more effective weapons? And why were they asking Tege and Ja to find out?

There was no way I could make any judgements about the big game, especially since Christopher was never willing to discuss it with me. It didn't stop me thinking about it though, and I reckoned that MI5 also drew their own conclusions from the Germans' questions, only with greater certainty. Perhaps my work was of use from that point of view. I mean, it's easier to divine one's enemy's intentions from the questions he poses.

Every now and again Christopher brought me a letter from Tor. It did not exactly make for uplifting reading. Tor still felt bitter and he was having difficulty coping with his unjustified imprisonment. 'I was a fool to try and help this country and my own!' he wrote. 'If I'd known I'd end up here, I would never have left Norway. The most surprising thing is that the people responsible for my internment are actually making use of what I gave them. That surely ought to prove that my intentions were honest.'

I wrote to Tor saying his honesty was not in question. The only reason he had been interned was his reckless behaviour. I don't know if that was of any comfort. The treatment he had incurred was scandalous, even Ted and Christopher agreed on that. However, they could not do anything about it. We did send him cigarettes, a book on chess that he had asked for, and money. It was all we could do, but it took a long while for the packages to get through. Sometimes even as long as a couple of months.

At first Tor was in a camp on the Isle of Man. After a few months he was moved to Dartmoor, where he was placed in a room in the hospital wing. That meant he was even more isolated but, despite that, the conditions were, on the whole, not too bad.

A couple of times I had tried blackmail. If Tor was not released I would not send any more messages. But Christopher had just smiled and shaken his head. I realised that someone else would just take over Ja's role during transmission, just as Ted would play Tege's part. Most likely I would end up on the Isle of Man or in Dartmoor. Such a sacrifice was absolutely pointless so I quickly dropped the subject.

In the early summer Ted Poulton and I travelled to the south of England. Once again the object of the mission was to try to contact Oslo. Christopher told me it was also important that I looked around the area. I might discover things that could be of use. If I really had been to the south and seen what was happening there, it would be easier to formulate my reports in a natural way. And, after all, it was my trustworthiness that was on the line.

As usual we travelled down by train. On arrival we were shown to a khaki-coloured car, complete with uniformed chauffeur from the Security Service. Two civilians interested in tall buildings and apparently travelling aimlessly around might arouse suspicion, especially since there were so many military installations in the area.

Vigilance was high, which was a good sign, albeit somewhat problematic for us. We had to be careful not to be stopped by an over-eager guard who was not aware of the significance of the code on Ted's identity card. A rumour might then spread that two suspicious-looking men had been arrested and interrogated. Perhaps someone with a German contact would react and thus destroy our little set-up. A military car and chauffeur provided a good camouflage against over-observant, curious soldiers.

We drove around the hilly countryside for a couple of days. Spring was evident everywhere: the fruit trees were blossoming and there was little sign of the war in these idyllic spots. We discovered a promising place — an abandoned water tower high up on a hill. It was completely isolated and seemingly ideal for our purposes. Ted and I climbed the tower, puffing our way up the narrow spiral staircase. On reaching the top we realised that we would have difficulty setting up the antenna. There was no door or hatch leading to the roof and we knew there was no point in trying to transmit with the antenna inside the thick concrete and stone walls.

We climbed back down and found ourselves right in the middle of a military exercise. A lieutenant was leading a small armed unit on the march but shouted 'Halt!' when he caught sight of us. The car was parked a bit away and our chauffeur was nowhere to be seen. We realised that the lieutenant could easily misinterpret the situation. What with two men in civilian dress, one short and fat, the other slimmer, both wearing trenchcoats, coming out of an abandoned water tower in the middle of a military area.

The lieutenant shouted something unintelligible. Ted swore. We both knew what was coming; we'd be stopped and taken away for questioning. Higher authorities would be called in and then, finally, a phone call from the Intelligence Service would put everything right.

We stopped and Ted reached into his inside pocket to get his ID. Then we hear our car starting up, accelerating and driving up to us. The corporal jumped out and opened the door for us. The lieutenant walked towards us, but obviously changed his mind on seeing the regimental emblem on the car and shrugged his shoulders. Our chauffeur drove away quickly.

We laughed about the episode afterwards. Our activities

were threatened more by our own side than by the enemy.

We returned to London without having managed to find a good place to transmit from, but the journey had been a welcome break in our routine. Perhaps that was the idea. However, life went on as usual, except that Andrew was moved and I was alone in the house. It felt empty without him. We had lived together for almost a year and had become good friends. I was sad when he left Crespigny Road, but at the same time I knew he would be of more use elsewhere. I was totally accepted by MI5 now and as free as any other man in their service. I no longer needed to be chaperoned.

After a while Christopher asked me if I had anything against moving in with the Poultons. Apparently they were having difficulty in accounting for the whole house just for me alone. I told him it was fine by me. I was already spending a lot of time with Muriel and Ted, so sleeping there as well did not require any big changes. Perhaps this was another part of the plan? After all, Ted was going to play a more important role than before. He was to take over Tor's role and try to contact the Germans.

One night I told the Germans that Tege had been granted leave from his post in Iceland. He would soon be in London and report his observations. We were anxious to see whether the Germans would react when Tor was replaced by another Morse hand. Ted had been practising very hard at Tor's particular style, but would he manage to fool the Germans?

Ted succeeded! The Germans welcomed Tor back in their reply. They didn't suspect a thing, so from then on Ted and I took it in turns to transmit.

From Christopher's behaviour I could tell something was on the go, but as usual I did not find out very much. I was told just enough for me to carry out my job but not to complete the jigsaw.

I installed myself at the Poultons' and tried to live as normal a life as possible. I asked Muriel and Ted to treat me as they would any other member of the family. Ted promised to do so, and the first proof of this was that I was appointed as one of the neighbourhood's Civil Defence deputies. Not as a regular, I was just to assist Ted whenever he was on night duty.

Civil Defence was organised so that every district had its own central authority and someone from the neighbourhood in command. All the regulars did night duty several times a month. They were equipped with sacks of sand and spades, so that when the Germans dropped the burning magnesium sticks, which they did in their thousands during an attack, they could rush out and extinguish them.

The bombings were less frequent now, and those times German planes dared to fly over England their targets were central London or harbour installations. Hendon was not attacked during this time and I was never needed to act as a fireman. During night duty I was, however, required to stay awake just in case anything happened. Whenever there was an air-raid and the sirens went off, I used to go outside and look up at the night sky. It was like watching a play: the searchlights, the rumble of planes, the sudden bursts of anti-aircraft fire. Then, suddenly, a plane would appear in a beam of light and was followed by it. Round the black silhouette of the bomber flashes of exploding shells would light up the sky, at times quite close to the plane and at other times far away. Sometimes it was a direct hit; the plane would suddenly spin round in the air, plummeting down to earth in a shower of flames.

Night duty was an enforced, yet welcome break. My only difficulty was in staying awake. Sometimes I dozed off and Ted would wake me immediately, informing me of my flagging sense of duty. I understood what he meant. Everyone sharing these night duties had daytime jobs too, so staying awake a couple of nights a month was but a small sacrifice to make to aid the war effort. Certainly no one should neglect his duty.

One day Christopher informed us of our next mission — Operation Triangle. I never found out which war operation had received the name, perhaps it was completely fictitious. Be that as it may, my job was to make sure that the Germans found out about the operation. I was to report to the Germans that during a visit to Scotland I had accidentally entered an empty conference room, where an important meeting of high-ranking officers had just drawn to a close. Obviously they had been planning an attack of some sort. I hadn't discovered where this would take place, but a lot pointed to the fact that it was imminent and that they would be using crack troops. I had also recognised one of the officers and which regiment he belonged to. Unfortunately, I couldn't pass on any detailed information, but one of the delegates had left his folder on the table and there had been a red triangular symbol on it. Surely Abwehr could work out what it stood for.

I summarised the information, coded it and sent it one night from the Poultons' house. The Germans' reply came the very next evening. They wanted further details. What did the red triangle stand for? When was the attack to take place? Was the triangle a symbolic reference to the destination of the attack?

We waited for a couple of days, then I replied that I had no further details to come back with. I had found the folder by accident and the only clue I could give them was that the operation was obviously symbolised by a triangle coloured in red. The Germans would have to try and discover its meaning for themselves.

Their reply was almost immediate this time too. I was to try to get more information, as it was extremely important. I told them it was impossible since I was no longer in Scotland.

A couple of days later Christopher came round to the house. He tossed a newspaper on to the table. 'Have you read the news?'

I had, but saw nothing I immediately associated with us.

'Operation Triangle was carried out successfully with only a few losses,' said Christopher. 'The Germans weren't prepared despite the clue we gave them.'

Christopher pointed to one of the headlines and

suddenly I understood. The planned attack had been for real and had now been executed. The Allied Forces had landed at Spitsbergen, not far from a place called Pyramiden.

'We couldn't tell the Germans the whole truth,' said Christopher, 'but we let you tell them about the triangle, which is very like a pyramid. That was enough to have solved the problem.'

He smiled. My position as a German agent had been further secured. I had discovered and reported a forthcoming attack. That the Germans had not worked out where it was directed was not my fault.

We followed up Operation Triangle by pretending to be very disappointed. I asked whether it was worth my while giving them important information when they didn't use it. The Germans apologised. Unfortunately they hadn't understood the symbol, but they were pleased by my diligence. Next time they would take my reports more seriously and make a conscious effort to follow them up.

We were happy. Christopher was positively beaming. Abwehr now trusted Tege and Ja so completely that even misleading reports would be believed. It suddenly struck me that nobody in MI5 seemed to remember that Tor and I had already succeeded in winning Abwehr's trust. If we hadn't, we wouldn't be here now. Our English friends also seemed to have forgotten whose idea the whole operation had been in the first place.

30

Our next transmissions were full of irony, but the Germans did not react. We wondered why. What had been the consequence of Operation Triangle? The person responsible for interpreting our information had failed miserably and had perhaps been transferred or demoted. If so, it boded well for us in the future, whatever that may be. We satisfied ourselves with this assumption.

It was my idea to carry out another act of sabotage. I had taken notes when Ted and I had travelled round the south of England. I had been both discreet and careful because I didn't want to end up like Tor when he'd been playing the spy in Glasgow. So, without arousing suspicion, I had jotted down my observations on the movement of troops, military exercises, which regiments were in the area, possible sights for sabotage, the conversations I'd had with people in the district — in fact, just about everything a real spy might find useful. The objective of the exercise was so that I could appear totally trustworthy in my reports. MI5 did not want me to report anything that I could not have possibly seen myself.

Every time Christopher brought an order from MI5 it was for me to decide what was to be sent. Could I have seen that? Was it believable for me to have overheard those precise words? MI5 deemed my analysis of every message to be of the greatest importance.

Now it was sabotage I was concerned with, and I remembered from our trip that I had on several occasions spotted a certain type of camp based on the military exercise areas. These camps comprised small groups of

Nissen huts with crescent-shaped roofs. They were light and cheap to construct but probably not particularly comfortable to live in. When the exercise had been completed the huts were left desolate. My suggestion was that we sabotage one of these abandoned camps. Christopher thought it a good idea as there were several advantages: firstly, the Germans would hold us in greater esteem; and secondly, a camp would prove an ideal object for sabotage, especially since I had access to military areas.

After a couple of days, Christopher reported that MI5 had approved the suggestion and that its planning was in full swing. They had even got as far as picking out a couple of abandoned camps and unguarded barracks in Hampshire ready for selection. Of course I was not allowed to be present during the preparations or the actual sabotage. However, I was allowed to inform the Germans that I'd found a suitable objective and that this time the effect would be more impressive than the fire in the provisions store. Besides, I had managed to get hold of some dynamite from an unguarded depot. The Germans' reply was heartening. I wasn't to act too hastily, but it would please them immensely if the sabotage was directed at a military installation.

The problem was the same as the time before — how to make the explosion look like an act of sabotage and get the newspapers to write about it.

Christopher relayed all the details of the carefully laid out plan. I was grateful; it made me feel a part of it all, that I was one of them, even if I was a silent member. Maybe I even contributed a point of view that had proved useful.

The Nissen huts were to be exploded by experts from the Special Branch, just as they'd done last time. To make it look like sabotage, fuses and a Norwegian-made compass were to be placed close by the barracks. When the local police discovered the compass they would hopefully put two and two together and come up with a Norwegian link, possibly the saboteur. The papers would write it all up, and from that the Germans would have concrete proof that Tege and Ja lay behind the whole affair.

I was at the cinema when the explosion took place. Like last time I waited eagerly to find out the results, so that I could prepare my report for the Germans. However, Christopher didn't call me, or Ted, for a couple of days. When he did appear his expression told me things hadn't gone very well. Apparently the explosion had been all too effective. Both the barracks and the fuses had been blown to pieces and someone had stolen the compass after the explosion. It seems that a flock of sheep were wandering over towards the barracks just as the explosion was about to go off, but luckily they were not harmed. The local police had arrested a soldier from a nearby camp and had kept him in overnight since he was unable to produce a plausible reason for being in the area. They were so convinced that he lay behind the explosion that MI5 had to step in and get the poor man released.

'What'll happen now?' I asked.

'We're in the process of distributing fresh clues,' said Christopher. 'Just as long as the local police find them. But we can't make it look too obvious.'

The next day I bought a copy of the local paper. There wasn't a single word about the sabotage. It wasn't mentioned the next day either. Then, finally, a week later there was a large article about the incident. The reporter had discovered through a well-informed source that it was a question of sabotage. It was a good feeling.

'We've succeeded at long last,' said Christopher. 'Mind you, it took long enough.'

'How do you mean?'

'Well, we had to send in the Special Branch to carry out an investigation. It was only then that the papers took any notice. According to journalists, anything has to be something when prominent men from London appear. Anyway, it was then that just enough information was leaked.'

I told the Germans that the sabotage had gone according

to plan and that there was a write-up in the papers, so they could read about it if they wanted. We also needed more money.

Further congratulations came. We were getting used to all this praise! Although new questions about troops and defence were posed, no word was said about more money. I promised to do what I could but, unfortunately, my work meant that I couldn't go and do what I pleased.

The summer drifted by and we lay low. Contact with the Germans was kept to a minimum. Tege returned to 'Iceland'. I became impatient and wondered why we weren't capitalising on the situation. MI5 had to admit that as an agent I was definitely in favour. Christopher calmed me down saying that something would happen soon.

However, it was not until the end of August before the next operation began. I did not find out what it was about, just that Ted and I had been ordered to travel to Scotland and it wasn't a joyride.

The train journeys were always pleasant. We always had a sleeping compartment reserved, which meant avoiding the crowds and the queueing. Our first destination was Glasgow this time and we arrived there early in the morning, having slept well and feeling refreshed. We were to continue northwards to Inverness, first by bus and then by connecting train. We had to keep our eyes peeled, note any military activities, which troops were based there, and what was happening on the roads, the railway stations and in the various communities.

We boarded the bus, sitting ourselves down at the back so as to be left in peace. We peered out of the window. There wasn't much to see but whenever the bus passed a military camp, or if there were manoeuvres on the go, I carefully noted it down in my notebook. In the evening we checked into a hotel. I transferred my notes into letter form, which I posted to MI5 in London the next morning. Then we continued by bus to the next town, observing, noting down and then sending these reports to Christopher.

I saw a lot of the Scottish countryside; the rain, the mist, the undulating moors, at times wonderfully green in the bright sunshine, flocks of sheep grazing on the hillside, crofts scattered about, the narrow roads which wove their way through the hills, and the sheer rock faces that dropped sharply to small lochs. However, we hadn't come to study the Scottish landscape. We were here to discover at first hand how much a Norwegian sergeant of the Intelligence Corps could possibly observe during his leave or, perhaps, on an official trip. What was possible? That was the continual question.

Well, we saw troops everywhere. Scotland was just one big training ground. A worthwhile observation was the number of different regiments in the area. The Germans were interested in names and emblems of regiments. On more than one occasion they had asked their agents Tege and Ja to enlighten them as to what a certain regiment's emblem looked like, or which battalion sported such and such an emblem on their uniform. From the bus we saw a platoon of soldiers being trained in the art of mountaineering. That also might prove important. Once when we had gone for a morning walk in a small coastal town, we had seen landings being practised on a beach nearby.

The railway stations were of particular interest, with all the goods trains and troop transport trains passing through. I noted what sort of things were being loaded on to the open waggons, and through conversations with thirsty soldiers in railway restaurants I learned where they came from. There were Frenchmen, Canadians, Australians; men from a variety of different nations were converging on Scotland.

After about a week we reckoned that we'd seen enough of Inverness-shire. We returned to Glasgow and stayed there for a couple of days. We visited the harbour together with one of Ted's relatives who worked there on the administration side. The visit formed a part of our preparations and whilst we were there I had to note down what I saw: what ships were docked there; the type of transport; the ships' home ports; and their destinations.

Then we returned to London and the old routine. I learned quite quickly the reason for our journey, and I guessed that the messages I'd been sending the Germans during the autumn had a completely different objective from before. I was no longer building up their confidence in Tege and Ja. Now the aim was consciously to deliver misleading information.

For greater scope we let Tor return from Iceland and join the Norwegian troops based in Scotland. Thus, both Tege, courtesy of Ted, and Ja could send reports. Christopher brought the first message. During a visit to Inverness-shire I had spotted a platoon equipped with skis and ski-sticks, both painted white — whatever that signified. Apart from the Norwegian troops I had also noticed an Austrian unit on manoeuvres. The Germans were curious and I received orders from Oslo to find out more of what was being prepared in Scotland.

The next transmission was from Aberdeen. Ted and I spent a couple of days there and were assisted by Ted Ingram in the radio room at the top of the police head-quarters. We reported fresh observations that I'd made during my temporary stay in Scotland. I'd seen both soldiers and officers in white anoraks, and I had overheard that landing craft would be arriving shortly.

After that I returned to London, where Tege took over transmission for a few weeks, reporting his observations when up north. He was on leave at the moment, he said, but he'd soon be returning to Scotland to a training camp. Up north they were eagerly awaiting the first snowfall so that winter warfare training could begin in earnest. We continued these reports on activities in the north throughout September and October. Thanks to my journey to Inverness my reports sounded credible with those genuine little touches.

After the whole affair I understood what it was that MI5, on orders from the highest war command, wanted the Germans to believe — a landing, somewhere on the Norwegian coast. We didn't actually say where in our reports but when the Germans had put all the small details together they'd be led to believe that an attack was being prepared and aimed straight at Norway. Skis and sticks were being stored in Scotland, along with anoraks and other warm winter clothes, skiing boots, woollen hats, 'pulkas' and tins of ski-wax. As soon as possible the troops would practise skiing, mountaineering and coastal landings.

A lot of the information I gave the Germans was perfectly true. There really were Norwegians and Austrian troops in Scotland; they were practising landings, mountaineering and skiing. However, this was merely routine training and hadn't been intensified during these past months. If the Germans checked our information they would find it correct. Mind you, we had grossly exaggerated the quantities of the various items of equipment, the intensity of training and the numbers of soldiers participating. Christopher reminded us that it was extremely important that we constantly allude to the fact that winter warfare and landings were being practised up north. These small details, some correct, others exaggerated or completely false, would create a picture of an imminent attack. An attack on Norway.

I understood enough to realise that an invasion was being prepared but that it wasn't aimed at Norway. I tried quizzing Christopher but his lips were sealed. He probably didn't know. His task was to mislead the Germans through Tege and Ja.

I wondered why Norway had been chosen as the decoy. Perhaps because the coastline was so long and if the Germans wanted to be prepared they would have to deploy a lot of forces in the strategically important towns along the North Sea coast. If so, Norway was more suitable than Denmark or Belgium. Or would the attack be aimed at one of these countries? When would the invasion take place? During these autumn months I did not receive an answer to my questions. I formulated our reports with great care, sent them or sat beside Ted when it was Tege's turn.

We thought the Germans had swallowed the bait. They were interested in our information, continually asking questions and encouraging us to continue our investigations to elaborate on information we'd already sent. As far as Abwehr in Oslo were concerned, Norway was definitely the object of the forthcoming attack. We hoped that this belief was shared by Berlin, the Military Council and, above all, by Hitler.

This wasn't a particularly intense period of work for me. There were more transmissions than usual but it was still just a question of a very sporadic contribution. I wrote out the text which was to be sent, coded it and tapped it out into space. Most of the time we transmitted from the Poultons' house, but we did go up to Aberdeen once more.

It was after that I started feeling less comfortable with the Poultons. I still got on well with Muriel but my relationship with Ted was not the best. We had been forced upon one another. We did what we had to do, but there was no contact beyond our special work. We were just too different, both in age and interests. Besides, I was not married. I was, more or less, going steady with Claire and I needed more privacy.

I told Christopher of my problem. He was very understanding and after talking to MI5 he told me they had agreed to my renting a room somewhere. And to start with I'd get an extra pound a day in my allowance. I was pleased. It meant that I was now being treated the same as any other employee and it felt good. I found a room in a small boarding house run by two elderly gentlemen, not far from Marble Arch. I settled in quickly. For the first time since leaving Stavanger I was on my own. I could divide my time as I wanted, meet whoever I pleased, do whatever I felt like doing; just as long as I did my work.

I followed the events of the war on the radio and in the papers. I often thought of what father had said — that the Germans would never win the war, it was just a question of how long they'd hold out. However, the war had lasted for three years now. The Soviet Union, USA and Japan had all entered into what had now become a World War. The Allied Forces' successes had still been somewhat limited. Yet all the British people I talked to were just as convinced as father had been that ours would be the final victory. Even though things looked black at the moment, events would soon turn.

Perhaps the turning point came in the autumn of 1942. At least I thought so when I read about the desert war and Montgomery's Eighth Army. Rommel was on the run; 9,000 Germans had been captured; 260 German tanks destroyed; and 600 aeroplanes put out of action.

On the 9th of November I was convinced that the war had entered a new phase. It was a Monday and the headlines on the front page of the *Daily Mirror* read: 'Our New Front Line has Opened in North Africa'. There was a photograph of General Eisenhower and the extra bold text told of an enormous armada, the largest the world had seen, which had sailed off to North Africa. The landing had been a success.

So, North Africa was the object of invasion. I wondered what effect my misleading information on ski-sticks and winter warfare had had. Had the Germans left their troops in Norway just in case? Had I, as a mere cog in the machinery, been able to influence the outcome in some small way?

31

Christopher was unsure. 'We'll have to check the whole thing,' he said. 'I don't know what influence Tege and Ja had. Perhaps the Germans were so convinced the attack would be in the north that they left several armoured units in Norway instead of sending them south, so that other units could be freed and sent to North Africa, where Rommel surely needed as much back-up as possible.'

I hoped that was the case; that Tor and I had played our part in the double-cross. If so, it had all been worth it.

I wished that I could write to Tor and tell him about our communications with the Germans during the autumn and the end result. The censor would never tolerate such information so I did not write about it but instead told him about my private life. Claire and I had a quiet engagement celebration in a little restaurant in the West End. Shortly after, she left London to start training to be an officer. For a couple of months she went to a cadet school and we could only meet at weekends.

I had met new people during the autumn and no longer relied solely on Christopher, Ted and the others in MI5. I often visited a Danish family called Berg and gradually I became like a son to them. The father worked in a restaurant, the oldest daughter was Christmas Möller's personal secretary with the exiled Danish Government, and the youngest daughter, Helle, was still at school. Helle and I would go to see a film together from time to time. We got on really well despite our age difference.

The Bergs lived in a residential area near Hendon Central. They owned a huge house with an enormous garden. Like so many Londoners they grew their own vegetables and also raised chickens. Since I did not have much to do during the day I often went over to the Bergs and worked in the garden. I took care of the chickens for the most part and became quite a good butcher. Sometimes I would wring the necks of as many as twenty or thirty chickens in a week. Berg then took them to his restaurant and exchanged them for butter and other foodstuffs.

Since I had moved away from the Poultons my life had changed. I did not feel as trapped as before. I could be by myself and do whatever I wanted. At the same time I had to do my work and carry out MI5's orders. As I now had my private life to myself, I felt more motivated. Perhaps it was because I now realised that the Secret Service saw me as an important piece in the game being played far from the battlefield. I did not want to betray their trust.

After the North African invasion Christopher and I discussed whether the Germans would still trust their agents Tege and Ja. Had our frequent misleading reports of the activities in Scotland made them suspicious? We had never actually said that they would attack Norway, we just reported details from which we hoped the Germans would be able to draw their own conclusions. In that respect we had not compromised ourselves totally. However, there was the risk that our reports would not carry as much weight in future.

'We'll have to ignore that,' said Christopher. 'All we can do is continue as normal. Tege and Ja can't possibly associate the landing in North Africa with what they saw in Scotland. We've decided to continue messages from there and to draw the Germans' attention away from it we'll prepare another sabotage attempt.'

'It's too difficult,' I said. 'There's no way we can get hold of the explosives.'

'We could break into a military supply depot.'

'Too risky — I don't think the Germans would want their agents to take unnecessary risks. Firstly, we ought to ask the Germans to equip us with a new transmitter. Since Tege and Ja work in different places they can't operate as successfully as they would like,' I said.

Christopher laughed. 'How would you manage that?'

'The Germans could send us more money. They've got grandfather's address. Why not ask them to send a transmitter to Manchester? Or we could refer to Müller's promise: "if there are any problems we can send an aeroplane across and drop whatever you need by parachute".'

Christopher thought for a while: it was a daring suggestion, but I could see he thought it was worth investigating. Did the Germans really have such an effective organisation in Britain that they could equip their agents with a transmitter? It might be interesting to find out. 'I'll take up the idea with the others,' said Christopher. 'But I doubt the Germans have such resources!'

'Through a neutral embassy?' I said.

'There aren't many neutral countries left.'

'Or by aeroplane. Let them decide.'

Christopher returned after a few days. MI5 had decided I was to ask for money and a transmitter. Then we would wait for the Germans' reaction.

I worked hard formulating the report. The problems were always the same. I had to choose my words carefully so that the Germans would not think me anything other than their loyal agent. I had to imagine myself in the part.

I had become a part-time Morse operator. I had a comfortable life; I got a small salary and daily expenses; met my friends and studied languages in the evenings. A couple of times a week I took on another guise and thought and acted as a sergeant of an Allied regiment's Security Service. An employee who, in his spare time, acted as a spy for the Germans.

The long talks I had with Christopher before every transmission were both useful and necessary. First of all we went through the fictitious situation. Then we read the reports beforehand so that our information would not be conflicting: it was only then that I started writing down the report. We changed it, condensed it, changed it again, substituting a word here and a word there until we were happy with it.

I asked the Germans if they could get the requested equipment for us and send it over. I explained that we really needed another radio and some money. The radio transmitter would have to connect to a standard wall socket because it was becoming much harder and more risky to buy batteries. In passing I pointed out that they had an address — my grandfather's address in Manchester — at which they could easily reach us if they wanted to make use of that route. The Germans' reply was evasive. They understood our problem but it was difficult to equip us with what we wanted. However, they would look into the matter and return to us.

They came back to us after a couple of days. They would see to it that we got the equipment. By parachute. An aeroplane would be sent over to drop what we needed. All we had to do was find a suitable place — isolated but still easy to find from the air.

'No one in MI5 thought the Germans would go this far,' said Christopher. 'I must admit I didn't think so either. But it just shows how established and respected Tege and Ja are. We're pleased.'

It was decided that a suitable place for the drop would be around Aberdeen. Logical really. My regiment was based in Scotland, so I could tell the Germans I was spending my leave in Aberdeenshire. Soon I was away on yet another journey and was once again installed at Aberdeen's police headquarters. I was becoming a well-known figure there and no longer needed to show my pass to gain entry.

The police headquarters was a large building of red granite with enormous steps of polished stone. The third floor was reserved for the highest-ranking police officers and there was also a guest room for visitors on official matters. MI5 had made sure that I had been housed there during my previous visits. It was seen to be safer than in a hotel where I might arouse unwanted suspicion. Otherwise

I could roam the city freely and mostly went out for lunch and dinner although I could have used the canteen on the ground floor of the police station.

John Westland was given the job of helping me find a suitable spot for a parachute drop. We set off round the east coast by car. We came to an area round Peterhead and Fraserburgh and drove along the 'B' roads of the open countryside looking for a place. It was not easy finding an ideal spot. It had to be far away from any buildings and there had to be a noticeable landmark for the pilot to locate us.

We looked around for several days. I contacted the Germans a couple of times, saying that I was preparing for the drop but that I did not have as much free time from my work as I wanted. They would have to wait for my instructions; as soon as I had anything I would contact them. All action was suspended for the coming weekend, the fourth Christmas since the outbreak of war.

I was invited to the Westlands on Christmas Day. It was a pleasant, happy occasion and I felt like a welcome member of the family. To start with the daughters were slightly reserved. After all, I was one of those two men who, on a previous visit, had taken over an upstairs room and done secret things. Perhaps they thought it was rather exciting, my being there for Christmas. A lot of attention was paid to me and I tried to contribute to the good atmosphere by playing the piano.

After the holiday we continued our search, and finally we thought we had found the right place. A couple of kilometres inland from the coast, between the two small towns of Peterhead and Fraserburgh, there was a valley with a small lake. Obviously there were plenty of fish in the lake; I had seen there were some fishing huts on the beach. You could not see the lake from the road, which was an advantage. Invisible to passing traffic, someone could deal with the parachute and hide it in the bushes which led to the water.

It was also important that the lake was marked on the

map. It would make it so much easier for a German pilot to find it even if it was in the pitch dark. If he plotted his course from a landmark on the coast he would easily see my signals. I could stand a bit up the slope on a path which headed off northwards from the lake. The pilot ought to be able to direct himself towards the path and drop the parachute a hundred yards north of our position.

John Westland and I wandered round the lake. The spot was ideal. We could not be seen from the road and if we needed to we could hide in one of the fishing huts that were used in the winter months. I noted down all the details and when we got back to the police headquarters I got in touch with Christopher. I told him of our discovery and Christopher said he would discuss the location with MI5 before I could give the Germans the go-ahead signal.

So far so good. Now all that was left was to see if the Germans really would dare to try. It was risky. The RAF were on constant reconnaissance of the coast and a lone aeroplane did not stand much hope of escaping observation. However, should the Germans take the risk it would serve to prove how highly they regarded our work.

The next day I had my breakfast in the police station canteen. A young policeman sat down at my table and started talking. He did not know who I was but had obviously seen me a couple of times and took it for granted that I was on the staff.

'Did you hear about the capture made last night?' he asked.

I had not heard of any capture.

'A German spy was dropped by parachute,' he continued. 'I was there when he was captured.' He was proud of it. 'He'd broken his leg so he could hardly go very far. He didn't put up much resistance.'

'Where was he from?'

'Norway, so they say.'

One of our followers, I thought. Probably trained by Andersen if he was still in Islo. I wondered what number in the series Hummer Nord the captured spy had been given.

I returned to London, stayed a week and received instructions from Christopher. It was now a question of convincing the Germans that the place was safe for a drop. I reported that I had found a suitable valley, described it and referred to the map.

The Germans came back after a couple of days and said that they had located the lake and that they approved of the site. Then they asked me to set a time. What day would be best for me? I had to be there in order to signal to the pilot and then take care of the parachute. Christopher told me to set a time. What day would be best for me? I had to be there in order to signal to the pilot and then take care of the parachute. Christopher told me to suggest a Saturday night. Normally someone in my position of work would be granted leave from Saturday lunchtime to Sunday night. The Germans could suggest a date but I had to know in good time so that I could prepare myself.

The preparations and contact with the Germans continued throughout the whole of January. The Germans were ready to carry out our wishes. Step by step the plan came together. Finally, the day for the drop was decided.

The afternoon before the great event would take place a large group was gathered in the Aberdeen police station at Lodge Walk. John Westland had chosen two of his closest associates as ground staff. I knew one of the men, Inspector Slatter, who said that he definitely preferred this job to escorting Tor and me to Scotland Yard. Christopher came up from London together with another MI5 man called Victor Rothschild. An American observer had also been invited, a Captain Fischer from G2, the USA's equivalent of the British Intelligence Service. We were introduced. Fischer was convinced that the Germans would never come and we bet each other a pound. Then we sat in the canteen waiting until it was time to drive out to the small lake between Peterhead and Fraserburgh.

32

I had put on a sergeant's uniform which was at least two sizes too small. The trousers were far too tight and the jacket was impossible to button up. But we had agreed that I had to be in uniform. It would simply have to do.

During the planning we had discussed all the possibilities. If the Germans did as we had asked them, they would be dropping a radio to us by parachute. If that were the case we could foresee no problems. But they might just send somebody down with it, another spy, someone who needed a contact to help him establish himself over here. If that were so, if they intended to take the opportunity of sending another agent, things would prove very difficult. I was told to behave as I would normally do in such a situation. I would signal the plane and wait on the side of the hill. I had to be in uniform as the German would think I was in the army. Whatever he was, he would have been well briefed. My appearance would reassure him.

I had been given strict instructions should another agent arrive along with the equipment. I would be armed, just in case, but was only to use it in an emergency. I would delay him as long as possible and help him bury his parachute. I had to give the aeroplane enough time to turn for home and disappear, so that no distress signals could be given to the pilot. Then the special force would move in. They would be waiting not far from the drop.

The American captain laughed at me in my ill-fitting uniform and smirked mockingly at the whole idea. 'The Germans will never do it,' he said.

'That's to be seen,' replied Christopher.

'What if the plane's shot down?' I asked. 'They might suspect that we had informed the RAF.'

'It won't be,' said Christopher. 'There will be no air reconnaissance in the area. It's all been cleared.'

John Westland went over the plans for the operation. He showed us how to get there on the map and exactly where his men would be posted. Slatter would be lying in wait up the road, fully armed for the occasion, and prepared to arrest me and the German spy that might be dropped.

I showed them the lamp I was to use to signal to the plane. It was just an ordinary torch to which Ted Ingram had affixed a cardboard tube through which the ray of light would be pointed at the approaching aircraft, ingeniously preventing anyone but the German pilot from seeing the flash. Christopher handed me a pistol and showed me how to release the safety catch. I hoped that I wouldn't need to use it.

I pulled my trousers up as high as I could and secured them with a belt. Then I put on the trenchcoat I had also been given. It was a better fit and helped to hide the unbuttoned jacket. I put the pistol into my coat pocket. We were ready. The Germans had said that the plane would arrive at two in the morning. We arrived in good time. At eleven two cars set off from the police headquarters in Aberdeen.

Christopher, John Westland and myself travelled in McConnought's large car along with the American. The chief constable sped down the narrow, winding road that led north. He kept his headlights on full beam; the authorities had exempted us from the usual restrictions. It was vital to avoid getting lost or having an accident in the dark.

In fact, we almost had an accident as it was. McConnought had turned off the lights as we drove through a small village so as not to disturb the villagers unnecessarily. It was pitch black and the car suddenly thundered into the pavement, thudding over the kerbside.

We were slightly shaken but the car was undamaged. We helped push it back on to the road and after some anxious moments McConnought managed to restart the engine.

We arrived at the fishing huts by the sea in good time. The car was parked beside one of the huts and covered with a camouflage net which was kept in the boot. We never saw Slatter and his men.

McConnought gave his last orders. Once I had taken my position on the steps, John Westland would make his way to the patch of cover further up the slope. He was equipped with a rifle and telescopic sight and would be on hand should anything go wrong. The others would stay hidden in the car. One person would take cover in one of the huts where he would be able to get a clear view of the steps.

'Do you have the pistol?' asked Christopher.

'It's in my pocket,' I replied, sticking my hand inside to feel the cold metal.

'You know how to unfasten the safety catch?'

'It's already off,' I replied. 'If I'm forced to use it, I won't have a chance to unfasten it. Seconds could make all the difference.'

'That's fine. We can't be sure that they'll send someone. They might just drop the radio.'

The minutes passed slowly. It was time to take up our positions. Christopher wished me luck and walked over to the cars. Westland took cover behind the bushes and lay down to give himself a better view of the steps.

'You'll be a pound worse off pretty soon,' I said to Fischer. He laughed and jogged over to the hut.

There was a fresh northerly wind blowing. The sky was overcast. Now and then I caught a glimpse of the stars twinkling through a break in the clouds. The wind blew noisily, drowning out the other sounds of the night. I tilted my head, listening carefully. The plane would have to come from over the sea, so I tried to position myself in such a way that I would be able to pick up the drone of the engine.

I saw a silent shadow glide inland from the sea. For a fleeting moment I thought it was the plane gliding with its engine out but I soon realised that it was just a gull in search of a resting place for the night.

Every now and then I called to Westland: I could not see him, but felt secure in the knowledge that he was there.

Then, the faint sound of a motor. It came from the sea, faded away briefly as the wind rose, but then returned louder than before. It was definitely a plane; right on course for the valley. I could soon see its silhouette against the grey clouds, a dark shadow slowly creeping towards me.

I lifted the long torch and pointed it towards the plane. Then I began signalling: di-da-da-da — J — the first letter of my codename Ja. I flashed at a calm, even rate, following the aircraft with the torch, raising it slowly as it drew nearer.

There was no reply, but I hadn't expected one. They were not expected to make themselves more conspicuous than necessary. The plane flew in very low, drawing closer. I continued to signal, pointing my torch straight up as it flew just a few hundred feet over my head. I turned as it continued over the sea.

For a second I thought that the pilot had not seen me. The plane carried on as if the pilot was still searching for his landmark. Then I heard the engine sound change and the plane made a sweeping curve and flew back. He must have spotted me.

I maintained the signals, and when the plane passed over for the second time I saw spouts of flame and heard the rattle of a machine-gun. I threw myself to the ground and rolled away from the path, covering my head. The rattling continued and as I turned to look up I saw a dark object falling through the night sky. The engines roared as more flame spouted from the plane and I lay on my stomach, burying my face in the wet, dewy grass.

Then the noise died away and I could hear the roar of laughter from where Westland had taken cover. 'Were you scared?' he shouted. 'It was just the exhausts.'

'I thought it was a machine-gun.'

'The ignition must have been faulty.'

I got up and looked towards the lake. Something lay down on the shore. It was a parachute resting on the grass. It lay still. The intruder I had been expecting was nowhere to be seen.

I heard the others scrambling down the slope.

'Be careful!' shouted McConnought.

They circled the parachute. I followed and stood between Christopher and the American captain.

Wc heard a series of muffled bangs come from the north. It sounded like explosions but it was somc distance away. The circle of men listened for a moment and then directed their attention to the parachute once again.

The Germans had done as we had asked; they had made the drop. A policeman lifted the material to reveal a large, dark-brown suitcase, its stout handle attached to the lines.

'How's that for accuracy?' said Captain Fischer as he paced out the distance between the landing spot and the steps. 'Twenty yards west of the road and about eighty from the lake. We could do with some pilots like that.'

'Success, once again,' said Christopher. 'Congratulations, John. You handled it well.'

'You'd better put the catch back on,' I said handing the pistol to him. 'I can't remember how to do it.'

As I spoke we heard the faint sound of an aeroplane engine.

McConnought, who was crouched over the parachute, stood up and listened. Christopher replaced the catch with a click as we all heard the distant rumble. It grew louder. The plane seemed to be moving towards the sea once again.

'It's going in the wrong direction,' said Christopher. 'It should have been on its way ages ago.'

However, it was not. It was coming from the direction of Fraserburgh and nearing the sea. The cloud cover had grow denser, which made it more difficult to tell.

McConnought cried out. Westland dropped the case and took cover by some bushes. Christopher buried himself beneath the parachute and the others rushed up the slope towards the huts. I was the only one left, but presumably that was where I was meant to be. I had nothing to fear — the pilot was probably on his way back to check that I had found the drop.

I took my torch and waited to signal but the plane never came. Instead, it banked away towards Peterhead. The engine's drone faded and I realised that the pilot had chosen a course south. He would perhaps follow the coastline and then fly over the North Sea at a low altitude to Germany.

McConnought called out his men when the coast was clear. Westland picked up the case he had dropped when he ran for · cover. Christopher finished folding up the parachute and Fischer helped him carry it back.

That was everything. The case and parachute were put in the car and the camouflage net was removed and stashed away in the boot. We all climbed in for the journey back.

Christopher was in high spirits and talked non-stop all the way. It was understandable. The success of the drop had been a triumph for him. MI5 had probably had to fight hard for the War Office's permission to go ahead with the attempt.

On the way back to Aberdeen we were stopped at a police check. McConnought grunted. The policeman recognised him and saluted.

'What's all this about?' asked McConnought.

'Fraserburgh was bombed last night,' came the reply. So that was what we had heard.

'The bastards,' muttered Christopher.

'Let us through.'

The policeman waved us on and McConnought zig-zagged through the road block.

So that was it. The plane had been armed and after its successful drop the pilot had set a course for Fraserburgh, attacking the defenceless town. Hopefully, nobody had been injured. Our happiness over our recent success was dampened by the news.

'It's too easy to be wise after the event,' whispered

Christopher. 'Perhaps we shouldn't have told the RAF to keep away, but then the Germans might well have suspected Ja, had their plane been attacked. We had no choice.'

'How were we to know that the plane was carrying bombs?' asked McConnought.

'We'll let the Germans know what we think,' I said. 'Surely they'll see the madness of risking their agents' safety for the sake of a couple of bombs.'

'What do you mean?' asked Christopher.

'Well, the bombing brought out the entire police force. The road blocks meant that I had real problems getting the radio to safety.'

Christopher nodded. It was a sound idea. We could accuse them of being clumsy. Dissuade them from doing it again, if they intended to do so.

The suitcase and parachute were carried round the back to McConnought's office. Slatter joined us and put the case in the middle of the table. It was an ordinary case, perhaps a bit worn and scratched. It wouldn't have aroused suspicion had I been travelling with it. I had to give the Germans some credit.

Christopher's colleague from MI5 took out some sort of instrument and placed it on the case, passing it over the leather and looking for any response on the dial. Then he put on a stethoscope and listened for any sounds.

I understood the need for precautions. It was not impossible that a bomb had been placed inside. The Germans might have discovered my double-cross and decided to put us out of action for good following our incorrect reports of the impending attack on Norway.

The MI5 agent worked meticulously, turning the case, testing each surface. Then he straightened up, put away his instruments, and looked at us. 'Everything seems to be all right. But just to be on the safe side . . .'

He pointed to the door. He wanted the room empty when he opened the case. We made our way out, shutting the door behind us and waited in the corridor. After a couple of minutes we heard him call out. We could go back inside.

The radio stood on the desk, beside it an envelope and a large package. Christopher examined the radio closely and then turned to his colleague. They nodded to one another. I reached for the envelope. It was unsealed so I could get to the contents easily enough. I began to laugh. The Germans had supplied us with a bundle of five pound notes. I counted them quickly — £1,500.

McConnought untied the package and removed the grey wrapping paper. Along with the radio and the money they had sent extra supplies of fuse-wire, detonators and the small pen-sized incendiary devices. It was more than we had asked for. The message was clear. The Germans had done us a favour. In return we were to increase our espionage activities.

'I think we all deserve a strong cup of tea,' said McConnought.

We left his office. He locked the door behind him and we walked down to the canteen. As we made our way down the corridor, Captain Fischer put his hand on my shoulder. 'I know you've just been given a cash bonus, but fair's fair. I lost. Here's your pound.'

33

The radio was sent to London by aeroplane to be examined by MI5. We took the night train back the following evening. Christopher was ecstatic over our success.

I felt pleased by the success too, but I still felt angered by the Germans' unnecessary bombing. The effect of the two bombs dropped on Fraserburgh had not been great, but houses had been damaged and a few families made homeless. So it said in the newspapers: it was lucky that no one had been killed, but the Germans would be told how amateurishly they had behaved. Even on the journey back to London I started formulating my thanks to them. It would consist more of the problems I had incurred than the parachute drop.

I worked on the report the next day too. I put myself nto the situation I would have found myself in had I been a real spy. I would probably have cycled to the spot. I would have collected the case and then, after burying the parachute, I would have tied the radio to the carrier and headed off. I would have had difficulty keeping my balance because of the weight of the case. Maybe I would only have been able to sit on the bicycle and pedal on the downhill slopes. Normally it would not have been difficult for me to get back to Aberdeen. Suddenly, however, the traffic on the roads had become livelier. Police cars screamed past and ambulances and fire engines thundered off towards Fraserburgh. A police patrol had set up a blockade in the middle of the road. I was forced to take a smaller road and hide the case for safety. Then I lay low until late in the morning. It was only then that I dared to go on the roads again. I did not know when I would get the chance to collect the radio. All these problems had been caused by their idiotic bombing run.

Christopher read my draft. He seemed pleased with it and took the text to MI5 for analysis. There was no hurry to send it as yet. The Germans would have to wait to hear the results of the operation. I had to be careful — after all, I had come close to being captured.

One thing worried me. It now appeared that the bombing really had caused a death. An eleven-year-old boy had been killed. Christopher tried to comfort me by telling me it was war and that the fighting claimed lives every day. You had to take that into consideration. What we had achieved was important and meaningful. The boy had not died for nothing. I did not agree with him, but there was not much I could do about it. I thought that I could send a letter of condolence at least, and I asked Christopher if that would be feasible.

He thought about it for a while. 'If you feel that way,' he said, 'write a couple of lines to the provost and express your feelings on the event. Anonymously. Do whatever eases your conscience.'

I wrote the letter and addressed it to the Provost of Fraserburgh. I do not know how he reacted or even if the letter got there. However, I felt better for having sent it.

After a week I was summoned to Hendon. It was time to send the first report to the Germans. The choice of words was almost the same as I had suggested. I condensed the contents; it had become routine for both myself and the Germans to use as few words as possible. Then I tapped out the number groups on the old transmitter. The new one was still concealed in the undergrowth outside Aberdeen.

Of course it was not really there. It was at the Poultons, and after the transmission we took a look at it. It was a transmitter and receiver combined, designed to be connected directly to the mains. At the back hung a flex and beside it there was an adaptor for different voltages. The set was smaller and lighter than our old one.

The Morse key was built in, which made it easier to handle and quicker to assemble the set for transmission.

It suddenly struck me that all the text on the indicators and controls was in English, not German, like the battery-run radio. I asked Christopher what conclusions he had arrived at.

'You would have realised sooner or later,' he said. 'It's one of our sets.'

'Ours?'

'One of our agents in France used it.'

'How did the Germans . . .?' I began

But of course. They had captured an Allied spy and confiscated his radio. Now they had sent it to one of their own spies. Müller and Andersen must have been rubbing their hands together with satisfaction when they packed the British agent's radio for our use.

After a few days the Germans replied to my angry report. They apologised for the incident. They had not thought that the bombing would have such consequences. They promised not to make the same mistake again. The damage had already been done, the boy was dead, but their reply had at least shown that they understood our point of view. The Germans had said 'again'. Did that mean they were prepared to make another drop if we asked?

'Aren't we going to press them to make another drop?' I said. 'We need sabotage equipment. We have to show them that we're being active.'

'Keep calm,' said Christopher. 'Let's take this one step at a time.'

The appraisal continued for a long time. During this period we stalled the Germans with other information. We let Tege report that I was up in Aberdeen collecting the radio and that next time we would try transmitting with it — if I found the place I had hidden it and if I was not captured. The Germans returned with cautious hopes that everything would go well. We were not to take any risks. We had already done Abwehr excellent service and their greatest wish was for us to continue as before.

We exchanged a further couple of meaningless messages, tried out the new transmitter, which had two different frequencies, and discussed the quality of transmission.

Everything went back to normal. The long, idle days, the discussions with Christopher before the transmissions and then the short, but intensive, clatter of the Morse keys.

Even before the planning of the parachute drop I had moved from my rented room at Marble Arch. It was too expensive. Almost all of my expenses went towards the rent. On a noticeboard in a newsagent's at Baker Street I had found an advertisement saying 'For Rent'. I wrote down the address and made my way to a huge house with thick walls. I entered through a solid door and found a room marked 'Information', knocked, and was admitted by a woman. There were two nuns in the room, drinking tea. I excused myself, saying I had probably come to the wrong place, that I was looking for a cheap room. I had landed in a convent. It was the right place though. There were rooms for rent and I was shown upstairs to a large room with a bed, table, some chairs, a hotplate and an electric heater. The walls were dirty and peeling. However, the rent was reasonable and I decided to take it. A double agent could not have a better cover address than a nunnery. Most of the nuns, in fact, had moved out to the country, looking after evacuated children.

I tried to make the room as nice as possible. I bought some paint and painted the walls, decorating one corner with the huge Norwegian flag I had been given by mother's friend just before we left Oslo. It looked quite comfortable once I had finished.

Claire was still attending her officer's training course so for company I visited the Berg family at Hendon Central from time to time. There was to be a party and I had to slaughter and pluck half a dozen chickens. I was also invited to stay for dinner.

Early in the evening one of the guests arrived. A car stopped in the street outside and a chauffeur rushed out and opened the door for a man in his sixties. His name was

Niels and he was obviously an old friend of the family. The reunion was a cheerful one. The conversation at dinner revolved around mutual friends in Copenhagen and the situation in their occupied homeland.

Late in the evening the uniformed chauffeur returned and the visiting Dane took his leave. In the hall he looked around for his briefcase. I remembered that he had put it down in the living-room and ran to get it for him. When I picked it up I looked at the name tag which was strapped to the handle — Niels Bohr. I recognised the name. At first I could not place it, then I remembered that a Dane of that name had received the Nobel Prize for physics several years ago. I remembered that he had something to do with atomic physics, whatever that was. I gave him his briefcase; he thanked me and left. After a while I returned to my room in the old convent near Baker Street.

I thought about Niels Bohr for a while. He was like so many other scientists who had left their country because it was occupied by the Germans. What was he doing? Was he engaged in a war project? It also struck me that if he was researching something his work would be marked secret. And if I had been a real German spy I could easily have found out about his work. Perhaps just by having opened his briefcase and looking through the papers inside.

I discussed this with Christopher. The Germans believed that their clever agents Tege and Ja could move almost freely through England and Scotland. Did they have several similar agents? Were there many German spies in London, people still unknown to the British Intelligence Service and who could get people to reveal secret information? I had shown how easy it could be if one was clever and had a bit of luck.

'We're aware of the risks,' said Christopher. 'And I think most British people are too. But there's no harm in reminding people that spies do exist, and that they could be anywhere at anytime.'

'I noticed that Selfridge's large clock is nine minutes fast,' I said. 'What if we told the Germans?'

Christopher looked at me, then slowly shook his head. 'I don't follow you,' he said. 'Why should that be of any interest to them?'

'We could suggest that they include it in their English broadcasts. Lord Haw-Haw could say that the Germans have ears and eyes everywhere, in Oxford Street one of the clocks is fast. We know that here in Berlin and we know much more.'

'I still don't understand what you're getting at,' said Christopher.

'We'd be even more respected by the Germans for a start, and the British would be given something to think about, thus increasing their awareness of the spy risk.'

Christopher did not like my idea. He did not even take it up with MI5. 'It could have very different results to those you imagine,' he said. 'There could be panic. The police would be inundated with reports. So-and-so has behaved oddly; so-and-so has asked strange questions and shown far too great an interest in such-and-such.'

We did not discuss the matter further. A couple of days later the clock in Selfridge's was spot on time once again.

It was spring. The wild rains spattered the pavements, the trees were budding and the sun was pleasantly warm — when it came out.

The Germans started to become impatient. They wanted results, not just talk. We had received both money and a new transmitter. Now we had to prove ourselves worthy of the goods.

'We've decided to plan another act of sabotage,' said Christopher. 'It's the best way of keeping the Germans satisfied.'

'What's the target this time?' I asked.

'Have you got any suggestions?'

I thought about it. I had found a suitable objective during the journey that Ted and I had made. A large abandoned power station.

The Germans had already told us in Oslo that power stations were some of the better targets for sabotage. I had suggested breweries. If there was anything that could lower the morale in England it was a shortage of beer. Andersen had not understood, so there had not been any further discussion about the consequences of empty pubs. That's why it was better choosing something more in the Germans' style. I told Christopher about the power station. I described where it lay, explaining that I had only seen it through the car window, but I had noticed several large pipes to which limpet mines could be attached.

'You and Ted can make a preliminary examination,' said Christopher after a couple of days. 'We've discussed the power station. It's not in use anymore and we think it could suit our purposes.'

Once again Ted and I took a train. We did not order a car this time, but bought tickets for the bus that passed the power station. Christopher had given me a camera, so when the bus chugged past the site I took a couple of discreet photographs of the outside from behind Ted's back. We returned on the same route and I took more photographs. To make the whole thing more authentic we borrowed two bicycles from the hotel where we were staying and set off on a little tour which ended up at the power station.

We gave an account of our observations on our return to London. Whilst we had been away Christopher had got hold of the designs for the building and we made a careful study of them.

'As an amateur, how would you go about it?' Christopher asked.

'I'd need explosives,' I said. 'And someone to explain how and where to place them.'

'We'll take the problem of explosives first,' said Christopher. 'Where would you get hold of some?'

We soon came to the conclusion that there was no way I would be able to get hold of, or make, explosives that would be powerful enough. The building was solid and compact; homemade incendiary bombs would have no effect.

'In that case the Germans will have to supply us with what we require,' I said. Christopher nodded. Even MI5 had come to that conclusion.

I relayed my problem to Abwehr in my next transmission. We were thinking of destroying a power plant. We had already made a careful study, but we did not have the right equipment. Could they send it by parachute? The Germans were willing to try and after a week they came back and said an aeroplane was ready to deliver what we needed on a Saturday night, in three weeks' time.

We did not want to make it appear too easy. Tege and Ja did not have unlimited possibilities of travelling around England, taking leave whenever they wanted. So we replied that that Saturday would not do, but that we could get leave on the Wednesday and Thursday of the following week. The Germans replied that they could make the drop on the Wednesday night. The time would be 2 a.m. as before, and they wanted to use the same drop zone.

We decided to make things difficult. We said we had found a better place. We described it and asked for their point of view. They explained that they trusted our judgement and that the pilot had nothing against it. I said I had understood everything loud and clear; but a couple of days later I cancelled it. Neither Tor nor I had got leave on that night. Instead I wanted to go back to the initial date the Germans had given us. The Germans realised it was difficult for me and that there was nothing I could do about my hours of duty. They would come on the night between Saturday and Sunday instead. They would also supply me with everything I needed to blow up the power station.

'It's just a matter of waiting now,' said Christopher.

We waited. As usual there was not much for me to do. During the day I went to matinées, but new pictures were few and far between. I soon reckoned that I had probably seen all the films showing in London. I watched some of them two or three times, sometimes with Helle, but when she got a temporary job at the Danish Embassy I was reduced to my own company.

Making the days pass was irritatingly difficult. I put on several pounds and my level of fitness dropped noticeably. When Tor and I had planned our operation, we had never imagined things to be like this. In fact, we had never discussed what would happen in Britain — well, nothing more than being greeted as heroes. I had never imagined that a double agent's life would be quite so dull.

And that Tor's vision of the future had not been fulfilled was substantiated by his letters which I now received almost every month. However, it seemed as if he had accepted the situation. He still felt bitter but his hatred of those who had interned him was of secondary importance. His thoughts had now turned to the trivial day-to-day problems. The spring in his gramophone had broken, could I get him a new one? The Red Cross, who had previously supplied him with cigarettes, had been forced to stop the service. Could I send him a couple of cartons? Sometimes the injustice he felt shone through. 'I'm looking forward to the day when I can make those responsible answer for their actions. I'll never forget how much pain the people in this country have caused me just because I was foolish enough to do everything I could to help them. When I get home to Norway I'll explain what the English mean by hospitality, fair play and justice. The biggest pack of lies I've ever heard. Maybe you think I'm exaggerating, John. I don't.'

I had tried everything to get him released. MI5 could not, or would not, do anything; the Norwegian Embassy had no authority as far as prisoners-of-war were concerned. All I could do was continually to remind Christopher and send Tor packets and letters.

Then came the day for the Germans' second drop. They had promised several times that this time the plane would not carry any bombs. Christopher believed Abwehr's promises and once again the RAF agreed to turn a blind eye and stay on the ground. This time the place for the drop was nearer the coast. We had given the pilot a landmark, a small village with a grove behind it. I would be on the other side of the grove, on a small hill. From there I had a good view in all directions.

The crowd assembled in the Aberdeen police station was smaller than last time. Christopher was not there, nor the American Intelligence captain. However, McConnought was in command once again, and Westland, Slatter and Ted Ingram were included in the chosen unit. We knew the routine now and none of us felt the same excitement as on the last occasion. However, I did feel a bit nervous as I scrambled up the slope by myself to take my position with my flashlight. It was a cold, damp night. A light mist was coming in from the sea but visibility was reasonably good. An experienced pilot would not have any difficulty locating the village, the grove and the hill.

I waited. It was 2 a.m., then 2.30, and still no sound of an aeroplane. I signalled, jogged around to keep myself from freezing, stopped and listened. Nothing could be heard from the sea. At 3 a.m. we gave up. The Germans were not coming, it was just a matter of confirming the fact. They had left their agents in the lurch.

'There's nothing we can do about it,' said McConnought.

'Something must have happened,' I said. 'I don't think the Germans would simply not have bothered sending us the equipment.'

We returned to Aberdeen, a quiet group this time. We were not stopped by any road blocks, which I suppose was a good sign. I went to my room and got to bed straight after I had finished off the little pocket flask of whisky that I had taken to help myself keep warm during my wait on the hill.

In the morning, when I passed the telephone exchange on my way to the canteen, I was stopped by the telephonist. McConnought wanted a word; he was waiting for me in his room. I walked upstairs to his office, knocked on the door and entered. McConnought sat at his desk. On the table was a case just like the one which had held the transmitter a couple of months ago! There was a folded parachute on the floor.

'It was discovered over a mile from the appointed place,' he said. 'In a potato field. The case is full of magnetic mines.'

34

The German pilot must have navigated wrongly or come into a high mist and dropped the parachute, hoping for the best. All we could do was say that we had not received the promised equipment, that we had waited in vain at the appointed spot. In our next transmission we told the Germans this. We said we had neither heard an aeroplane nor had we seen a parachute. Had the Germans forgotten about it or had there been an accident? We still needed the supplies and asked them to suggest another time.

The Germans replied honestly. They had sent an aeroplane but the pilot had not been sure if he had found the right village and grove. He was sorry we had not found the parachute. We suggested the valley for the next drop since it was obviously easier to find from the air. We also said that at least I would probably be able to get leave the night the Germans chose.

The procedure was repeated a third time. I went to Aberdeen, got the loan of a sergeant's uniform which fitted me better than last time. I was also equipped with a pistol. Then we set off, with McConnought in the lead. I got into position on the slope, Westland crept under his bush. After half an hour's waiting we heard a lone aeroplane. The drop was undramatic. I signalled, the aeroplane circled the lake and then the parachute floated down to land about a hundred yards from the path. The aeroplane disappeared out to sea and we rescued the heavy suitcase. No bombs were dropped. The Germans had kept their promise not to make matters more difficult than necessary for their agents.

The case contained magnetic mines, detonators and small incendiary bombs, exactly the same equipment that they had sent the last time. There was also an envelope containing two hundred pounds. The Germans would be expecting a spectacular result.

Once more we had proved that Tege and Ja were highly thought of by the Germans. They had dropped equipment and money for us three times now. I felt enthusiastic and eager to get to work. We ought to exploit the situation and do something special, something new, something out of the ordinary.

'What?' asked Christopher.

'You lot in MI5 are far too passive,' I said. 'I'm beginning to understand how Tor felt.'

'Don't do anything stupid, John,' said Christopher.

Of course I was not going to do anything by myself. That much I had learned. But I wanted to achieve more than what MI5 had decided. After all, Tor and I had set the whole thing up. I ought to be able to get my ideas accepted sometimes without them being eaten away by bureaucracy.

'I've thought about buying a house,' I said.

'A house? In London?'

'Scotland. By the coast. I think I've found what I want. It's situated in an isolated spot, the beach is stony, the land is barren and only good for the sheep. I could use it when I'm on leave.'

'Are you serious?' asked Christopher.

'I can get it for £1,500,' I continued. 'I'll ask the Germans for the money.'

'What are you hoping to achieve?'

'We could set up an operation base, a sort of sabotage group. I could enlist some reliable Scots. The Germans might want to enlist a couple of specialists and I can take care of them.'

'Do you really believe the Germans will take the bait?' said Christopher.

'So far they've swallowed just about everything,' I said.

'This is far too big.'

'That's precisely why they'll think the suggestion is perfect.'

'What's the idea behind it?'

'The Germans might send people who would be of interest to MI5. I've written an initial report about my idea. Will you take it with you?'

Christopher promised to let his superiors know, but he was very reluctant, I could tell.

MI5 said no. I ought to have realised they would. 'There are more important things for us to do,' said Christopher.

I was disappointed. I had thought the idea of creating a German spy and sabotage organisation within the framework of the British Intelligence a stroke of genius. However, after mulling over why MI5 had so categorically refused to discuss the idea, I understood how they viewed my role as a double agent. The plan was to use Tege and Ja for something important, something that could influence the outcome of the war. Pretending to buy a house in Scotland, and trying to entice German agents there, was just a waste of energy and effort. A plan like that would not influence the war. I might as well forget it.

Yet another act of sabotage had to be planned. The Germans were expecting it. On this occasion the target was to be the power station at Bury St Edmunds. Ted and I went out on another reconnaissance trip. We cycled out to the power station, studied the building carefully, examined the high fence round the station, and sat out one night in the bushes to see if there were any guards.

It was an easy task. The power station had obviously been abandoned for quite a while as no one paid any attention at all. There was an American air division based in the area, but all we saw of them was a jeep with a couple of American military policemen in it, which drove past on its way into town. The jeep returned after several hours. We could hear bawling voices from a long way off and when it passed us we saw that the policemen had found some female company for the home journey. A German saboteur could hardly have had an easier task.

We returned to London and reported our observations. MI5 sent out a couple of staff members to gather even more information on the power station and I started to prepare the Germans for what would happen. I sent a short message saying that I had found a hole in the fence, that I had plotted the guards' nightly rounds and that I was convinced the destruction of this vital power station would succeed.

'You've got some very powerful magnetic mines,' said Christopher. 'Now the question is where to put them.'

'How do you know if they're effective?' I asked.

Christopher smiled. 'We made them. The mines in the case had been taken from our own agents. Or they were found in some potato field somewhere. We send equipment by parachute too and it doesn't always end up in the right hands. But apart from that, you can't possibly know where to place the mines for maximum effect.'

'I'll have to ask someone then,' I said.

'Who? You can hardly ask one of your friends in the army to help.'

That was true. Abwehr in Oslo knew that my knowledge of explosives was minimal. The sabotage would have to be very amateurish if it was to appear authentic. Or could I learn somehow? I thought a while before I came up with the solution.

'I'll ask the Germans,' I said.

Christopher nodded. It was only natural. If an agent was faced with a far too difficult situation for him to cope with, he would naturally turn to his own colleagues for help and advice. I described the power station to the Germans, told them about the large water pipes which I'd seen outside and asked how many magnetic mines I should use and how closely I should place them for maximum effect. The Germans came back, wanting additional information. I replied with what information I could easily have gathered during my reconnaissance.

In the meantime, MI5 had made their own investigations. The American jeep passed the power station regularly every night and returned equally regularly after a couple of hours with the beer-swilling military policeman and a host of laughing girls. Contact had also been made with the brigadier-general in command of the air force. He was told that there would be an exercise in the area and that there would be a large explosion, but that the police were in full control. He did not need to step in.

As usual, I was not allowed to be in on the actual sabotage. It was carried out by the Special Branch and it was only the day after that I heard the result.

Christopher phoned in the morning and asked me to come into the office at Regent Street. I got there as quickly as I could, gave proof of my identity and was shown into the inner conference room. I could see immediately from Christopher's face that he was very pleased.

'It worked,' he said. 'A large part of the installation was destroyed. The local firemen and police arrived en masse and even during the clearance work there was talk of sabotage.'

'And the press?'

'They were given as much information as we wanted them to have.'

I was told to wait a couple of days before reporting to the Germans that their confiscated mines had been used successfully. First of all we would wait for the reaction in the press.

It was reported extensively. Several newspapers wrote about the event. The material damage had not been large but it was a question of sabotage and that was serious enough. Then I sent my report to the Germans and boasted of yet another successful mission. As before, they sent their congratulations and greetings.

I was surprised that the Germans still had confidence in us. Tege and Ja were clearly well-respected agents in the Germans' eyes. However, there was always a slight uncertainty with MI5. Were the Germans also playing a double game? Did they know that the British Intelligence Service lay behind the sceness, directing everything their spies reported?

I discussed this with Christopher on several occasions. I understood from him that the same discussion was being carried out by MI5's command. Tege and Ja had kept up transmissions since the summer of 1941. For more than two years they had managed to avoid discovery. They had carried out three successful acts of sabotage and taken care of two parachute drops. Was this possible? Did the Germans truly believe that the enemy's vigilance was this slack?

'Let's test them,' I said to Christopher.

'No more of your isolated houses.'

'I've got a completely different idea,' I continued. 'We've got two transmitters, but there is always the risk that we'll have to get rid of them or dump them into a river.'

Christopher agreed. In a critical situation an agent must first of all think of his own safety.

'If that should happen we would have no way of contacting the Germans. We could perhaps continue to be of use, but without a transmitter we can't communicate with them. We can't even tell them that we've lost our "voices" and that we need them to deliver another transmitter.'

'Have you thought of how to solve the problem?' asked Christopher.

'We'll ask Abwehr for a contact address in a neutral country. Then we can send a postcard with a mutually agreed message should anything happen to us. The Germans know they can contact us through grandfather. Now we want an address for Abwehr.'

Christopher took up my idea with MI5. 'No one thinks the Germans will give us a contact address,' he said after the meeting. 'But we've got permission to try. Let's get going.'

I prepared a message trying to make the Germans realise the implications, the disastrous situation we would be in if we were unable to contact them. I tried to leave them with the impression that they would be the real losers.

'The Germans will never give an address,' said Christopher. 'You just don't do that sort of thing.'

After a week we received a contact address in Lisbon — a street number and the name of a woman.

'What will MI5 do now?' I asked.

'Not much,' said Christopher. 'We'll watch the house discreetly, see who visits, but we can't do any more than that. If we do anything the Germans will know that Tege and Ja leaked the information and we just can't take that risk.'

So the secret address in Lisbon was not of much use. Perhaps, however, it could provide a small piece of the puzzle when the Intelligence Service tried to map out the German spy network.

The green of summer slowly changed to the yellow and brown of autumn. We had played our part for the time being and so I tried to occupy myself as best I could. I wrote to Tor, sent him books and other things he wanted. He seemed a bit happier; in fact in one of his letters he was unbelievably optimistic. He had received a spring for his gramophone after waiting almost a year. Now he wanted something to play on it. I sent him some classical records. My economic resources were not large, but I had a couple of pounds left over and invested them in Tor.

One morning Jock's Citröen parked outside No. 35 and he sauntered in accompanied by Christopher. I had spent that night at the Poultons after listening in on the SOW frequency in case they had something for us. Abwehr would often send a message, preceded by their call-sign SOW. They realised that although we might not be able to transmit we would be able to listen and copy their message and find out what they wanted us to do. They did not realise that this extra time was instead used by us to prepare the answers we would be giving. This was particularly useful when MI5 had to consult High Command before we sent our replies.

'The Norwegian Foreign Minister wants to see you,' said Christopher.

What does he want?' I asked. 'To give me another job?'

'No idea. I was just told that he's waiting for you at lunchtime.'

Jock drove us into London and the same procedure as before was repeated. Christopher went ahead and announced our arrival and then collected me. I was shown into an office, waited a while, but then Uncle Trygve came in. He looked tense but he smiled when he saw me. He came over and hugged me. He asked me to sit down, looked at me for a couple of seconds and then cleared his throat.

'It's probably best if I get straight to the point,' he said. 'I've received reports from Norway. Your father is dead.'

I stared at him.

'I understand that it'll come as a shock to you,' Uncle Trygve continued, 'but I wanted to tell you personally, rather than you hearing from someone else.'

'How did he die?' I whispered. 'The Germans?'

'No. He was released from Grini prison several months ago. It was his heart. You knew he had problems with it, didn't you?'

I nodded. I knew about it. His illness, his nitro-glycerine tablets, his slow movements.

'You can be proud of him,' said Uncle Trygve. 'Helge did a lot for his country.' He looked at his watch. 'You'll have to excuse me,' he said, 'I have to get back. It's just that I wanted you to know as soon as possible.'

I got up. He held out his hand. Then he hurried off. I walked slowly out into the corridor to Christopher who was waiting.

In the car I told Christopher and Jock what had happened. I had prepared myself for father's sudden death. Our family doctor had told me before the war. I was still surprised. It was a bitter feeling knowing that I had not been able to help him, that I had not seen him or talked to him before the end, that I could not even go home for the funeral. Father was gone and I could not say a last goodbye to him.

35

Tege — with Ted Poulton taking his place at the Morse key — took over the transmissions with the Germans for several months. I did what I had to do, translated the text that Ted was sending and coded it. However, I did not have the same motivation that I felt previously. Had I done the right thing leaving Oslo? Should I have stayed and looked after the firm? It had been father's greatest wish. I had let him down. Was there any purpose to what I was doing now? Was I really making as great a contribution as I had thought I would when I decided to dupe Abwehr?

When I asked Christopher he replied honestly. 'I don't know,' he said. 'You can't just point to someone and say that he's more important than the next man. We're part of an Allied war force. We carry out whatever orders we're given. It's all these small contributions that will decide the matter. I still think that what you and Tor have done can be rated higher than many other things. I don't like talking about it in these terms. Basically, the girl who examines cartridge cases in an ammunition works is just as important a cog as a general.'

It sounded rather lofty but it was just Christopher's way of expressing himself. Perhaps it was thanks to these long conversations with him that in the late autumn I managed to drag myself out of the depression which father's death had caused.

War continued. In the east the Soviet troops slowly broke down the German lines. On the newspapers' maps the front line was being pushed even further westwards towards Germany. In the south, Italy had been beaten, even though the Germans continued to oppose. In the Pacific the Americans forced the Japanese from island to island.

Father was right. The Germans would never win the war. But how long would it take? What would happen next?

I realised in the late autumn of 1943 that something was about to happen from the questions the Germans asked and from MI5's actions. One night we received an inquiry from Abwehr. The message started with 'Important! Important!' and then continued with the Germans wanting to know if we could get information about events in Scotland. They were interested in knowing which troops were on exercise in the north; which ships had been gathered in the Scottish ports; which aircraft types were based at the aerodromes? We were to report troop movements, material transport, in fact they wanted information on every kind of activity.

MI5 took the Germans inquiry very seriously. It took a couple of weeks before they decided how I was to act, what messages I was to send and how I was to formulate my reports. Obviously many of the questions were difficult to analyse and had to be referred to the war command for final decision. I recognised much of the information they wanted me to pass on to the Germans from those months prior to the invasion of North Africa. Bit by bit Tege and Ja would once again sketch a situation similar to that of the autumn of 1942. Troops were gathering in camps in Scotland, skiing equipment was being shipped there, they were being trained in mountaineering and winter warfare; landing craft practised on the rocky stretches of coastline. I realised that MI5's job was once again to make the Germans believe that an attack on Norway was imminent. It was up to Tege and Ja to make sure that the right information was sent to Abwehr's radio room at the top of Klingenbergsgaten in Oslo.

The Germans were interested in everything I told them. Every report was followed by new questions. Each question was answered, at times vaguely; at other times I apologised that I could not get hold of the information. I was ordered to describe the emblems the soldiers in a certain area were wearing and which regiments were based in a certain training camp in a certain town. MI5 decided what I could inform the Germans, although I noticed Christopher now frequently would refer to requests made by someone higher up.

Sometimes I had a stroke of luck, or so I told them. An NCO whom I had got to know had invited me home for the weekend. He lived in an area restricted to everyone except the local inhabitants. However, he managed to get permission to take me with him to his home town on the coast. There I saw a small fleet of landing craft which had been camouflaged on a beach. I also heard soldiers speaking Norwegian in the pub, and that one officer had said they would be home soon.

Everything had to be believable, plausible, possible. Christopher placed even greater importance on my sending the Germans only what I possibly could have seen with my own eyes. We discussed every single word in the messages. We went carefully through every detail.

It was only afterwards that I realised that an attack on the Germans was being planned, and that it was not aimed at Norway. It would be aimed elsewhere: at the Balkan Peninsula, France or, perhaps, directly at Germany. The English and the Americans were preparing a final blow at Hitler. It was a matter of concealing their intentions. Misleading information had to be spread about. Tege and Ja had been selected for that job.

Like the last time Christopher had little to say about the real operation's objective and meaning. His oath of silence included me. Perhaps he was also being kept in the dark as to what was going to happen; perhaps in that respect we were on an equal footing.

The transmissions continued until Christmas 1943. I told the Germans that my weekend leaves had been cancelled and that this was happening in many units based in Scotland. Military personnel were not too happy about the sudden confinement to barracks or camps in the north.

This meant a break in transmission and I took the opportunity to go to Manchester to visit my grandparents.

Grandfather's attitude towards me had not changed. I was still in civilian attire. He asked me again and again why I had not received a commission. As usual I replied evasively but I could tell that he thought me unenterprising. A simple detail like that could hardly cause any problems if the determination existed. After all, many of my ancestors had been officers.

Grandfather was ashamed of his grandson. I realised that when he refused to take me to The White Lion. He took it hard that I had let down the family tradition. One evening as we sat silently beside one another after dinner, I decided to tell him the whole story. He was an officer and I ought to be able to rely on him to respect the fact that this was to go no further. I started at the beginning, describing the situation in Oslo after the occupation, about Tor and the post censor and the names we had managed to get to the resistance. I tried to make him see how Tor and I had become trusted by the Germans, explaining how we were trained as spies and finally put down off the coast of Scotland by a German seaplane.

'So, you're a German spy,' grandfather stated.

'Of course not,' I said. 'Tor and I only pretended to work for the Germans. It was really our intention to become double agents and get in touch with the British Intelligence Service. We succeeded. I think we've been of great help to the Allies.'

'But you were trained to be a German spy?' said grandfather.

'To be able to get to Britain and do our part for the war,' I said.

'You were recruited by the Germans.'

I continued the argument, telling him about Christopher and our constant radio contact with Abwehr. I described the parachute drops and explained that the Germans trusted us, which meant a great deal.

'Do you send secret messages to the enemy?' asked grandfather. His face had gone red and it was not because of the whisky. He was outraged, morally indignant. First of all I thought it was because things like espionage and counter-espionage had not been part of his generation's idea of how to conduct a war. He belonged to those commanding officers fostered in the traditions of the Crimean War and the Boer War, a sort of sport for gentlemen. A play where the extras were sent on to the battlefield to prove a tactical theory. There were always plenty of extras.

I tried explaining to him that the war in Europe was not the same as the campaign at Gallipoli. Weapons were different; this was a world war. A bomb could be dropped even on the quietest part of Manchester. In this use of every resource, counter-espionage was also used, a conscious misleading of the enemy so as to achieve an element of surprise.

He was not listening. I could tell that he quite seriously believed me to be a German spy, a traitor. Hadn't Hitler taught me the Morse alphabet? Hadn't Hitler sent a transmitter to Scotland for me? These facts which I could not deny were enough for him.

That was not all. I had put him in a moral dilemma. I was his grandson. The boy who had spent every summer holiday in his house had become a German messenger sent out to damage his Empire. I realised that I could not get through to him. He was convinced by his own interpretation; he had decided what he believed. That I was not in uniform had been bad enough. But that, besides, I was on the German side was far worse.

He kept all that to himself. It was as if he felt guilty that he had not been able to raise me to be a better person. He kept up a reserved, polite friendliness towards me, but he was no longer open.

I felt unhappy when I left. I was alone. I had lost the two people closest to me — my father and my grandfather. For one horrible moment I was terrified of what would happen after the war, after the victory. Would others see me as grandfather did, as a traitor to his country? What would they say when I returned to Oslo? Would they believe me when I told them what I had done? Would I be allowed to tell them? Or would my work be stamped confidential even after the war? How would Tor be greeted? Tor who'd been interned.

However, the war was not over yet. Germany had not been beaten. Hitler still controlled most of Europe. Soon an attack would take place in an area that only the highest war command knew about. My job was to make the Germans believe it was Norway.

When I returned to London I reported that large troop forces were being gathered in Scotland. On the airfields were troops from the USA and Canada. A lot of them had been equipped with white anoraks, and skiing was being practised on the snow-covered mountains. I had not seen any of this, but I guessed that much of the information was true. Soldiers were being trained to ski, though perhaps not several platoons, whole regiments and army corps as I said in my reports.

There were troop transport ships in Scottish ports, but they hardly had room for the millions of soldiers I told the Germans about. Aeroplanes did land on the Scottish grass-covered airstrips, but not in the numbers I reported to the Germans.

At the beginning of February 1944, I went to Aberdeen. For the first time I made the journey alone. As usual I got a ticket for the overnight train and arrived early in the morning in the city that by now I knew quite well. A police car took me to Lodge Walk where I met McConnought and John Westland, and then I started working on the report I would send in the night.

I had received my instructions from Christopher. I had not made any spectacular observations in Scotland. There were troops everywhere, on their way to training camps, I wrote. More importantly, I had received new orders. I was now permanently attached to a battalion in the north as security officer. It was said the war was entering a sensitive phase and I could not be sure of getting any leave for several weeks, perhaps months. That was why I had decided to take the transmitter to my camp. It was risky — vigilance was great. The preparations were secret and we had all received strict orders not even to reveal where our base was, and certainly not what exercises we were engaged in. In the meantime, I hoped everything would go well and that from time to time I would be able to send reports. However, I was afraid it might be difficult. I had learned that we were going to practise winter warfare and to keep ourselves prepared for action. I did not know any more about our duties.

I worked on the text for a couple of hours, cut it down and finally had the line of words I knew the Germans would understand. Then I translated it into German, coded the message and went up to the radio room where Ted Ingram was sitting listening to the radio traffic from the police cars on patrol. He said hello and I listened for a while to the happenings in rowdy Aberdeen. Then I asked him to fix the speech distortion device on the telephone. I wanted to call Christopher and read the night's message to him.

Ted Ingram was used only to being trusted until the device was set up. He did not ask why I wanted to be alone in his radio room. He just did what I asked him and then crept out.

I dialled Regent 6050 and asked for Christopher's extension. When I heard his voice I connected the scrambler. I read out the text and after a while Christopher replied that it was fine. I could send it as it stood.

I went down to the canteen and had a couple of cups of strong tea. Then I made my way to my room and rested for a couple of hours.

At midnight I traipsed up the stairs again to the radio room and asked Ted to leave. I got ready for the transmission, waited for a while and then turned the wireless on. I tapped out the calling signal, waited a while and then repeated it.

The Germans replied almost immediately. They had done so recently, perhaps because they were more excited than ever to hear what news Tege and Ja would come up with. As soon as I got the go-ahead signal I began telegraphing the coded group of letters. The routine was so well ingrained that I was calm and sure of what I was doing. I ended the message and left the airwaves free for the Germans.

A rush of Morse code poured from the loudspeaker. I wrote the letters down and when the Germans had finished I decoded it and dialled Christopher's number to tell him the report. New questions, new orders, a new request for further details on something I had told them about earlier. Then good luck and out.

The next day I relaxed. I wandered around the city, paid the Westlands a short visit and then found my reserved overnight compartment on the London train.

Christopher met me at the station. It was unusual. He had never done that before.

'I want to talk to you,' he said.

He looked serious and I could tell it was something important. During the taxi drive to Regent Street he didn't say anything except a few words about the changeable February weather. It was only when we got to his office that he told me why he had come to collect me.

'We've decided Tege and Ja are to go out of business,' he said. 'That was your last transmission to the Germans. We can't carry on.'

I was not surprised. I had an inkling it would happen when I had been sent alone to Aberdeen. But I wanted to know why.

'We've given them enough bait,' he said. 'If we continue there's a risk they'll be mistrustful. We can't exaggerate the importance of the troops gathering in Scotland.'

'I could lie low for a while,' I said, 'and then return.'

'You're not going to return, John. The Germans can think what they want. They'll probably think you've been caught at last.'

'Have I done something that's annoyed MI5?' I asked.

'Completely the opposite. All the leaders are very pleased with your work. But the decision stands. For tactical reasons we mustn't exaggerate. It's better that the Germans live in uncertainty about what's happening in Scotland.'

'So I'm fired?' I said.

'Not fired,' said Christopher. 'More like used up, if you'll pardon the expression. You've played your part, John, and you've played it well.'

'Thanks.'

'You've got to realise it's not you this concerns. I'm not talking about John Moe, but the agent the Germans call Ja. The hand that operates the Morse key.'

'What'll happen?'

'What do you want to do?' asked Christopher. 'Do you want me to contact the Norwegian Foreign Minister and ask him to organise a job for you?'

'Let me think about it.'

'We'll help in any way we can. Just say what you want to do.'

'What about Tor?' I asked. 'Since Tege and Ja don't exist any more he ought to be set free.'

'MI5 can't do anything about the internment authority's decision,' said Christopher.

He said it in such a way that it was obvious that the subject had been discussed and that MI5 had definitely decided not to meddle. Then he got up, put out his hand and laid it on my shoulder.

'It's been interesting,' he said. 'You can be pleased with your achievements.'

His words were kind but I still felt empty. I realised that I ought to feel happy and relieved. I had been released from a situation that I had landed in without thinking of the consequences. But at that precise moment I just felt that something in my life had suddenly ended, and I did not know what would follow.

'One more thing before we part,' said Christopher. 'We

don't want you to reveal one word of what you've been doing during this time. The war isn't over. MI5 has a one hundred per cent secrecy policy.'

'And after the war?' I asked.

'Even after the war. We don't know what will happen in the future, do we? What enemies will we be pitted against in five or ten years' time? We've got no intention of telling the world how we operate.'

'I promise,' I said.

'A promise isn't enough, John,' said Christopher. 'It's a command for total silence, forever. That's what we want. And there's no alternative.'

'I understand,' I said.

At that time the command seemed unimportant. I had nothing against having four years of my life eradicated.

'It's not enough that you understand,' said Christopher. 'MI5 require complete loyalty. There are no exceptions and no compromises.'

'Otherwise what?'

Christopher did not reply, he just smiled and it was a smile I understood.

Epilogue

I had come to a decision by the end of a week. I told Christopher that I wanted to be transferred to a regiment and do my military training. I was in bad condition. The boredom and the many night passes had made me sleep badly. I had also started to lose my hair. I needed a job that required physical exertion so that I could get into shape.

It was not on account of the work I had done that I felt completely worn out. On average I had not been at work for more than a couple of hours a week. However, I had lived in a state of tension the whole time. I had pretended to be someone else, living a double life with two cover stories to balance out against one another. My relatives and friends in England thought that I lived a comfortable life as a translator at the Ministry of Information. The Germans believed me to have a subordinate, yet important, military post. Every second I had to be sure with whom I was dealing and constantly play the role expected of me. If I was accepted as a recruit in the military at least these problems could be forgotten. I would be an ordinary soldier and if asked what I had done before I could say I had sworn an oath of silence.

Christopher understood my reasoning and promised to organise it for me. However, there was one thing I had to realise and that was that I would never be enrolled in a fighting unit or take part in a mission outside England. At all costs I had to avoid being captured and questioned by the Germans. I was aware of this, but people were needed on the home front too. After my basic training I might be able to work in a depot or as a troop trainer or something else.

After a couple of days all the formalities were cleared and the papers signed. I signed on to serve in a regiment based in York and was given my first leave a month later. I went to visit my grandparents in Manchester. At last I would be able to get my grandfather to change his mind about me. I had fulfilled the wishes he had had of me. I was in uniform and doing my duty.

Grandfather was happy to see me, but we still did not go to The White Lion. There were no marks of rank on my uniform and that was as much of a disappointment to him as my arriving in Manchester dressed in civilian clothes and when I had revealed what role I really played. I was relieved when my leave came to an end and I had to return to my regiment.

The weeks passed by in montonous repetition but I felt myself becoming both physically and psychologically stronger. Military life was good for me, even if it was incredibly boring. Then came the reports of the Allied landings in Normandy. The end of the war was in sight.

I realised that the last reports I had sent to the Germans had something to do with the planning of this enormous invasion. I did not know what importance those misleading reports about the gathering of troops in Scotland had. Neither did I know why MI5 had suddenly decided that I should stop my transmissions. I puzzled over this from time to time. Did they want to make it look as if I had been captured? And would this increase the strength of my position in Abwehr? Would the Germans be worried by the silence, causing them to believe that Norway really was threatened and despite the loss of information from their reliable agents, count on an assault on the north? Had they prepared themselves for such an attack? If this was the case, then perhaps I had been of some use. Perhaps German resources had been kept in Norway; perhaps the landing in the north of France had been easier thanks to Tege and Ja?

Eventually I became a troop trainer. The job was a varied one and I was happy. The atmosphere in England became lighter and happier the closer to Berlin the Allies came.

Then the Germans capitulated. Norway was a free country once more and I would have given anything to have participated in the celebrations on Karl Johan. I learned that the Allies were going to send a force to Norway to disarm the Germans and liquidate the occupation. I asked my superiors if there was a possibility for me to serve in Norway. After all, I spoke Norwegian and knew Oslo well. I got help with my application. It was granted and I got on board a troopship in Liverpool. A few days later we glided into the harbour at Oslo.

I did not kiss the ground when I disembarked. I thought about doing it, but we marched down the gangplank in unison and then continued through the city to a school where we were billeted. It was situated just a few minutes walk from the flat on Therese's Gate where we were living on the day of the invasion — 9 April 1940 — barely five years ago.

We were given leave that evening and I rushed off into town. I phoned a couple of old friends and learned that my mother had moved. I got her new address and went there. It was a moving reunion after four years. We sat chatting for a long time. She told me about the dark years, the friends who had gone, father, and the salon which had been confiscated by the Germans and during the last years of the war had been frequented by the prostitutes the Germans had brought over from Paris for the enjoyment of the occupation troops.

Then I called on Gerd, Tor's fiancée. She had not received any sign of life from him and she had no idea when he would come home. I told her about our time in England, of Tor's treatment and what we had achieved thanks to him. His internment was unfair, a miscarriage of justice, but it was all over now. He would be restored to his former position and receive all the recognition he so rightly deserved. He would soon be back in Oslo a free man. Gerd took comfort from this.

I was transferred to an American detachment, 28th Mobile Disarmament Unit, whose job it was to disarm the Germans who were still left in Norway. My duty was to receive officers at Fornebu, check their luggage and confiscate any weapons before they were sent to Britain.

After a while Gerd told me that Tor had arrived in Oslo, but he was not a free man. On arrival he'd been put in prison, accused of being a traitor to his country. He would soon be put on trial. At first I did not believe her, but I soon received confirmation. Together with other interned Norwegians, Tor had been taken to Oslo to be judged by a Norwegian court. That was the agreement between the exiled Norwegian Government and the British.

What could I do? I could not reveal what Tor and I had done in Britain. MI5's activities were confidential and even if I broke my promise and told the truth, no one from MI5 would substantiate what I said was true.

I looked up the chief of the Norwegian Intelligence. His office was at Akerhus. I was worked up and told him as much as I dared and it seemed as if he really believed me. He promised to investigate the case and check my statement with the British authorities.

It did not help. Tor was put on trial at the beginning of September 1945. He declared himself not guilty of the charges of being a German spy. He told them what had really happened, that we had devoted ourselves to causing the greatest possible harm to the Germans. They did not believe him. The judge, Valborg Platou, was not convinced of Tor's intentions. The newspaper account was ironic — the headline read: 'Norwegians as German spies. They did it to "sabotage".'

Even my name was made public, but I did not care at all. Now it was a question of Tor and his trustworthiness. No one from the British Intelligence Service came to his defence. That really disappointed me. Could Christopher or someone else from MI5 not have stepped forward as a witness so that Tor could receive an official pardon? The war was over. Germany lay in ruins. Was it truly necessary still to keep our activities in the dark?

Of course Tor was set free, but he never got redress. We were still mistrusted and anyone who did not know the truth would believe Tor to be guilty, since there was no concrete proof that would hold up in court.

I met Tor as he left the prison gates. It seemed that, despite everything, he had received help from England. A man from the Special Branch had travelled to Oslo and, in secret, explained to the surprised authorities that people in London had nothing to accuse Tor of. That was why he had been released.

It was a difficult reunion for both of us. Tor did not have much to say. All he wanted to do was get away to a quiet place in the country to rest.

We parted. We had done our bit and we had come back alive. Perhaps we ought to be grateful for that.

As for myself, I wanted to leave the army,. I handed in my resignation and got a note from the Minister of Social Affairs, Doctor Sven Oftedal, who had been one of my father's fellow prisoners at Grini, saying that I was needed to take over the remnants of Helge K. Moe & Son. My resignation was accepted. I was demobbed and received a bonus of a hundred pounds. It struck me that it was the same amount the Germans had given me to take to Scotland over four and a half years ago. The amount made no difference, neither did the fact that the family business could not be put back on its feet.

The thing that hurt me was that Tor had been branded a traitor. It hurt me more when I realised that a brand like that is almost impossible to eradicate.

THE SECRET HUNTERS

ANTHONY KEMP

'Missing in Action'.

That was the official line. World War Two was over, Germany was in chaos and the British authorities preferred not to stir up more trouble — or make more work for themselves.

But the British SAS and Special Operations men — and women — were not 'missing in action'. They had been killed: shot as saboteurs on Hitler's orders or murdered in concentration camps.

The Secret Hunters is the story of how a small, dedicated group of their ex-comrades refused to accept that official line. Starting with a suppressed report into the horrors of the Nazi camps, they searched relentlessly for the truth, uncovering the grisly evidence and tracking down the war criminals responsible: the men who gave the orders, who pulled the triggers and operated the gas chambers.

Based on the TVS film, *The Secret Hunters* reveals in detail for the first time the heroism and the barbarism that lay behind that bland, official untruth: 'missing in action'

Post·A·Book

A Royal Mail service in association with the Book Marketing Council & The Booksellers Association.

Post-A-Book is a Post Office trademark.

THE CLIMATE OF TREASON

ANDREW BOYLE

'The natural and marvellous follow-up to le Carré ... as compulsive as a spy thriller, its greatest value is its sheer readability'

Oxford Mail

THE CLIMATE OF TREASON is the sensational book on the background to the Burgess, Maclean and Philby affair that led to the exposure of Anthony Blunt as the 'fourth' man. Brilliantly researched and compulsively readable, it shows how four upper-class Cambridge-educated Englishmen could work for Russia and consistently betray their country.

Andrew Boyle has completely revised and rewritten his book for this edition to give the definitive account of perhaps the greatest of all espionage mysteries.

'The story of Burgess, Philby and Maclean has never been better told ... the tone is calm, the research deep and the presentation very exciting'

Daily Telegraph

CORONET BOOKS

THE SECRET OFFENSIVE

CHAPMAN PINCHER

The Russians call them 'active measures': words that describe the Kremlin's unceasing challenge to the basic tenets of freedom in the West. Using manipulation of the media, blackmail and terrorist tactics, the Communist offensive goes on, virtually unchecked.

In his controversial new book, investigative writer Chapman Pincher exposes the full force of the Soviet threat, a threat which for often dubious diplomatic reasons the governments of the West chose to ignore.

Via our newspapers, our trade unions and even our churches, covert Russian aggression is growing, while our ability to withstand it is undermined. Here we learn how this has been allowed to happen, and why we must take action before it is too late.

'Frightening'

Daily Mail

'Fascinating new material ... from a distinguished journalist'

Sunday Telegraph

'Pincher has gathered together a remarkable amount of material about KGB activities'

British Book News

NEW ENGLISH LIBRARY

THE LAST SECRET

NICHOLAS BETHELL

In 1945, some 50,000 Cossacks, men, women and children, found themselves in Nazi Germany: some prisoners of war, others refugees from the tyranny of Stalin's Communism. Many of them had ended up fighting for Hitler, believing that when the war was over they could throw themselves on the mercy of the Allies. None could have guessed that at Yalta, Churchill and Roosevelt had already signed their death warrant. For between 1944 and 1947 the Cossacks were systematically and forcibly repatriated, at rifle and bayonet point, clubbed and herded into trains, many of them committing suicide rather than face Stalin's revenge. This, told for the first time is the full terrible story of what Solzhenitsyn described as the war's last secret.

'This is the story of one of the most tragic episodes of the last war . . . Lord Bethell's book could not be more timely'

Observer

'Lord Bethell has told this shameful, horrifying and very difficult story with great restraint and balance'

Daily Telegraph

CORONET BOOKS

ALSO AVAILABLE FROM
HODDER AND STOUGHTON PAPERBACKS